There was nowhere to go, nothing we could do. We had only two or three seconds to be frightened, for our guts to clench in that final knot of fear. The giant wall of water came out of the darkness without warning, drowning out all other sound. Its roar overpowered the scream of the wind generator outside, the howl of the wind, the crashing of the sea against the trimaran's hull and decks. It drowned out the sound of the radio playing in the cabin. It drowned out the heartbeat thudding inside our heads.

The wave hit *Rose-Noëlle* side on and she did not hesitate. Six and a half tons of boat flipped over sideways as if it were a toy plucked from a bath by a child's hand.

THE SPIRIT OF ROSE-NOËLLE

119 Days Adrift: A Survival Story

John Glennie and Jane Phare

Sketches by Joan Grehan
Line drawings by
John Glennie

FAWCETT CREST • NEW YORK

A Fawcett Crest Book
Published by Ballantine Books
Copyright © 1990 by John Glennie and Jane Phare

ISBN 0-449-22082-6

This edition published by arrangement with Penguin Books Limited London

Manufactured in the United States of America

First Ballantine Books Edition: April 1992

Cover photo by John Selkirk

This book is dedicated to the memory of Rose-Noëlle Coguiec, who died tragically on 23 July 1973, aged 19 years . . . and to my young son Geordie, who I hope will grow up to a life of dreams and adventure.

There is no such thing as a miracle to those who know how it is performed.
                                                    —Joan of Arc

CONTENTS

FOREWORD

I heard the news that the crew of the *Rose-Noëlle* were alive and well on Great Barrier Island on the radio as I was preparing my yacht *Endless Summer* for another season of sailing.

Later that evening I watched on television as Paul Holmes interviewed John. He looked gaunt and tired, slumped in the studio chair under the bright fill lights.

"Did you have doubts you would make it?"

"No, not one."

"What was the secret?"

"Faith, just faith."

That is the cornerstone of this remarkable saga. It's John's great battle cry, hard won and built up over thousands of ocean miles. That faith comes out in this book. It will mean different things to different people, depending on where they stand and look. But like all strong faith, it comes from within and is a special power.

What is the secret ingredient of survival against great odds? It is an attitude, an intention of harmonizing with nature and tapping into its universal force, a commitment which, once made, holds the key to the tools of discovery.

I first met John twenty-six years ago in the Bay of Islands—just yachties drifting about and dreaming. Since then we have crossed tacks on many occasions, both in New Zealand and among the islands of the South Pacific.

It was with despair that I heard of his disappearance somewhere off New Zealand in June 1989, and it was with great joy I heard the news of his homecoming 119 days later.

This is a very readable book about a remarkable sea saga and a voyage of personal discovery, and it gives me great pleasure to pay tribute to *Rose-Noëlle* and her skipper, a very dear friend.

Penny Whiting

ACKNOWLEDGMENTS

I could not have survived the first few months after coming ashore nor worked on this book without the help and support of some very special people. They are too many to name, but I would like to mention a few who went out of their way to show their friendship. To them I owe a big thank you.

To Penny Whiting for looking after me, understanding me, helping me with decisions and protecting me in those early days. She and her husband, Doc Williams, always made me so welcome in their home.

To my coauthor, Jane Phare, for being my minder. I couldn't have asked for a better friend and writer; I will miss her very much. She and her husband, Byron Ballan, made me part of the family for the five months it took to write and research this book.

I was indeed blessed in having friends like Penny, Doc, and Jane around me during those early weeks to share the funny side of life.

To my sister Christabel and Malcolm Tomes for their love and support; their belief that I would come home never faltered.

To Elizabeth and Geordie, Danielle and Alexandra for their love and faith.

To all those who prayed for us and believed we would return, especially Pat Hanning, Rose Young, Rod and Karol Lovatt, Maureen and Russell Foley.

To Shane Godinet for making our homecoming special from the moment he appeared at the Scrimgeour house.

To Television New Zealand and Action Downunder for the new clothes they so generously gave me. At Action Downunder I had to face my first decision: what would be the colors in my new life? Before, it had been yellow. Without realizing it, I chose green, for balance.

To Ray Richards for relieving me of the burden of book-publishing arrangements in those early days and the subsequent film arrangements.

To Joan Grehan in her studio nestled among the tree ferns overlooking the Bay of Islands, where I watched the sketches take form.

To Gavin Ellis for his computer knowledge and help.

To all those friends from around the world who wrote to me and gradually helped to fill my new address book.

To my fellow crew members, Rick Hellreigel, Jim Nalepka, and Phil Hofman, for being out there with me.

PROLOGUE

The death of *Rose-Noëlle* came quickly. The wave hit her like a freight train roaring out of the darkness toward us, the terrified passengers stalled in its path and trapped inside. There was nowhere to go, nothing we could do. We had only two or three seconds to be frightened, for our guts to clench in that final knot of fear. The giant wall of water came out of the darkness without warning, drowning out all other sound. Its roar overpowered the scream of the wind generator outside, the howl of the wind, the crashing of sea against the trimaran's hull and decks. It drowned out the sound of the radio playing in the cabin. It drowned out the heartbeat thudding inside our heads.

The wave hit *Rose-Noëlle* side on, and she did not hesitate. Six and a half tons of boat flipped over sideways as if it were a toy plucked from a bath by a child's hand and dumped unceremoniously on its head. It was six A.M., 4 June 1989, midwinter in New Zealand and still dark.

The capsize toppled me onto the roof of the cabin above the dinette seat where I had been curled up under a rug, listening to the storm. Two of my crew—New Zealander Rick Hellreigel and American Jim Nalepka—were lying in their sleeping bags on the opposite starboard double bunk. When the wave hit they hurtled up in the air and crashed down onto the dinette table below. They landed in a bruised heap on the skylight hatch in the ceiling. I crawled across the roof—now the floor—to join them, water swirling up around our legs.

The third crew member, New Zealander Phil Hofman, was missing, and we could hear him screaming out in the

1

darkness. He had been lying in a single bunk up behind the dinette seat on the port side. With the back of the dinette seat forming a side to the bunk, it resembled a cot; the moment we turned upside down it became a coffin with seawater pouring in. He was trapped in his sleeping bag, lying on the roof above the bunk with the mattress and bedding on top of him. We called out, hoping that he would crawl toward our voices.

Phil Hofman was a big man; at 1.71 meters he weighed 89 kilograms. Rotund or not, sheer panic and terror gave him the temporary agility of a gymnast. He scuttled through the water, across the roof, and under the dinette table as if his life depended on it. It did.

The cabin was fast filling with water. I knew the trimaran would reach its state of equilibrium, and the water would rise no further. My crew were not quite so convinced. Phil rushed for the companionway doors and kicked them open—a mistake, understandable in his panic to find an escape route, that was to cost us dearly. The sea surged in . . . and out, taking with it equipment and provisions that we could never replace. I had read about the danger of this surge in accounts of other multihull capsizes. The emergency flares were the first to go.

The instant we turned upside down, I knew it was the end of an era. The boat was not insured, and the thousands of dollars' worth of equipment on board was irreplaceable. Regret flashed into my mind; then it was gone as quickly as it came. There was no room for blame, fear, or indecision; there was a job to do. Instinctively I knew we had to move quickly to save anything we could before it, too, was plucked out by the surge. I told the others to grab everything they could find floating around and throw it into the aft cabin, which by its very design would end up the highest level above the seawater.

We worked feverishly; by now the water was waist height at the front of the main cabin where the bows rode high and chest height back aft by the galley. It stopped rising, and the level was to remain that way for the next 119 days.

Phil Hofman was calm now, but already there was warning of an attitude that was to become a real concern to Rick, Jim, and me during the coming weeks. "We're doomed," Phil kept saying. "We're bloody doomed."

I had waited nineteen years for this dream voyage, and so had *Rose-Noëlle*. I was full of expectation, a sense of adventure and anxious to leave, but in just four days my dream had gone horribly wrong. This trip to the exotic islands of the South Pacific was, I thought, the key to my happiness. "I'll be happy once I get back to the islands," I kept saying. Those close to me said I sounded like a cracked record. I will be happy once I get back to the islands. . . .

It was this urgency to leave that caused me to set sail with three crew members whom I did not know and who, between them, had very little sailing experience. I had met Phil Hofman a few weeks before we left, when he stopped by one day to chat. He was one of the "live-aboards" at Picton, a bunch of cruising families who live on their yachts and combine their home with their lifestyle.

Phil, his wife Karen, and their two teenage children had spent the past three years aboard their thirteen-meter ferrocement yacht *Toroa*. He was interested in multihulls, so I took him out for a short sail on *Rose-Noëlle* with a couple of other locals; he was impressed with her speed and performance.

A few weeks later I had the trimaran lifted out of the water to paint her undersides with antifoul in preparation for my long-awaited cruise of the Pacific. Phil wandered over, and I told him I was looking for crew to sail with me to Tonga.

Ideally I wanted friends along, people who would appreciate the trip and have fun, but at the last minute my prearranged crew—all friends and all good sailors—had to pull out. Two of them, Alan Barnes from Picton and Terry Dedden from Mooloolaba in Queensland, Australia, planned to join me in Tonga for the next leg of the cruise. I was disappointed and kept hoping right up to my eventual

The capsize. Desperately we grabbed everything we could salvage and threw it into the aft cabin.

departure that one of the three would become free of the commitments that had delayed them. Many times in the next four months I was to regret deeply that I did not have at least one friend out there with me.

I spent the next couple of weeks readying the boat for the trip and asking everyone I knew in Picton and my hometown of Blenheim if they would like to sail to Tonga. I even advertised in a local newspaper, but without success. Most people were committed to jobs, families, and mortgages and at such short notice could not, or would not, take the time off.

My plan was to catch up with the South Seas Cruising Club flotilla that had left the month before for a fun regatta in the Pacific Islands. I had joined the club, a newly formed organization to promote cruising in the Pacific, earlier in the year, but as the regatta drew closer I knew *Rose-Noëlle* would not be ready in time. I wrote to the regatta organizers enclosing a photograph of *Rose-Noëlle* and told them I would catch up with the other yachts in Tonga.

By the end of May I was desperate for crew, and Phil Hofman was keen to try bluewater sailing. He went home that night and discussed the trip with Karen. The next day he returned and said he would love to go; he seemed excited at the prospect. Phil had never been out of New Zealand before, and he had to catch the ferry across Cook Strait to Wellington to organize his first passport.

He offered to help me antifoul the boat, a gesture for which I was grateful. He spent the next couple of weeks helping and, once *Rose-Noëlle* was back in the water, gave me a hand to stow all the gear back on board. Phil and I struck up a reasonable working relationship during this time, but we never became close. We simply did not have enough in common. I found I had to be careful what I asked him to do on the yacht because he was slap-happy, a little rough; but then I was difficult to please when it came to *Rose-Noëlle*. I am a perfectionist, and I like to do things myself. However, Phil was well meaning, and I felt I owed him.

A few days before I planned to leave, Rick Hellreigel arrived at the wharf. He had heard I was looking for crew and, having experienced a disastrous trip to Fiji some years back, he was keen to give ocean cruising another chance. Thinking back, Rick spent most of the time interviewing me about my sailing experience and generally checking me out rather than the other way around. He asked if he could bring a friend to meet me who might also be interested in sailing to Tonga.

The next morning Rick dropped in on his friend Jim Nalepka, an American cook working for the Cobham Outward Bound school at Anakiwa in the South Island's Marlborough Sounds. Rick lived nearby at Mahakipawa with his wife, Heather, and their eight-month-old son, Matthew.

Jim had planned to spend his holidays with his partner, Martha Bell, an instructor at Outward Bound, but when Rick breezed in, announced he was sailing to Tonga, and invited Jim along, Jim didn't hesitate. Sure, he'd give it a go.

That day at work Jim hesitated, wondering if he had made the right decision. The kitchen workers and instructors at Outward Bound egged on their American cook. "Don't be a wimp, Jim, give it a go. You'll kick yourself if you don't."

Jim had never been sailing, but he was surrounded by gung-ho workmates vying to outdo each other in terms of outdoor adventures. Little did they know he was about to outdo them all. He drove in to Picton the following day and came down to meet me on *Rose-Noëlle*. I was a little uneasy about taking two close friends on as crew. I always remember meeting an experienced American cruising couple, Dr. Bob and Nancy Griffith, on their yacht *Awahnee* in Hawaii years ago. They warned me never to take on husbands and wives or buddies as crew.

"They have already formed a relationship, their own system," they used to say. "When you are sailing there is only one system, and that is the boat's."

But Jim seemed a nice-enough sort of guy with an open, friendly face—and I needed crew. I told him I planned to leave on 1 June.

*   *   *

The day before we left I was flat out doing last-minute chores aboard *Rose-Noëlle*. As always when leaving on a cruise, there never seemed to be enough time. Phil arrived and asked if there was anything he could do to help. I left him to untangle and repack the ropes for the new sea parachute I had just bought for $800. It was a magnificent piece of silk—8.5 meters in diameter—an acquisition of which I was quite proud. I had never used one before and was intrigued to know how it performed. Like many bluewater sailors, I've always believed the best way to handle a bad storm is to sail through it. Still, it didn't do any harm to have the parachute on board, although I hoped I would never need to use it.

My sister and brother-in-law, Christabel and Malcolm Tomes, arrived from Blenheim armed with a basketful of walnuts from the trees in their garden, trays of kiwifruit, and bags of Granny Smith apples, which local orchardists had offered them free for the picking. I'm very close to Christabel and Malcolm, and it was good to see them. They were always so cheerful and helpful—just the sort of people I needed around. The week before they had driven the 115 kilometers from Blenheim to Nelson to fill up the four nine-kilogram gas bottles with LPG and to organize a set of charts of the South Pacific to add to those I already had on board.

A friend from Picton, Rose Young, sat down at the dinette with Phil and started on the tedious job of cracking open scores of walnuts. Rose had made up a large plastic container of homemade muesli, and she and Phil added the nuts into the mixture. Rick and Jim arrived and asked me what they could do to help.

"You can help them crack nuts if you like," I said, nodding toward Rose and Phil in the cabin.

I think they were a little taken aback at such an odd chore the day before leaving on an offshore cruise.

Rick had a list of safety aspects that he was checking on the boat. Phil told him that in the past few weeks he had examined every inch of *Rose-Noëlle*, and he was satisfied she was well built. Rick asked me where I kept the life jackets and, still busy with last-minute chores, I replied, "That's the least of my worries right now."

Gradually I made progress, stowing gear I would not need on the voyage to Tonga in the two floats, leaving the lockers in the crew cockpit free. In these I stowed neatly coiled sheets for the sails and the plastic sea squid, a small sea anchor. That night I worked late checking and rechecking the navigation coordinates for the trip and feeding them into the computerized satellite navigation system.

Rose brought her electric sewing machine down to the boat, and we spent the evening making up a small cockpit suncover, essential for the helmsman and quickly erected while sailing in the tropics. It was never to see the sun.

The next morning I woke feeling out of sorts. Everybody seemed ready to leave except me and *Rose-Noëlle*. There were still lots of little niggling jobs I wanted to finish, and I wasn't happy with the weather conditions. I didn't really want to go; other local yachts wanting to sail had been held back by three weeks of unfavorable weather, and today, 1 June, was not much better. I wandered over to see a neighboring yachtie, Jim Bramwell, on his boat the *Argonauta*. He had a sophisticated weather facsimile on board, and I wanted to know the latest. Still not good. He suggested we keep a radio schedule each day at 8:15 P.M. during which he would give me up-to-date information from his weather fax. I thanked him for his offer and agreed to listen out for him each night on my ham radio.

I was undecided about whether or not I would reply, because I did not have a license to use the ham radio. I told Jim Bramwell that I might reply briefly but would not identify myself or the *Rose-Noëlle*. I did not have a high-frequency (HF) radio, which the New Zealand Ministry of Transport recommend but do not make compulsory for a New Zealand yacht going offshore. For a start, I did not have the $6,000 needed to buy one, and I felt that if I waited to earn the money I would never get to sea.

I have nothing against accumulating safety equipment and gadgets; by all means, if you can afford them, buy them and use them. But you have to draw the line somewhere—stop accumulating and start sailing. Besides, too much equipment can lull you into a false sense of security. To rely on radios and gadgets to get you out of trouble is dangerous. Similarly, if you rely on an engine to get you off a lee shore and it fails, then you are in trouble.

I still believe that if you choose to go to sea, you should be prepared to get yourself out of any trouble you might find yourself in. I do not expect authorities to spend large amounts of money and possibly risk lives to come looking for me.

Later in the morning Phil, Rick, and Jim arrived to stow their personal gear. Rick and Jim had a large tramping pack each, so I suggested they take out what they needed for the trip and stow the packs in one of the floats. They were well prepared for wet weather and had each brought their own life jacket. We were all dressed warmly against the midwinter chill, and Phil, obviously prepared for the worst, had boots and wet-weather gear on over his clothes.

Rose had made a large fruit cake and jars of tomato soup. She was a great cook and in the months to come, I was to dream more than once about some of her delicious recipes.

Christabel and Malcolm arrived with my mother, Jean. At the age of eighty-four, she lived in a Picton rest home but still enjoyed the odd outing. Ever since I was in my early twenties she had been farewelling me on some adventure or other, usually to do with the sea. She never was one for last-minute "Be careful" instructions, and today was no different. She figured that at forty-seven I knew how to look after myself. Mum sat in the car above the wharf and enjoyed the chaos at a distance.

Christabel had made chili con carne and a fresh batch of scones for us to eat on the way. *Rose-Noëlle* was well stocked, for I knew I could be cruising for up to a year and had stacked the lockers full of tinned and nonperishable foodstuffs. I was proud of the range of seasonings and spices on board, and the galley was certainly better equipped with gear than the average kitchen. Knowing that groceries were expensive in the Islands, I had even bought a bulk supply of toilet rolls.

Rick and Jim had paid $150 each to cover the cost of food on the trip; Phil had paid $100 because he had helped prepare the boat. I had promised each of them they could stay on board for a week once we reached Tonga, before they flew home. I was then expecting friends to join me for the next leg of the cruise.

Rose-Noëlle was looking her best. The paint gleamed on her bright yellow hulls and white cabinsides and cockpit. Inside, the main cabin was decorated with the garlands of artificial flowers and bright Hawaiian tapa print curtains I had kept as mementoes from my last trip to the islands.

Usually I had bunches of cut flowers from Christabel and Malcolm's garden in vases that rarely toppled, even under sail. I was raised in a family that adores flowers, and I could not remember a day when our home was not adorned with fresh blooms from the garden. Today there were no flowers, but I did have a fine collection of potted plants on board, including my prized raphis palm.

Everyone was waiting expectantly on the wharf for our departure. Heather Hellreigel was there, but Karen Hofman had already gone to work, confident she would see Phil again when he flew home from Tonga in two or three weeks. Heather asked me where I kept the life raft, and I told her there wasn't one. I explained that I did not believe they were necessary or even desirable on a multihull. It was too tempting for a panicking crew to abandon the yacht and set off in a life raft. Life would be cramped and uncomfortable; food and equipment would be limited, and the raft could easily flip in a storm. There were no guarantees how long a crew might be floating around before they were rescued or hit land. In the meantime the raft could well disintegrate. I have always practiced and preached "stay with the boat"—providing it is still afloat, of course. It is the biggest piece of flotsam around, more likely to be seen from the air, and provides a source of shelter and food. Unlike a monohull, which will sink quickly once holed, taken down by the weight of the lead keel below, a multihull will not sink if built with sufficient positive buoyancy materials. Upside down, it will float just fine once the water and the boat have reached a state of equilibrium, as we were about to prove.

Short of a violent gas explosion, in which case the life raft would be blown to smithereens, too, there was very little that could sink *Rose-Noëlle*. The hulls, deck, and interior fittings were built of Airex PVC foam-sandwich core, laminated on both sides with fiberglass. The material was light, buoyant, and extremely strong. Even if I had gone completely bonkers at sea—a condition that has been known to happen to lone yachtsmen under stress—and drilled hundreds of holes in her sides, she still would not sink. I pointed out to Heather that I did have a fiberglass dinghy lashed on the cabintop and an inflatable dinghy stowed in one of the floats.

I still wasn't happy about the weather prospects and had almost decided not to leave that day. Privately the thought of crossing Cook Strait in a fierce southerly with three inexperienced crew was not my idea of a fun time. But suddenly Jim Bramwell appeared alongside waving one of his famous weather facsimiles. A light northeasterly to get us comfortably across the strait, changing to a southerly for a fast trip up to Tonga. Ideal. A Customs officer from Nelson had visited earlier in the morning and cleared us to leave. It was time to go.

Everything happened in a rush after that. I raced up to the Picton Ferry Terminal shower block, remembering that it would be a week or two before I could indulge in a hot freshwater shower. It was a moment to be alone, to collect my thoughts and savor the warm water pounding on my back—all for fifty cents. I might have splurged a second fifty-cent piece had I known it was to be my last shower for four months. On the way back to the boat I stopped to give Mum a last kiss and hug in the car before joining the others clustered around *Rose-Noëlle*.

My friend Alan Barnes had come to say good-bye, and
Ricky Bugler, a local boatbuilder, was there to wish us well.
That morning he had patiently spliced two big loops on each
end of the bridle for the sea squid, ready to slip over the
big winches on either side of the cockpit should we need
to slow down the trimaran.

I remember shaking hands with people, hugging Rose, and
turning the key to start the 9.9 Yamaha outboard mounted on
the stern. What luxury an electric start was after years of
manual pullstart outboards. *Rose-Noëlle* represented everything I had always dreamed of in a boat.

As we pulled away from the wharf, I turned to look
back at the small band of well-wishers. I spotted Christabel
smiling and waving. Somehow in the last-minute rush I had
forgotten to give her my forwarding address in Tonga and,
more important, to say good-bye. The thought bothered me.
Standing next to Christabel, Rose raised her camera and
snapped the last photograph ever to be taken of *Rose-Noëlle*
the right way up.

ONE

The Storm

Leaving on a journey and arriving at a new port or island is for me the best part about the cruising life. In fact, if I am honest, I dislike sailing; it bores me to tears. I suspect that if pressed, many bluewater sailors would admit that at times they, too, feel the same way.

Sailing across an ocean out of sight of land for a month is fun—at first. But I found the novelty soon wore off. So did the prospect of hour upon hour at the wheel, getting seasick in bad weather, changing sails and being soaked by unkind waves, and keeping watch through the night.

Cruising is a life of extremes. You cannot appreciate those highs if you don't go through the lows. At times you are putting your life on the line, pitting yourself against the elements. For me, it was the only way of seeing the world and taking my home with me. And those hours alone on the helm gave me time to think, time to dream up new dreams. While I did not build the trimaran in response to a nautical yearning, I did enjoy being at the wheel of *Rose-Noëlle*, for she handled beautifully under sail.

In the top pocket of my shirt was my business card: "John A. Glennie, Yacht *Rose-Noëlle* . . . yacht deliveries, yacht builder by profession, adventurer by choice." I had waited a long time for this adventure. I wasn't sharing the first leg of the voyage with those I would have liked, but at least I had a crew. I am not a lone sailor; I like company and have never sailed on my own. A four-man crew meant that we could share a comfortable watch routine of two hours on the wheel and six hours off. Although *Rose-Noëlle* had an automatic steering system and was rigged for single-handed sailing, I was mindful that the low winter sun would not generate enough power through the solar cells to drive the autopilot without draining the batteries. In fact, the two banks of forty-two-watt solar cells were not generating enough power for the satellite navigation system.

Rose-Noëlle had no engine, apart from the outboard. From my observations, engines always break down just when you most need them. In addition, I was determined to have nothing on board that I could not easily fix myself, not being particularly mechanically minded. However, I did have alternative power sources.

Mounted high on an aluminum-pole structure on the port side was a wind generator, which trickle-charged the batteries in winds of more than seven knots and energetically overloaded them in winds of forty knots. The outboard's generator was wired into the boat's electrical system to help charge the batteries, and as a backup, though I rarely needed it, I had a little Honda petrol generator. This gave me 240-volt power when in port, and the crew could revert to the luxury of hair dryers, beaters, and blenders—all of which I had on board.

The double-pole structure mounted aft behind the steering cockpit was my own design and was handy as a Christmas tree from which to hang things. Mounted on the port pole with the wind generator was the aerial for the very high frequency (VHF) radio and the wind-vane for the autopilot. On the starboard pole was the color radar scanner, wind instruments, the satellite navigation aerial, and an aerial for both a standard CB and a marine CB radio. I had a little hand-held CB radio to take ashore with me whenever I left *Rose-Noëlle* at anchor. It was useful to check with crew for forgotten grocery orders or to plead for a lift back to the boat if I had been left behind.

Running between the two poles was a pipe supporting the two solar banks. The structure doubled as tent poles to hold the sun canopy over the crew cockpit, essential when in the tropics.

Before leaving for Tonga I had rigged double safety lines from the starboard float, around each pole and across to

the port float behind the steering cockpit. The greatest
danger when sailing a multihull—apart from turning upside
down—is being thrown backward off balance and overboard when the boat surges forward as the wind fills her
sails. Unlike a monohull, which gradually picks up speed,
a multihull gives no such gracious warning. Acceleration
is immediate and, for the uninitiated, the experience can
be alarming.

Running up behind the pole structure was the backstay,
which held the insulators for the ham radio aerial. While
I did not have a ham radio license, the set was useful
to have aboard in case of an emergency. A ham radio is
considerably cheaper to buy than an HF set and, if need
be, I could talk to anywhere in the world on just about any
frequency. Not that I did chat on the radio. I used to listen
in sometimes to the endless and often inane chatter; it was
a source of great amusement and entertainment. Cruising
yachties these days seem to suffer from verbal diarrhea,
particularly Americans. The radio is their social link with
the outside world; it is their television, transistor, video,
telephone, and fax machine all rolled into one. For me a
ship's radio is to be used only when absolutely necessary.

As we headed out into Picton Harbor, Phil and I hoisted the
mainsail—a large, curved, and fully battened sail that gave
Rose-Noëlle plenty of power under the right conditions. But
in the flukey winds of the harbor, the outboard would have
to help out. Rick, Jim, and Phil stood up on deck looking
at the beauty of the Marlborough Sounds and familiarizing
themselves with the motion of the boat. We didn't talk
much. Each of us was thinking of the trip ahead, wondering
what it would be like, if the weather would treat us kindly.

Once we passed through the entrance to Picton Harbor,
I set the new roller-furling headsail. I was pleased with
this new addition to *Rose-Noëlle*'s sail wardrobe, hoping
it would save me hours of sail changes. As the trimaran
began to pick up speed in response to the sail, I cut the
engine. Peace at last. A little further and we would begin
to glimpse the full glory of Queen Charlotte Sound.

I regard the Marlborough Sounds, with their miniature fiords and valleys, as one of the best-kept secrets in the world. The smells and sounds are so special to me—water, always trickling and gurgling; the sweet, peaty smell of the bush, so lush and clean that its dankness does not repel; the rasping sound of nocturnal opossums gorging themselves on ripe berries; the orchestra of native birds.

I am passionate about sharing these secrets with visitors who might appreciate them. I used to watch tourists get off the interisland ferries at Picton and prepare to take off down south, turning their backs on the breathtaking scenery just round the corner. Sometimes I would offer to take visitors aboard *Rose-Noëlle* for a scenic cruise and a bushwalk on one of the many headlands. They always accepted, and they always enjoyed this treat. Often our different languages meant we couldn't communicate very well, but the sights, sounds, and smells of the Marlborough Sounds spoke for themselves.

As *Rose-Noëlle* rounded the headland into Queen Charlotte Sound, I looked north across to my treasured Kumutoto Bay. This place more than anywhere in the sounds was special to me. As a family we often holidayed across from Kumutoto at Sunshine Bay. I remember my late father, Bill, rowing two or three miles in a clinker dinghy with my younger brother, David, and me to Kumutoto. We would pitch our tent near the beach and wait for darkness. Spearing garfish (like miniature swordfish) was our purpose, and a dark, moonless night ideal for covering our tracks. Dad would wedge an old car battery in the stern of the dinghy to power the spotlight, and while he rowed backward, David and I would take turns at hurling the spear at our prey. The spear was fashioned from a cluster of bicycle spokes and sometimes it went astray, causing the frightened garfish to flutter and flap across the water, leaving a trail of confused phosphorescence in the darkness. David and I would collapse in laughter, the reason for our mission temporarily forgotten.

Back on the beach we would light a fire and throw the garfish—barely an hour out of the water—straight in the pan. The backbone and small bones attached peeled easily away. The rest were so fine we ate them without noticing, hot butter and fish juice dribbling down our chins. For David and me, there was nothing more precious our father could give us than his time.

Years later, Kumutoto Bay continued to be a place of good memories in my adult life. On the New Year's Eve before my fateful trip to Tonga, I sailed *Rose-Noëlle* across there to celebrate the arrival of 1989 with Alan Barnes at his family's holiday home. It was there I met Alan's younger brother, David, who skippered New Zealand's challenge boat *KZ1* in the 1988 America's Cup against Dennis Conner's catamaran. We lost on the water, and the battle continued in court. Nevertheless, David Barnes came home a hero. New Zealanders never conceded defeat. They just figured Dennis Conner had cheated.

Alan, David, and their father, Bob, used to entertain a houseful of guests with recitals on the piano and organ. They were all musically gifted and learned to play by ear. The rest of us sang along from songbooks, a pleasure I will long remember.

As we sailed past Kumutoto Bay, Christabel, Malcolm, and Rose watched our progress from across the other side at Karaka Point. *Rose-Noëlle* was scudding along and made a pretty sight against the deep blue of Queen Charlotte Sound.

It was an ideal time to get cracking on those chores that had been bothering me before leaving. We took turns on the wheel and spent the afternoon lubricating the blocks and fittings to make sure everything worked smoothly. I hoisted Rick up the mast in the bosun's chair to thread a new Kevlar rope down the outside, ready to use as a spare mainsheet should the one inside the mast break.

We snacked on tea and gingernut biscuits and Christabel's scones. No one usually feels like eating for the first day or two at sea; it takes a while for the stomach to get used to the motion of the boat. Although I have spent much of my life in and around boats, I get seasick just standing on the edge of a wharf watching a yacht bobbing up and down alongside. I well remembered the agony and misery of dry retching in rough weather just hours after leaving port. This time I had taken some wonderful English seasick tablets, guaranteed not to let the skipper nod off while on watch but effective enough to quell the dreaded queasiness.

I felt a lingering regret as we cleared Tory Channel and headed out into Cook Strait. My last link with home. But ahead was a new adventure and to me that was what life was all about. Overhead a float plane flew in low, returning on its regular afternoon flight from Porirua, near Wellington, to its base at Picton. Leaving Phil on the wheel, I ducked below and switched to channel sixty-three on the VHF radio.

"Float Air, Float Air, this is *Rose-Noëlle*, do you read? Over."

The pilot did not reply, but back at the airline's Picton base, secretary Rebecca Downes answered almost immediately. She recognized my voice from the many times I had dropped in for a chat with the float plane crew on my way to the shower block. Rebecca had also been aboard *Rose-Noëlle* on the day I first took Phil Hofman out for a sail.

"Gidday, what can I do for you, John?" she said casually.

I asked if she would call Christabel in Blenheim and pass on the Royal Sunset Island Resort in Nukualofa as my forwarding address.

"No problem. Whereabouts are you?"

"Just clearing Tory Channel," I told her.

"Have a good trip. Catch you later," she replied chirpily.

That was at 4:15 P.M., 1 June 1989—the last radio contact I had with anyone while aboard *Rose-Noëlle*.

Back at Glenrose, our old family home now owned by Christabel and Malcolm, the telephone rang. It was Rebecca passing on the address and our latest position, the last message Christabel was to hear for more than four months until I rang her on 2 October and said simply, "I'm back."

Once out in Cook Strait the wind picked up a little, and Phil and I put a reef in the mainsail. I went below to bring up our first way-point on the satellite navigation and to check my bearings with Baring Head at the eastern entrance to Wellington Harbor while there was still light. Everything lined up, and I was satisfied that my calculations of the night before were correct.

Up on deck Rick was at the wheel. Even with a reefed mainsail, *Rose-Noëlle* was skipping across the Strait . . . eight, ten, twelve knots and sometimes peaking at sixteen in winds of fifteen to eighteen knots. Rick and Phil could not believe the speed.

Sailing a multihull when you have been used to a mono-hull is like accelerating in a Porsche after driving a Morris Minor. I've always loved the feeling of speed, and my crew seemed to be enjoying that same thrill. That appreciation of *Rose-Noëlle*'s speed and performance was to turn to fear, and in one case panic, within a couple of days.

As the sky began to darken on that first night, one of the Cook Strait ferries came up behind us. I checked to make sure all our navigation lights were on and, when the ferry was quite close, altered course thirty degrees to starboard and waited until it had passed before resuming our course. Weeks later when we were reported overdue, a passenger from the ferry rang Christabel and said he had noticed the four of us up on deck looking at something, and he wondered then if anything was wrong. There wasn't, apart from the crew getting edgy over whether the ferry had seen us.

Just before 8:15 that night I tuned the ham radio to six megs and strained to hear any message from Jim Bramwell. I sat for about ten minutes turning the dial backward and forward a little to make sure I didn't miss the channel. Nothing. I switched the set off and closed the door to the radio locker.

A few minutes later in Picton, Jim Bramwell tuned his radio to the six-meg band and began calling *Rose-Noëlle*—he was convinced that 8:30 P.M. was the time arranged for the radio schedule. Jim called repeatedly and after hearing nothing, read out the latest weather fax forecast and signed off.

* * *

That night we took a second reef in the mainsail as the wind picked up and the seas grew choppy. It was dark as we sailed past the mouth of Wellington Harbor, and the lights of the city winked a reassuring message. I thought of all those people sitting down to dinner or stretched out in front of the fire watching television with their families. For a moment I wished we were already in Tonga. I shivered in the cold and went below to make a cup of tea. No one felt like eating much. We nibbled on Rose's fruit cake, our stomachs not yet ready to face a full dinner.

We were in for a long night. Jim had already taken an unsuccessful turn at the wheel, and I realized that teaching him to steer would have to wait until lighter and brighter conditions. I explained to him that steering *Rose-Noëlle* was no different to steering a car except that the trimaran responded more slowly. He tried but kept going off course and he obviously was not happy with the responsibility. He had never sailed a boat before, so I didn't push the point.

From then on Rick, Phil, and I took two-hour watches with four hours off. *Rose-Noëlle* surged ahead in the darkness, leaving behind her a streaming wake lit with phosphorescence. The hiss of the hulls cutting through the water and the whirling of the wind generator were the only sounds above the wind.

Later I dozed fitfully in the aft cabin, snuggled fully clothed beneath a duvet. I knew that with an inexperienced crew on board I would have to be on the alert if something should go wrong. By raising my head and peering through a small window in the aft cabin I could see out into the cockpit to check on the helmsman.

I heard Phil call Rick to take over the helm. Rick fumbled in the dark for a torch to find his boots and coat. Phil came down below, pulled off his wet-weather gear, and crawled into his single bunk. I don't like to use the cabin lights at night: it wastes power, and I think it wise that crew should get to know the layout of a boat in the dark. That first night Rick, Jim, and Phil were constantly switching on torches to find their belongings and get dressed.

The cold hit me in the face out in the cockpit when it was my turn on watch. I closed my eyes for a moment and imagined the heat of the sun warming my skin as I lay on deck in the islands. I checked my bearings and realized we were approaching the second way-point off Cape Palliser. Ducking below, I used the satellite navigation to bring up our new compass bearing. After rounding Cape Palliser, I adjusted the sails to follow the Wairarapa coastline. The wind had risen to around twenty knots; *Rose-Noëlle* picked up her skirts and fairly flew in this sort of weather. I hoped for a steady southerly to push us to Tonga. It would only be a matter of time and the right conditions before the crew came to love the experience of being at the wheel and feel as exhilarated by the speed as I was.

The next morning the winds were still northerly, and we gradually headed out to sea. We could still see the Wairarapa coast, but the further we got from land, the more I relaxed. The wind had eased a little, so we shook a reef out of the main. Finally we lost sight of New Zealand completely. Ahead of us were sunshine, palm trees, and smiling Polynesian people with bronzed skins.

That evening I heated up Christabel's chili con carne. No one really felt hungry, but once it was on a plate in front of us, we ate it. Rick had trouble at the helm in the dark that night, and I suggested he take off his balaclava and steer by the feel of the wind on his face. He did so and later said it was the most useful piece of advice on sailing anyone had given him.

During the night a foreign fishing boat slowly gained on us, but it took three two-hour watches before it finally caught up. I was on the helm around midnight when it passed, and the others came up on deck to watch. It was well lit, and we could see its superstructure clearly. We watched with detached interest as it passed. The next time we saw a ship we would desperately try to make ourselves seen, but in vain.

On the morning of 3 June, I came off watch at six o'clock and wrote the last entry I was to make in *Rose-Noëlle*'s log. I noted that the barometer was dropping but that the winds were still light to moderate northwesterlies. We were steering magnetic north and making good progress. Exactly twenty-four hours later, the logbook was upside down and underwater.

Around midmorning the wind suddenly changed to a southerly, and a strong one at that. It caught us all a little unaware. Rick and Phil reefed the mainsail, and I came up on deck to give them a hand. As the day wore on, the wind strength grew and so did the alarm of the crew. I reefed down again and finally dropped the mainsail altogether. *Rose-Noëlle* was running with the waves under a partly furled headsail, but she wasn't yet surfing. The conditions were no different to those I had sailed through many times before.

Phil was on the wheel but was having trouble steering. He seemed really frightened by the strength of the wind and the speed we were doing, yet of the three crew he had the most experience as a sailor. I took the wheel, and the steering felt fine to me, but Phil's alarm had unsettled the others. I guess to them it felt like being a passenger in a racing car.

Rick and Phil wanted to lay the small sea squid to help slow us down and, even though I wasn't at all alarmed by our speed, I agreed. It was the beginning of a series of events over which I should have taken more control. It was my boat, and I was by far the most experienced person on board. I had sailed forty thousand miles in my cruising life and had encountered conditions in the Roaring Forties that made this storm seem like a Sunday afternoon cruise. I thought we should sail through the storm as I have sailed through countless others. After all, running with the wind is the ideal condition for a multihull in a storm. But I had an extremely nervous and vocal crew and, instead of telling them to shut up, I bowed to their demands.

We laid the sea anchor out astern and it did slow us down, but not enough. An hour or so later, Rick and Phil wanted to reduce sail still further. Neither of them was happy steering, and they were becoming more nervous by the minute.

The roller-furling headsail was still new to me, so rather than experiment by furling it in to create a small spitfire jib, I rolled it in completely and reverted to old habits. The wind had come up even more and was gusting up to forty knots. I left Phil on the wheel to steer the boat downwind while I went for'ard to hank a storm jib onto the inner stay.

I jumped down into the security of the for'ard cockpit, a waist-deep hole covered by two hatches. It wouldn't do for me to topple overboard right now. The storm jib ready, I shouted back toward the aft cockpit. Rick uncleated the halyard and hauled the sail up. Unfortunately no one thought to grab hold of the jib sheet. Within a matter of seconds I was staring up at a twisted, tangled mess of sail and rope. The wind had whipped at the sail, pulling the sheets free and sending them cracking into the air before winding themselves firmly around the flapping jib.

The noise of an out-of-control sail in a storm is a little like gunfire; it can be very frightening if you are unused to it. I yelled for Rick to drop the jib and then began to untangle the mess in order to try again. But the incident had unsettled the crew still further, and they were no longer willing to steer the boat.

Rick came for'ard and told me that they wanted to lay the big parachute anchor. Suddenly Phil lost control at the wheel and *Rose-Noëlle* rounded up. We were lying ahull to the storm, massive green waves heaving and rolling toward us. We were drifting sideways at a rate of knots, over swells capped with foam. I still wanted to try and set the storm jib so that we could take advantage of the tail wind and make some headway, but again I bowed to pressure.

We pulled the sea squid into the cockpit, and Rick and I went for'ard to lay the parachute anchor from the bow over the main hull. Phil had told me the day before we left that he had trouble getting all the kinks out of the parachute warp. Now Rick and I were sitting up on deck, harnessed on, trying to feed the parachute out while *Rose-Noëlle* tipped and slewed sideways across the waves.

As soon as the huge piece of silk hit the water, it took off and the rope tore through our hands. I took a turn round a bollard, but the rope reeled out so fast it chafed and threatened to crush our fingers at the slightest lapse in attention. Whenever we came across a tangle in the rope I would whip an extra turn on the bollard to give Rick time to sort out the snarl. We worked for more than an hour, and by the time the job was done, we were exhausted, wet, and cold.

Once the parachute was set, *Rose-Noëlle* behaved beautifully, turning into the wind and slowing right down. We stopped slamming sideways, and the boat held steady. I was impressed with this new piece of equipment. The orange buoy marking the trip line bobbed seventy meters out in front of the boat. When the storm died and we were ready to bring the parachute in, we would simply haul on that trip line and back it would come.

I lashed the wheel, and we went below to ride out the storm, knowing there was nothing more we could do. We were about fifteen miles off our third way-point, which put us about 140 miles off the coast. I considered that gave us a good safety margin for lying ahull.

We crawled into our beds and lay listening to the tons of angry water heaving around us. I curled up on the dinette seat and grimaced as the storm sporadically dumped a load of seawater on our topsides, but I wasn't worried about the pounding *Rose-Noëlle* was taking. I knew from having the hull stress-tested during construction that this would not trouble her. I was more concerned about my soaked bedding in the aft cabin. Every time one of those massive waves filled the steering cockpit, the water overflowed through a hole for the steering cables, sending streams of cold seawater through the hollow coamings and into the aft cabin. The windows were also leaking, the first time I had experienced that problem. Jim and I had tried to seal them with silicone, but without much success. I decided to head to higher ground until the weather improved.

During the evening the motion of the boat changed. Once again she was shuddering as waves slammed into us from side on; we were lying ahull. Unbeknown to us while we were resting in our bunks, dozing and listening to the stereo, the trip line had gradually become entangled with the parachute anchor rope. As the tangle worked its way down seventy meters of rope, it finally fouled the parachute.

I struggled into a safety harness and clambered out on deck to inspect the parachute. As *Rose-Noëlle* was pushed sideways up to the crest of each huge wave, the partly opened parachute would grab in the water, jerking her back and allowing the full force of the water to slam against her resistant hull.

I was about to clip my safety harness on when I heard a roar above the noise of the storm. I had a split second to turn and register the size of the wave before grabbing for the for'ard rail. Water thundered down and washed quickly past. I took one look at the heaving rope holding the parachute and realized there was nothing I could do to untangle it; nor could I pull it in with the fouled trip line. There was a risk we would get our fingers or feet caught and crushed if we tried to tackle it. But I was unwilling to cut $800 worth of parachute silk and line completely adrift when I had only just bought it; moreover, up until that point, I had been pleased with its performance.

As I turned to go below, I noticed the trampoline on the starboard wingdeck (between the main hull and the float) flapping. It had been ripped from its frame by tons of pounding water. I pulled the material free and dropped it in the cockpit, intending to restitch it during a leisurely moment in Tonga.

Down below, Jim and Rick were still recovering from being hurled from their bunks into the dinette table by the force of the wave. They were to be turfed out of bed several more times that night. I told them my reasons for leaving the parachute where it was. No one seemed particularly keen to go up on deck and attempt to free it, so after some discussion we decided to sit tight.

Apart from the occasional very large wave, the seas were not too steep, and I had convinced myself that *Rose-Noëlle* would never turn over. I was sure of that even when I was building her. So confident was I that I decided not to build

escape hatches in the main hull. In hindsight it would have
been wiser to cut the $800 parachute adrift and save my
$250,000 boat. However, thinking back on the size and
velocity of the wave that capsized *Rose-Noëlle*, I suspect
it might not have made much difference.

That night I made eggs with chili for dinner. Again none
of us really felt hungry—in fact, Jim was feeling quite
seasick—but we ate it. It was the last hot meal we were
to have for a long time.

Later we lay in our bunks, listening to the fury of the
storm lash out at *Rose-Noëlle*. The wind generator was
spinning at a nerve-racking, high-pitched scream—eeeh,
EEEH, EEEEH—as it struggled to respond to gusts of
between fifty and sixty knots. I was worried about the
batteries overloading, because there was no regulator on
the wind generator system to prevent overcharging, so I
turned on the stereo and tuned in to a local radio station to
use up some power. The music seemed to calm our nerves
and take our minds off the storm.

All except Phil. He had steadily worked himself into
a panic. Nothing Rick, Jim, or I could say or do would
calm him down. He was absolutely convinced the boat
was going to capsize. He was terrified and at times close
to hysteria. He would lie for a few minutes in his bunk,
then leap up, peer out the window, and call out, "We're
going to flip over. We're going to flip over." Finally Phil
got out of his bunk and strode over to the radio locker
next to the chart table and pulled it open. He switched on
the VHF radio and began calling on channel sixteen: "This
is the *Rose-Noëlle*, this is the *Rose-Noëlle*, can anyone
hear me?"

Phil kept calling over and over again. When there was
no reply, I reminded him that the VHF was a line-of-sight
frequency. We were too far out to be heard by anyone
unless there happened to be a ship passing close by. Phil
then demanded that I tune the ham radio and call for help.
He had watched me tune it each night at 8:15, listening for
Jim Bramwell's radio schedule. I told him that I was not

The wave hit *Rose-Noëlle* like a freight train roaring out of
the darkness.

licensed to use the ham radio and that I would only use it in a real emergency.

I did not consider a storm an emergency—a yacht cruising in the Pacific could expect to encounter five or six storms before reaching a destination. I also pointed out that even if we did call up on the ham radio, no one in their right mind would come out in those sorts of conditions in the middle of the night. Any rescue would be left until the morning or until the weather subsided a little. But Phil was adamant. He wanted a helicopter to come and take him off *Rose-Noëlle*, and he wanted it now. He was like a man possessed—gripped by an uncontrollable fear that was distorting his logic. I thought it possible that in his panic he might try to do something stupid. He was fully dressed, ready for what he considered was inevitable. In the end he was right.

Phil's terror was contagious. Rick and Jim wanted to know where all the safety gear was kept. They got out life jackets and the emergency flares, which were later to be washed away after we capsized. Rick removed the electronic position-indicating radio beacon (EPIRB) from the radio locker and put it in a waterproof bag. All this activity made Phil even worse. He was almost at the stage where he needed a straightjacket.

The night seemed to stretch on forever. Jim had brought some cassette tapes with him, and we played a selection—Bob Dylan, Eric Clapton, Bruce Springsteen. We tuned in to several radio stations and listened to the news—mass killings in China's Tiananmen Square. I put on a tape of an Australian comedian, Kevin Bloody Wilson, in an attempt to lighten the mood on board. I've had people roaring with laughter when listening to the tape, but this time nobody smiled. We heard a marine weather forecast telling us what we already knew: a gale warning with winds averaging thirty to forty knots—and, I knew, capable of gusting to fifty knots or more.

I don't think any of us really slept that night. Around four A.M. the wind began to drop, and the fear on board began to evaporate with the diminishing sounds of the storm. The waves were no longer topped by boiling white foam, and Rick thought that was a good sign. Phil was calmer because he knew that shortly it would get light and he would no longer have to lie in the dark waiting for the end. By six o'clock we had had enough of being at the mercy of the weather. We decided to have breakfast and get under way again. But privately I knew that the seas would not die as quickly as they had come up. Huge waves can roll for miles and suddenly join together to form one massive wall of rolling water, nine to twelve meters high.

It was then we heard the roar of that final wave, which set us neatly on our heads and continued on its way. Our lives would never be quite the same again.

TWO

A Matter of Days

As soon as the boat capsized, Phil's fear was gone. He had been more terrified at the thought of turning upside down than when it actually happened. But in the place of his fear was an attitude far more dangerous. He was convinced he was going to die, and there was nothing he or anyone else could do about it. Phil was adamant we were doomed, and weeks later he still thought the same way. He just didn't seem to care about survival, and that made him a dangerous person to have on board.

The water level in the cabin had stopped rising. Because the aft cabin, in behind the galley, had been the lowest level on the boat, it became the highest once we capsized. But it wasn't high enough. Water sloshed over the ceiling, now the floor, soaking the bedding and mattress that had tumbled onto it. We would have to build a platform to keep ourselves dry until we were rescued.

But first there was a more urgent problem. The two batteries that powered the boat's electrics were stored in the bilge locker of the aft cabin, and the capsize had tipped them out of their boxes, leaving one dangling in mid-air and leaking battery acid. I had read about the dangers of battery fumes in accounts of multihull capsizes, so I wasted no time in cutting it down.

I waded through the main cabin and threw the battery out through the open companionway, stopping to peer below in the half light at the tangle of rigging wires and stays attached to the remains of the mast. The mast had snapped off at the first spreader. What a mess; what a waste. I shook my head clear. There were hours of work ahead of us before we would be allowed to wallow in our misfortune. Even with the offending battery buried three miles down, the acrid smell lingered for hours.

The other battery had fallen out completely and seemed okay, so I stored it in what was the bilge locker below the galley floor, now with its hatches hanging open. This space was to be used as our cockpit and equipment cupboard over the coming months. There were so few places above the water-level in which to store anything, and very little space in the aft cabin. Only food and equipment essential for survival would have the honor of sharing that tiny space with us.

There was a third battery up for'ard to power the electric capstan for winching in the anchor, a luxury I had conceded after injuring my back years ago. Again I waded through the main cabin and found that this battery, too, had fallen out. It did not appear to be leaking, so I propped it up in a hanging locker on one of the few shelves above water.

The water inside the main cabin had quickly turned to a murky soup after we capsized. Rose's large container of muesli had spilled everywhere, and a five-kilo bag of wholemeal flour had split open when it toppled out of a locker beneath the dinette seat. I asked Jim to feel around with his feet and try to save anything he could find. There was no point in diving until the water had cleared.

At one stage Phil watched his camera float past in its case and out through the companionway. Much later he cursed himself for not scooping it up, because tucked inside the case was $400 in cash and his new passport. Right then he didn't think there was much point.

For the next few hours we worked solidly on the aft cabin; even Phil did. I just told him what to do, and he followed orders in a dazed sort of manner. Rick, although a wiry build, was strong and used to physical exertion. We salvaged everything we could find to pack down on top of the mattress and bedding to build a platform. I asked Phil to pull out two large, deep drawers in the galley which we could use as a base. I soon realized that I should have attended to it myself, because all the contents dropped into

the water and washed away. We could have done with some
of the items in those drawers later on.

We grabbed blankets, wet-weather gear, boots, clothes,
cupboard doors, and sleeping bags—anything to plug up
the space. From the lazaret cupboard at the foot of the aft
cabin I pulled all sorts of gear and stuffed it down the space
beneath us—even two dozen toilet rolls. Rick and Jim each
had a synthetic groundsheet, and we laid those across the
top of the platform.

One by one we crawled through the tiny entranceway and
lay down. Everything, including our clothes, was soaking
wet. We huddled like sardines in a tin in a space the size of a
queen-size bed. We had to lie facing the same way, nestled
against each other like spoons, wet spoons, in a cutlery set.
Above us we had just twenty centimeters of headroom. It
was like being trapped in a dark, wet cave. Suddenly I
remembered the words of a clairvoyant I had visited shortly
before leaving on this trip: "You will have an adventure in
an underground cave." Was this it? I wondered.

At that stage we still believed that our "adventure" would be
short-lived. We had the EPIRB and we figured it was only
a matter of days before we were rescued. Rick had grabbed
the EPIRB bag as soon as we capsized, and it was now
stored safely in the bilge space overhead in the aft cabin.

We lay wedged together for a while, trying to warm up
before realizing we had not eaten since the day before. Rick
and I waded into the main cabin in search of food. The
green apples Christabel and Malcolm had collected kept
bobbing to the surface, and we tossed these back to Phil
and Jim. I knew there was a good supply of canned food in
one of the lockers beneath the dinette. The hatch had come
off and a lot of the cans had toppled out, but there were
still plenty jammed in there, enough to make it an important
cache. I paused over the split bag of wholemeal flour but
then pulled it out of the way and let it fall into the water.
What possible use could it be? I was to remember the flour
that I had tossed away so extravagantly when, weeks later,
food became the most important and valuable commodity

on board. I retrieved a three-liter cask of orange juice, a few 1.25-liter plastic bottles of soft drink, and an assortment of canned food from the locker and waded back to the aft cabin. Meanwhile, Rick had been raiding the fridge, which was upside down and underwater. He rescued a block of cheese, butter, two liters of milk, and two legs of smoked mutton ham.

It was a bizarre picnic, lying soaking wet in the dark with the sickly smell of battery acid still in the air, listening to the fury of the storm. We sliced off pieces of ham with my fishing knife and ate it with cheese and English mustard. The spice and condiment cupboard was in the galley in reach of the aft cabin, and although its contents were upside down, they were mostly dry.

We drank juice and milk until our thirst was quenched and the taste of salt had gone from our mouths. The meal, though cold, helped to warm us. Later on that night we ate more of the mutton ham and cheese. Rationing didn't even occur to us, so convinced were we that rescue, hot meals, and hot baths were only a matter of days away. We decided that we should set the EPIRB going as soon as possible before we drifted further away from land. Phil and I waded into the for'ard cabin to cut an escape hatch. I had a large range of tools on board; fortunately they were still trapped in the for'ard hanging locker. Using a chisel, a hammer, and a keyhole saw, we hacked a hole through the side of the hull leading out onto the wingdeck. The toilet was in the way and, as we couldn't think of a use for an upside-down porcelain pan, we smashed it out with the hammer.

Rick and Phil clamped the EPIRB to the side of the hull with the aerial poking outside and switched it on. The red light flashed straight away, signalling a message to the outside world. We were elated. Now all we had to hope was that we would drift beneath a commercial airline flight path in the next week or so and that the flight crew were listening. Jim, Rick, and Phil were sure we would be rescued within a couple of days, so the mood in our cramped quarters lifted immediately. I thought it might take a little longer because of our distance from the coast.

When we capsized I estimated our position to be 179° 30′ east longitude, 40° south latitude—about 140 miles off the Wairarapa coast on the east coast of the North Island. We were well outside the range for domestic aircraft flying the length of New Zealand and would need to pin our hopes on an international flight.

Rick and Jim huddled together on one side of the cabin, Phil and I on the other. I thanked my lucky stars Phil was carrying all that weight. He was like a big, damp, soft hot-water bottle. Although we were cramped and uncomfortable, we needed the warmth and closeness of four bodies in those early weeks. It was midwinter, and we were wet for much of the time. We would have shivered uncontrollably if there had been just two of us in the cabin, and if I had been on my own, I do not think I would have ever warmed up. I was thankful for the layer of wool next to my skin; even though it was wet, it was warm.

In those early, dismal hours, Rick suggested that we talk aloud to keep our minds active and to stop us dwelling too much on our plight. I guessed this was a technique he had learned as part of bush survival. First we played games, mostly word games. At one stage Rick and Jim bet Phil and me that we couldn't spell their surnames. Phil and I spelt out N-A-L-E-P-K-A without too much difficulty. Rick's name we knew we would have more trouble with. As I lay on my stomach pondering in the semidarkness, I caught sight of something that brought a smile to my face, even in such gloomy circumstances. Unbeknown to Rick, I was leaning on his life jacket. There, written clearly on the collar, was Rick's surname.

I nudged Phil, pointed, and he grinned. "Oh, I don't know . . . this is a tough one," I said, scratching my head. "What about if Phil and I guess a letter each at a time?" Phil played along admirably. He and I struggled through, letter by letter, slyly reading it off the jacket. Rick couldn't believe his ears. No one ever spelled it correctly, he said. When Phil and I finally owned up, the sound of our laughter was, just for a few seconds, louder than the storm. It was one of the few times during the entire 119 days that we did laugh together.

When we ran out of word games, Rick wanted us to talk about ourselves, about our childhoods, families, friends. We lay there in the dark and, one by one, told our stories—mumbling into the back of the person jammed in front. No one really wanted to talk or play games—me least of all, I dislike games of any sort—we just wanted to sink into our own miserable thoughts; but we went along with the idea because we knew we had to keep one another's spirits up.

I found it difficult to talk to three virtual strangers about private and precious parts of my life, so I tended to hold back. As time went on, we would gradually discover more and more about each other. Rick and Jim, already friends, were to become particularly close, effectively shutting Phil and me out.

Phil was forty-one years old, an easygoing guy who enjoyed a few beers with friends at the local hotel and followed a simple, straightforward life. He and his wife, Karen, had been together since they were teenagers, and they had rarely spent a day apart. Their two teenage children, Chantelle and Dion, lived with them on their yacht at Picton. Three years earlier Phil had undergone a triple heart bypass. About a year later he gave up smoking but still had trouble keeping his weight down. Karen was very much the breadwinner of the family, leaving Phil to do odd jobs around the yacht and casual work around the wharf area. Phil grew up in Auckland but moved to the South Island when he was twenty and worked as a powerhouse attendant at Aviemore, near Timaru, then as a Railways storeman in Dunedin. He was a fairly quiet sort and rarely showed any emotion during our time adrift, apart from his initial terror during the storm.

Rick was thirty-one and he, too, had fought a battle with his health. Three years earlier doctors told him he had a brain tumor and gave him two years at the most to live. But Rick never believed he would die. The tumor affected the right side of his body, making it difficult for him to run or even walk. For someone used to a physical way of life, it must have been hard to accept. The tumor defied medical opinion by disappearing, only to reappear in a sad twist of fate barely three months after our safe return.

Rick was a fairly dominant character, testy and quick-tempered. At other times he could be gently spoken and loved talking. In contrast to Phil, he was a good communicator and was to spend hours chatting with Jim in the coming months about what he felt or thought. He had worked as a policeman in Auckland and as an Outward Bound instructor in the early 1980s. He was very capable and practical, and if ever I needed a hand to do a complicated job I always asked Rick to help. During the summer Rick and Heather ran a sea-kayak business with their friends, neighbors, and business partners Peter Brady and Jenny Jones. In the off-season Rick ran bush-survival courses for young people, and I surmised he must be used to dealing with those who followed his instructions and advice without question. He and I were to clash more than once in the coming months when he could not accept what he saw as my dogmatic views on how things should be done.

In the first few weeks Rick seemed to be looking for a fight, and the aggression in his eyes made me want to say, "Beam me up, Scotty," to quote *Star Trek.*

He seemed to be convinced that he had to take action and *force* his way out of the capsize situation. He could not accept that none of us had any control over our circumstances—we were being taken for a ride, and the only control we had was over ourselves.

I realized that if we were all to survive, I could not counter or dispel Rick's feeling of resentment and aggression. He, most of all, had to have his own truth. Even so, tension between us grew. I could not tell whether he resented me personally as well as the situation we were all in—probably both and more. The tension led to a showdown, much as I tried to avoid conflict. I've always considered that I win most of my fights because I can run faster, but this time I couldn't walk away. I had to state my mind.

"I don't know whether it's your police background," I began, "or that your time at Outward Bound made you a sort of overlord to a bunch of teenagers, but on board this boat you're acting like a little Hitler."

He was taken aback, became more agreeable for a time, and then lapsed into his independent, forceful ways. I had to wonder how he ever managed to relate comfortably to his former colleagues in the police and at Outward Bound.

Perhaps Rick had grown up to see himself as a leadership person, whereas his former employment and his circumstances on *Rose-Noëlle* called for joint responsibility, mateship, sharing, call it what you will.

Jim, a thirty-eight-year-old, was from Minneapolis, Minnesota. He, too, had won a personal battle, a struggle to kick a ten-year drug habit. Jim joined the U.S. army when he was seventeen and was sent to Europe. It was while in the army that Jim began smoking marijuana and using other drugs. He later trained as a cook and worked on construction sites and in restaurants, but it wasn't until his late twenties that he realized his drug habit had become a crutch. With the help of his ex-wife, he straightened himself out and started a new life. Jim had come to New Zealand originally on a cycling tour and later returned to work at the Outward Bound School.

Jim was baby-faced with a charming smile and a gentle manner to match. He was very much the diplomat of the four of us; I found I could relate to him better than I could to Rick or Phil, particularly if we were on our own.

I talked about my father, Bill Glennie, and my admiration for a man who set his mind to a task and did it well. He was competitive in cycling, rowing, and shooting, kept racing pigeons, played and taught the bagpipes and painstakingly nurtured new varieties of rhododendron in the garden at Glenrose.

Mum grew roses until our huge garden was just a mass of blooms. She, too, was musical, teaching the piano and pipe organ and coaching choral singing. My parents always encouraged us to set goals and work toward them.

As a teenager I was obsessed with the idea of becoming a top cyclist. I cycled hundreds of gruelling kilometers each week in training, determined one day to represent my country at the Olympics. I left school to train as a boatbuilder at Morgan's boatyard in Picton, cycling twenty-seven kilometers each way between work and home in Blenheim. My younger brother David and I used to race on Saturdays and take part in a 160-kilometer training ride on Sundays with friends from the local cycling club. We used to hurtle down the Grove Track above Picton, bent low over the handlebars, the wind whipping at our hair and stinging our eyes, daring each other to keep up the speed without touching the brakes. Occasionally one of us would end up in a heap at the bottom of the hill with the bike bent round our ears.

Racing was a different matter, something that I took seriously. If there was an audience watching, nothing could stop me from winning. I had learned I could do anything at all if I set my mind to it. There was nothing, I thought, that would keep me from reaching the top. Then one day as I was cycling home along a country road, I crested the brow of a small rise and came face to face with a car on the wrong side of the road. We hit head-on, and the accident left me with a badly injured leg, wiping my hopes for the Olympics and leaving me wondering "Why me?" All I had was a scrapbook full of newspaper clippings covering the cycling careers of myself and David and a collection of cycling medals I had won over the years. The scrapbook and medals, some belonging to my father from his days as a cyclist, were tucked away in a locker on *Rose-Noëlle* with other sentimental treasures from my past.

In a way the accident gave me a chance to switch dreams—from reaching the ultimate as a cyclist to building my own boat and sailing away. One of my favorite books as a teenager was Eric Hiscock's *Beyond the West Horizon*; I used to look at a photograph of his yacht anchored at Moorea and imagine visiting exotic places. But there was always one nagging doubt, one problem. I suffer from chronic travel sickness, whether I go by car, boat, plane, or train. I knew that if I sailed to the South Pacific, I would be sick all the way. The thought of disgracing myself while crewing on someone else's boat was more than I could bear. From my years of cycling, I already knew how to ignore pain, tiredness, frustration, and discomfort in order to get to the top. I reasoned that seasickness was something that I would have to suffer in order to reach the pot of gold at the end of the horizon. There was no doubt about it, I would have to build my own boat.

THREE

Survival

The southerly storm that had capsized *Rose-Noëlle* blew for
four days. Wind and spray lashed the upturned hull, and
huge waves tipped us up on the starboard float time and
again, raising a new fear. What would happen if another
rogue wave tipped the boat back the right way up? The four
of us were wedged tightly on our sides, and if *Rose-Noëlle*
flipped again, the drawers, mattresses, and assorted packing
would fall on top of us. With the hull already two-thirds full
of water, we would be trapped below the waterline in the
dark with water flooding in through the aft cabin entrance,
just big enough for one man to crawl through.

I didn't think we would flip, because the flooded hull was
so heavy and had become part of the wave; but Rick, Jim,
and Phil weren't convinced. I knew they were remembering
my assurances that the boat would not capsize in the first
instance. I think they lost confidence in me then; and as
time went on, Rick used to say, "When the boat tipped
over, everything changed."

In terms of who was skipper, who had the say over
the boat, the food, the equipment, things were becoming
difficult.

Food was a top priority at all times, and a basic irri-
tant as well. Even though the boat, gear, and supplies
were mine and continued to be my responsibility, I always
asked the others to join me in a snack whenever I felt
peckish.

Not so Rick and Jim, who simply reached for what
they wanted, a discourtesy that I felt keenly. When I
remonstrated, Jim accepted the breach, but Rick could

not. "Everything changed when the boat capsized," was
his expressive judgment.

Phil was terrified at the thought of being entombed underwater in the aft cabin. We discussed what we would do
should the boat turn over again. The person lying nearest
the opening—which was offset to one side—would crawl
out first, followed by the next closest. We were continually
changing positions so we all had turns at being nearest to
the entrance.

Phil just could not control his fear. He lay listening, his
eyes wide open, and when he felt the yacht roll sideways or
heard a crash, he would be off, our escape plan forgotten.
He would jerk his head up, bang it on the cabintop, and head
for the entrance, no matter what position he was in. We tried
to convince him that if two of us got jammed in the doorway
while trying to get out, we would all be doomed. But it was
no use.

The noise was frightening for all of us, particularly during
the long, long nights, when we counted the hours until day-
light. As *Rose-Noëlle* wallowed up and down in the swell,
the loose cupboard doors would bang . . . bang . . . bang,
setting up a rhythm that made sleep impossible. Although
two-thirds of the mast had broken off, the boom was still
attached to the rigging. It swayed and swung below us and,
as the trimaran rose and fell in the waves, it crashed against
the main cabin below, the boom reverberating through into
our tiny, cramped, miserable world. We lay for hours,
resting, waiting, thinking about home, hoping.

We found a single foam mattress floating in the main
cabin and, after folding it several times, jammed it across
the cabin entrance to stop the surge from washing through,
particularly on a stormy night. The last person in at night,
and so lying nearest the door, would spend ages arranging
the mattress and padding the corners; he knew that without
this protection he would get soaked.

My cotton jeans were cold and wet, so I found a spare
jersey in my locker in the aft cabin, sewed up the neck,
and stuck my legs through the armholes. They made a sort

of crude woollen underwear, and I wore them on cold days throughout our time adrift.

Already a tight unit was forming between Rick and Jim. The cabin was split in half, with Rick and Jim on one side, and Phil and I on the other. When we changed positions, we changed as pairs rather than as individuals. Phil's terrible claustrophobia meant that in those early days he refused to lie in the position furthest from the entrance. That was the worst spot—jammed up against the side of the hull with a panicking Phil jammed on the other side. There was no light and very little fresh air. But I felt protective toward Phil early on, because he had helped me prepare *Rose-Noëlle* for the trip. When it was his turn to lie on the far side of the cabin, I would take it instead.

During those first five days we lay huddled together, trying to keep our spirits up. The thought of the little red light flashing on the EPIRB was a comfort; it was our beacon of hope. We would only have to endure this misery for a few days before we would hear the comforting sound of a Royal New Zealand Air Force (RNZAF) Orion circling overhead, letting us know that help was on the way.

I found a black indelible marker pen floating in the main cabin and tossed it to Rick. Above our heads in the aft cabin were the two empty fiberglass battery boxes, and on the wall of one of them Rick drew three strokes to mark the number of days we had been adrift. In the other battery box we drew up a calendar, noting the day and date of the month. From then on one of us would ceremoniously fill in the details each day. At some point during the four months two of us must have filled in the same day, because when we came ashore we were convinced it was our 120th day adrift, not the 119th.

We soon got sick of wading chest deep in water every time we wanted to look outside through the hole up for'ard, so we decided to cut another hole in the top of the hull, nearer the aft cabin. The ideal place was above the galley, about a meter away from the cabin entrance. Above were the two large hinged hatches, which were now hanging down and flapping as the boat moved in the swell. We clamped the port hatch shut to create a cockpit floor and removed the starboard hatch to give us access. Phil and I hacked the new hole through the port slope of the hull so that once the weather improved we would have easy access up onto the keel.

I had always kept an orange plastic distress V-sheet tied to the top of my mattress in the aft cabin to keep it dry. When we capsized, the V-sheet ended up buried by the mattress, and we didn't find it until a few days later. During a break in the weather we went up on deck and tied it down over the keel. The sight of this lifted our spirits. Should an aircraft pick up our EPIRB signal, Search and Rescue would instantly recognize the V sign.

I was still worried about the possibility of leaking battery fumes and now decided to throw away one of the two batteries I had saved. They were both well topped up, and I thought it possible that I could wire up the EPIRB to one of the batteries should it run out of power before an aircraft picked up the signal. I took one of the batteries, waded forward, and heaved it out of the hole we had cut up for'ard. It bounced heavily as it hit the wingdeck, leaving a black mark. That mark was to be a constant reminder of my foolish haste in throwing out an item we badly needed later on.

I wondered about a safe place to mount the EPIRB, ideally on top of the keel. When I noticed that its casing was tapered, I knew there was a chance it would fit, and it did. It was almost as if it were made to jam in the centerboard slot. It was safe and high up.

The next day I was in the main cabin salvaging gear when I noticed an open locker with equipment jammed inside. I pulled out the hand-held compass and radio direction finder. Then I noticed an electric cord leading from the cupboard into the water and dangling out the companionway. It was the spotlight I used up on deck when coming into port at night. I peered down into the dark blue depths below and pulled on the cord. It was caught on something below, so I worked it carefully until it pulled free. What a prize.

If I could get it to work, we could signal passing ships at night.

On day six, 9 June, the weather calmed, and we were able to go out on deck for the first time to breathe fresh air, feel the weak winter sun on our faces, and ease our cramped limbs. We crawled out of the aft cabin, stepped across the water onto a shelf in the galley cupboard opposite, and hauled ourselves up into our new cockpit. One by one we emerged on deck, climbing through the hole in the top of the hull. It felt good to be out of our tiny, wet cave, but when we stood up and looked around, we realized just how small and alone we were. Everywhere we looked there was sea; not a sign of land nor any sound of aircraft.

Jim was very unsure of himself out on deck during those early days. He felt very vulnerable on the sloping curves of the upturned hull and preferred to sit still rather than move about and risk slipping. I explained to him that even if he did fall in, the boat was drifting at perhaps quarter to half a knot, so he could easily clamber back on board. The water was level with the wingdeck, and there would be no great effort needed to haul himself up. Later on he clambered about the hulls quite confidently, laughing at his early cautiousness.

That first day out on deck we peeled off our damp clothes and inspected our bodies. Saltwater sores had begun to fester on our bodies. I seemed to suffer least from the sores, and I suspect that was because I had a layer of wool against my skin. Rick and Jim still had grazing and bruising on their thighs from hitting the dinette table when *Rose-Noëlle* capsized. I dived in the forward cabin, found the medical kit, and took out some antiseptic cream and another tube of cream for the saltwater sores. Within a couple of days the sores had cleared up, and from then on any tiny cut or abrasion was treated with great success with the cream.

Apart from bruises, we were all in good shape, and I prayed that we would remain that way. Phil was still taking medication for his heart condition, and Rick, who suffered from asthma, had lost his inhaler when we capsized. If either of those two conditions worsened, we were in trouble. Our spirits sank a couple of weeks later when we realized that our precious medical kit had been washed away in the surge by one of the countless storms that plucked and pulled at possessions stored seemingly safely in the main cabin.

I brought the spotlight up on deck that first fine day, squirted it with electrical contact cleaner, and left it to dry out. I then connected it to the remaining battery and found it worked perfectly. However, the process was fiddly, and I knew it would be time-consuming for us to fumble around in the dark trying to connect up the spotlight. The solution was to wire it directly into the battery with a screw-down disconnect switch so that it could be easily and quickly used.

When night fell we shared a can of cold mushroom soup mixed with long-life milk. The sea was very calm, and we decided to stand watch right through. The plan was for Phil and I to share three-hour watches one night and Rick and Jim to share the watches the following night. I took the nine to midnight shift the first night and sat in our new cockpit scanning the blackness, straining to see that first pinpoint of light that signalled human life.

Suddenly I saw something that left me puzzled for the remainder of our time adrift and still does. A great shaft of light, which appeared to be between three and five miles in diameter, shot down from the sky. It went behind the clouds and emerged at eye level, where it flashed and spread, lighting up the whole horizon. I considered the possibility of a meteorite but discounted it because there was no round shape and it left no trail. Whatever it was made no noise and was gone as quickly as it had appeared. When Phil hauled himself up into the cockpit to take his watch, I told him what I had seen, but he saw nothing, and I did not witness such a vision again.

The next night we were hit by another storm, so we abandoned the three-hour watches and lay huddled in our tiny space. We never did resurrect the system. Instead, on fine nights we took turns every hour to scan the horizon before crawling back into the warmth of the cabin.

We soon realized that our soggy sleeping platform in the aft cabin was not good enough. During the gales that hit us every few days in those early weeks, water sloshed up under the platform and surged through any gaps. At times the whole platform floated. We were continually wet, and it was only the fact that our four bodies were jammed tightly together that prevented us from freezing. If the surge didn't get us from beneath the platform, the condensation dripping from above would.

Used to the comfortable beds we had left just days ago, our hips suffered from lying on boards, and we were forced to turn over every hour. When one turned or moved, we all had to move. Just as we seemed to get comfortable, someone would move a foot or an arm, letting in freezing air or encroaching on someone else's space. There were a lot of arguments in those early days. Nobody had enough room. Nobody was happy. Nobody wanted to be there.

Eventually we dismantled the sleeping platform, heaving the sodden packing out through the little opening into the main cabin. There was nowhere to store anything. All the surfaces, benches, and shelves were upside down and underwater. We had to let things float around until we needed them. I had warned the others about the surge in the cabin, but still we managed to lose irreplaceable items through the open companionway. I was particularly dismayed to find some bright orange wet-weather gear had disappeared. I thought it might have been useful to signal planes.

We repacked the aft cabin, and I tried to plug the holes and gaps with clothes, cotton blankets, and life jackets. The result was a little better, and for the moment it would have to do. We were exhausted from the hours of work and once again wet through.

That night as I lay in the darkness I imagined sipping a hot cup of tea. I could almost smell the aroma and feel the hot liquid in my mouth. Phil stirred and raised his head. Strands of wispy hair tickled my face; the cup of tea disappeared. This was something that was to become more annoying as the weeks passed, and Phil's hair grew longer.

The food we had salvaged on the first day was soon finished, but rationing still did not occur to us. I thought there was enough salvageable food on the boat to keep us comfortably fed until help arrived. Although I was reluctant to get wet and cold once again, I had no choice; I was the only one who knew the layout of the boat and the position of the food lockers, and I was the most confident in the water. I stripped off, put on a mask and snorkel, and plunged into the chilly depths of the main cabin.

The suspension of muesli and flour had long since washed away, making it easier to see underwater, but I couldn't help regretting that I had not stored the muesli in a locker so that we could now be enjoying it for breakfast. These hunting expeditions became my responsibility throughout the trip. Rick, Jim, and Phil were reluctant to join me on dives and rarely got in the water even to wash.

After I had been on a long dive I would climb exhausted into the aft cabin, suffering from mild hypothermia and shaking with a deep chill that would stay with me for hours. Phil, Rick, and Jim would take turns sandwiching their bodies against mine while I huddled beneath a single woollen blanket, the only one we had managed to salvage.

Soon after we capsized I found a twenty-liter container of water taken from the tanks at Glenrose; but I was more concerned with finding food in the early days, because I knew *Rose-Noëlle*'s water tanks were full when we left. I always liked a supply of rainwater to drink on a trip rather than rely on the 360 liters of chemically treated water in *Rose-Noëlle*'s tanks taken from the wharf at Picton. We also had several 1.25-liter bottles of lemonade, 7-Up, and Coke safely stored in our makeshift pantry.

With the milk, water, and fruit juice gone, we started on the soft drink. I thought it was time to siphon some water from the boat's main supply, so again I stripped off and waded into the main cabin with the empty water bottle and a funnel. One of the water tanks was beneath the floor in the main cabin by the dinette, and it was now above my head. I unscrewed the cap carefully, wondering how I was going to stop 140 liters of fresh water gushing down on top of me. I held the funnel and bottle ready and pulled the cap off. A trickle of water poured down my hand, and I felt my chest tighten with disbelief. The tank was empty.

I waded back toward the aft cabin and checked the second water tank above my head. Nothing. Jim, Phil and Rick had heard my involuntary "Oh no!" when I discovered the first tank empty and were now silent and watchful. I crawled back into the cabin and inspected the third water tank above our heads. Not a drop.

I knew then what had happened. Like most water tanks on boats, they were fitted with plastic air-breather hoses to release air as the tanks are being filled. When *Rose-Noëlle* capsized, the water had slowly drained away through the hoses while we were building our sleeping platform in the aft cabin.

The loss of water was a blow to our morale, but the EPIRB was still flashing a comforting signal, and we still had several bottles of soft drink left. In a strange, fatalistic sort of way I wondered whether it was such a bad thing that the water had gone. Maybe it meant we would be rescued all the more quickly.

As I lay curled on my side that night with Phil wedged on one side and Jim on the other, I mulled over the problem of the breather hoses in a capsize. Suddenly it was obvious. Next time I would fit a tap at the end of each hose that could be closed once the tank was full. If a multihull turned over, the tap would become a useful siphon by which to drain water from the tank overhead. I made a mental note to hunt for a pencil and paper on my next dive expedition to begin to write down these ideas. Someone stretched and moved; suddenly the four of us were uncomfortable again. It was time to change position.

Eight days after we capsized, the EPIRB stopped transmitting. The beacon had done what the manual said it would do; now we were on our own. We were silently despondent, each thinking private thoughts. I wasn't altogether surprised the signal had not been picked up. We were 140 miles off the coast when we capsized and, as each day passed, we were drifting east, away from New Zealand, at a rate of about twelve to fifteen miles. The EPIRB had a radius of one hundred nautical miles, so it was likely that local aircraft would be too far away to pick up our emergency signal. We might have been lucky enough to have been picked up by an international aircraft, although flights over the area in which we were drifting were infrequent. Even though the beacon was useless, it still represented a lifebuoy to us, and we carefully stowed it in the aft cabin.

Phil seemed once again to have resigned himself to our plight. I couldn't decide which version I preferred—the Phil who panicked or the Phil who stared blankly out to sea and seemed disinterested in our plans for survival. There was, however, one thing in which Phil was always interested—food. If rationing had been left to him, our supplies would have dwindled rapidly.

At first we shared a can of food among the four of us. But after the EPIRB stopped transmitting and we had to face the possibility of drifting around for longer than a few days, we began to ration what we ate and drank. A single can began to last four meals. We would put the food in a bowl and hand it round, savoring the two or three spoonfuls that made up a meal.

We seemed to be always arguing about what and how much to eat. The only solution was to vote. Gradually we developed a workable and fair democratic system, where each of us spoke before we voted. If the subject was to do with food and whether or not we should eat something, Phil would say, "Well, it's no good asking me. You know what my opinion is." These discussions would become quite intense and sometimes argumentative; if nothing else, they helped to pass the time. Jim was a careful thinker. He would speak slowly and deliberately and often was the most conservative voter of any of us. Rick and I were somewhere in the middle, although Rick used to fluctuate, voting against

eating a food item one day then voting in favor of eating
something else the next. Somehow we rarely had a tied
vote, and if this did occur, we opted for the conservative
decision.

Above our heads, in the space that had been a bilge locker, we stored our precious food supply and any item important to our survival. Much of the foodstores aboard Rose-
Noëlle had washed away after she capsized or were sodden
with seawater, but we still had a reasonable cache: cans of
corned beef, mackerel, baked beans, beetroot, sweet corn,
fruit, condensed milk, reduced cream, and coconut milk.
These I had gradually retrieved from the locker beneath
the dinette floor.

In the adjoining locker were the six trays of kiwifruit
Malcolm and Christabel had picked. The fruit in the top
tray had toppled out and were long gone, but fortunately
the tray itself had jammed. Behind were the other five trays
of kiwifruit, upside down but still intact. Carefully I reached
in and took out four of the green, succulent fruit. We would
feast on one each after dinner. Those kiwifruit, stored in
the dark and rationed out, in fact lasted us for one hundred
days, giving us a much-needed source of vitamin C.

I had stored supplies of food in several other lockers, and
whenever I made a dive I usually came up with a treasure—
a packet of biscuits, a container of rice, a pot of jam, or
more apples that had bobbed to the surface. One day shortly
after we capsized, I came across my prized raphis palm and
pulled it out of the water. It had been dislodged from its
pot and the soil had washed away, but I didn't have the
heart to throw it out. It was a pity we couldn't eat it. I put
the limp palm carefully in a for'ard hanging locker above
water level, but after a couple of weeks I noticed it had
disappeared. One of the gales that hit us every four or five
days during the early weeks had claimed another prize.

On 14 June I turned forty-eight, but nobody felt much like
celebrating a birthday. We had a little chocolate liqueur as
a treat. I thought of the roast meals my mother used to cook
at Glenrose. I could almost smell the roast lamb, new peas,

potatoes, gravy, and mint sauce. I had never worried much about celebrating birthdays, because I have always believed you are as young as you feel. My attitude to life is to have fun, no matter what your age; as time went by, Rick would talk about my "Peter Pan attitude" and claim that it was time I grew up.

I decided, however, to make this birthday memorable; I would have a go at connecting the EPIRB up to the main battery. I became quite excited at the idea. The beacon drew very little power, and I thought it would continue to transmit for weeks off the big battery. I dived in the main cabin to locate the tools and a bucket of electrical gear I would need. The four of us concentrated for hours on the task, lying in the aft cabin with the tools and the EPIRB spread about. Our tiny bedroom, living room, galley and, in rough weather, bathroom, now became our workshop.

I was delighted to find the beacon worked off small twelve-volt batteries, knowing that I would easily be able to connect it up to the large twelve-volt battery. My plan was to connect the EPIRB by drilling a small hole in the beacon case and running a wire down through the saltwater inlet in the centerboard case to the main battery, sitting in what was a bilge locker. That way the wire was out of harm's way; no one could trip over it or damage it. We ran a wire from the battery in the cockpit to the aft cabin, but the red light on the EPIRB refused to flash. We were so convinced it would work, clinging to this last thread of hope, that we were not prepared for failure. Rick simply could not accept the battery was flat, and he thought I must be doing something wrong. I tried again, this time placing the EPIRB in the centerboard well on the keel and connecting the wires directly to the battery.

As I worked, I already suspected what had happened. Someone had put the spotlight in a bucket to make it easier to find in the dark up in the cockpit. During a storm, waves coming over the top had swamped the bucket, shorting out the spotlight and draining the power from our one remaining battery. I looked at the black mark on the wingdeck made by the fully charged battery I had thrown overboard and cursed my earlier decision.

Two weeks after we capsized, we decided to erect a mast and hang up my string of bunting flags to make the wreck easier to spot from the air. I crawled along the wingdeck and felt underneath until my hand touched one of the five-meter spinnaker poles. It had come adrift at one end and was banging against the float deck in the surge. I released the other end and passed the pole back to Rick.

We stuck our new mast firmly in the centerboard casing and secured it with rigging made from ropes. Then we draped the line of plastic flags over the top of the pole and ran them either side to the stern and bow. We tied an orange buoy and a life jacket onto the mast and prayed that someone on a passing ship would be scanning the horizon at the right time. Tasks such as this served two purposes: they made us feel as though we were doing something constructive to help ourselves, and while working together as a team, we got on well and the mood aboard lifted. There is much truth in the saying that a working crew is a happy crew.

As the weeks wore on, we began to ration our food supplies more and more. For the first time in our lives we knew real hunger, the empty cramps in the stomach, the feeling of lethargy, the endless dreams about food— lots of it. The nights were the worst, particularly when we couldn't sleep.

More urgent than the hunger was the overwhelming desire to gulp fresh, cold water. Once we realized our water supply had disappeared, we began to ration our liquid until we were down to just three ounces—measured out carefully in a little spice jar—a day. We usually drank it at night, and sometimes we would vote on whether or not we could do without it. Down in the stuffiness of the aft cabin, our mouths became unbearably dry in the middle of the night. Fortunately I discovered the packets of sweets I had on board ready to help pass the long, dreary hours on watch during the voyage. We would suck on a fruit jube or a jellybean to get us through the night. Occasionally we treated ourselves to sharing a juicy kiwifruit, a slice of apple, or took a spoonful of powdered orange juice to dissolve in our parched mouths.

We always looked forward to breakfast in the early days, when it was our main meal. I had stored unopened packets of rolled oats and other raw ingredients for muesli in airtight plastic containers in the galley, and I found them under-water but unharmed during one of my initial dives. Break-fast became quite a ritual. Each morning we mixed up a bowl of bran, oats, wheat germ, sultanas, nuts, and perhaps a spoonful of jam or honey. Then we cubed an apple and mixed that in. The bowl was passed round and we each ate a dessertspoonful. The idea was to ladle as much as possible onto the spoon and cram it into our mouth before any of the muesli dropped off. Rick used to complain about this method, claiming that his mouth wasn't as big as ours, and he was therefore not getting his fair share.

As the days passed, we began to cut down the amount of muesli we made up and ration the apple, using only one quarter each morning. Eventually I dived down to the galley cupboards and found a set of dessert plates so that we could serve equal portions onto individual dishes. Using teaspoons to convince ourselves we were eating more than we actually were, we could proceed at our own pace and savor each mouthful rather than gulping it down like wolves.

Phil was always very worried about the lack of water and fretted about his liquid intake. He would eat all his muesli but leave the juice in the bottom of his dish; then he would carefully pour the liquid into a cup and drink it, a ritual he found comforting for some reason.

I was the only one left with a wristwatch after we cap-sized, and I hung it up in the empty battery box above our heads so that we could all see it. In fine weather we kept a watch every hour; we would take turns to crawl through the cabin opening and up into the cockpit to scan the blackness outside for any sign of ships' lights. But before long my watch disappeared; it probably dropped down into the bed-ding and was accidentally dragged out by someone crawling out of the cabin. We also lost balaclavas, hats, and socks in this way; to protect our heads and necks on cold days we cut a tartan cotton blanket into strips to wear as scarves. Socks and scarves were secured by tucking them down the front of our shirts, and we began to tie down loose items, even the dishcloth. I used a punch-and-die set to insert eyelets in larger items like our precious woollen blanket so we could tie it down while airing it up on deck.

After we lost the watch we had to rely on guessing the time. We would lie there in the dark and someone would ask, "Whose turn is it on watch?" Another voice would answer, "Mine, but I don't think an hour is up yet."

When one of us had been up on deck, we would drop down into the cockpit on our knees and call out, "Coming down!" The other three in the aft cabin would roll over and climb on top of each other to make a space so that the fourth person could drop down on the plank and crawl backward into the cabin.

In rough weather there was no point in keeping watch, because visibility was too poor and we would end up soaked through by the midwinter gales that hit us each week for the first month. It was hard enough keeping dry inside the cabin. As the waves built up in a storm, the surge would roar through the boat and into the aft cabin, sloshing up the sides of our sleeping platform and through the entrance.

The nights were always very long and very dark during storms. We had two torches, but the batteries soon went flat. I had a so-called waterproof torch, which I used to search underwater during one dive, but water leaked in and it refused to work after that.

The cupboard down behind the oven was tricky because it was stacked full of dried food. The moment I touched anything, it would dissolve and send a cloud of fragments into the water until I felt as if I was swimming in cold soup. I salvaged some packets of sweet and savory biscuits that were still edible, but there were several packets soaked through. I was about to throw them away when I thought we could toss them into a plastic container with a packet of wet cocoa and any other ruined food to make ground bait,

"Coming down!" Crawling backward into the warmth of our tiny aft cabin.

or burley, to attract fish. However, those fish we did attract by this method took one sniff and swam away, so the burley was abandoned to pickle itself in its briny syrup.

Quite a few items would just float around the main cabin for weeks on end, whereas other things would be plucked away by the surge overnight. Rick used to like watching a red packet of special coffee he had brought aboard because it reminded him of time spent with Heather, drinking coffee by the fire. We didn't bother salvaging it because at that stage we had no water and no heat. Like so many food items in those early days, we wondered, "What's the point?" only to kick ourselves later.

"See if you can find that jar of peanut butter, John," Jim pleaded with me one day when I was about to go diving. He had brought aboard a large jar and was now suffering withdrawal symptoms through not having tasted peanut butter for so long. With Jim kneeling on a plank above me, I dived down to the jam locker in the galley and found that some of the contents had already spilled out. Holding my breath and peering through my mask in the gloom I started pulling out jars of mayonnaise, jam, honey and, finally, a small jar of peanut butter. I emerged shivering from the water with my prize. Jim was naturally disappointed at the disappearance of his supply but delighted at what I had managed to salvage. Once my head was wet I began to get cold quickly and it was not until later on I remembered all the jars I had pulled out of the cupboard and left on the floor of the cabin. When I next dived down they were gone.

Although the battery we had hoped would power the EPIRB was useless, we kept it and pondered over ways to recharge it. There were the solar cells mounted on the poles aft behind the steering cockpit, and we wondered if we could connect them to the battery. Through the companionway hatch I could see something dangling below in the water, but when I dived down I found all the solar panels had gone. The color radar was still there, and the wind generator was drifting around attached to a wire. I didn't bother about the generator, for it was too complicated to rig up. It generated 240-volt power, and this needed to be converted to 12 volts for the beacon; all the necessary equipment was underwater. It was eerie swimming around down there, in the midst of all my beautiful equipment bobbing silently beneath the water.

I kept thinking about the battery and ways to generate power. The outboard was too difficult to salvage because it was firmly bolted on, upside down and underwater. Then I remembered the Honda generator; if I could get it out of the port float we might be able to get it working. I dived down with a length of rope and climbed into the pontoon. The generator was still there, so I tied the rope around it, heaved it into the water and Rick, Phil, and Jim pulled it up on deck. Phil and I took it apart and cleaned it up. I didn't think we stood much of a chance, because it was already partly corroded. But it was full of petrol and when we put it back together and pulled the starter we managed to coax a spark from the sparkplug. Where there is life, there is hope, we thought.

The two of us spent hours on the generator, trying to get it to start. We could only work on it in fine weather, either crouched in the cockpit or up on deck. I wondered if there was water in the carburetor, so once again we pulled it apart, but still it wouldn't go. We sat up on deck for days, pulling the starter and trying this and that to coax the wretched motor to life. I suggested to Phil that he dismantle the carburetor again to see if the jets were blocked. He set to work quite happily, but for some reason stood on the plank over the water to do this job. A little spring from the carburetor dropped into the water, so I had to make a replacement from a piece of copper wire wrapped around a nail. It worked only for a couple of pulls before the carburetor flooded.

I left Phil to fiddle about with the generator; I had lost interest in the project. Even if we did manage to get the motor going, I did not think we stood a chance of getting the generator to work, because its electrics were so corroded. Eventually even Phil gave up, and the Honda generator sat in the cockpit for weeks before we stored it up on deck. We were fast learning not to throw anything away, and I thought there could well be some useful parts inside. Besides, the petrol would come in handy to light a signal fire if we saw a ship.

FOUR

Highlight

One of my favorite photographs aboard *Rose-Noëlle* was of *Highlight*, the eleven-meter trimaran on which my brother David and I spent seven years exploring the South Pacific. The photograph showed the boat just off the beach on Moorea; our two pet chickens are perched on the mizzen boom, and David is sprawled on the sand in the foreground.

I framed an enlarged version of the photograph and fixed it to the bulkhead above the dinette on *Rose-Noëlle*. I often used to look at the picture and smile; it always brought back good memories. Weeks after we capsized, I dived down specifically to look at that photograph. It was still there inside the frame, but all the color had washed away, leaving a blank piece of sodden paper.

There was no one in our district I could ask for advice about yachts when David and I decided to build *Highlight*. Very few people sailed in Picton or Blenheim in those days; there wasn't even a local ship chandlery. While I was recuperating from my cycling accident I studied boating magazines and began sketching plans for a monohull yacht. Eventually I spotted a photograph in *Seaspray* magazine that was to change my thinking on yacht design forever. It was a Piver Lodestar, an eleven-meter trimaran, and to me it represented everything I had ever dreamed of. From that moment on, the monohull seemed wrong. I looked at the multihull and thought to myself, "Here is a boat that doesn't lean over and is not going to make me seasick." The trimaran was designed to skim across the top of the water, looking like a space-age airplane. To me, the design made sense.

I sent away to the designer, Arthur Piver in San Francisco, for a copy of the Lodestar plans after selling my motorbike to pay for them. My brother David, then a refrigeration mechanic, was keen to join me, and two other friends pitched in to help after hearing of the adventures we planned. There was plenty of space at Glenrose, and my ever-tolerant parents allowed us to dismantle an old shed used for drying onion seeds and reconstruct it as a boat-building shelter. The skills learned from my boss, Jack Morgan, stood me well. During the day I was handcrafting kauri clinker dinghies and whale chasers. After work and on weekends I was building a space-age yacht from plywood covered in fiberglass. It took us eighteen months to build the trimaran, which we named *Highlight* after a deep red rose growing in our garden.

The launching, on 16 May 1964, was a grand affair. Hundreds of locals lined the banks of the Opawa River in Blenheim while a cousin of ours towed *Highlight* down to the river with his tractor. The local newspaper and television reporters turned out to record Dr. Claudia Shand, wife of the Member of Parliament for Marlborough, Tom Shand, break the champagne over *Highlight*'s bow. David and I thought Claudia Shand, dressed up in a suit and hat, did a splendid job.

I can't say that our first attempt at sailing was at all memorable, nor would I recommend any young would-be sailors to learn the same way—by jumping in the deep end. I cringe to think of how David and I first set sail, if you can call it that.

We decided to take the boat across Cook Strait to Wellington so that we could learn how to rig and sail her properly. We also needed to arrange visas for Japan in order to sail there in time for the 1964 Olympic Games, the first stage of our adventure. At the last minute David caught pneumonia and was confined to bed, so Dad, Graham—one of the friends who had helped us build *Highlight*—and his cousin joined me for the trip. The mainsail, mizzen, jib, and genoa had been made in Auckland by Chris Bouzaid, but the sheets for the sails were made from clothesline and we weren't sure where they were supposed to go anyway. There were no handrails, cleats, or winches on deck; in fact, we sailed for seven years without winches. We had no life jackets or flares because you could not buy that sort of equipment in Blenheim.

The day we left, the weather was so calm we needed to be towed out past the Wairau Bar and into open water. We headed for Port Underwood to spend the night, ready to face Cook Strait in the morning. The sea was glassy, and we had to motor much of the way with our little outboard. To my dismay, I was chronically seasick. By the time we got to the mouth of Port Underwood it was dark and we hit a reef, wrecking the fin beneath one of the floats. We had also run out of petrol for the outboard, so we had to listen helplessly as the swell ground the fin off before we floated free of the reef.

Our trip across Cook Strait wasn't much better. We found ourselves in the middle of a howling gale with huge waves crashing on top of us. *Highlight* lurched and plunged until I became so frightened I forgot to be sick. We were forced to tow the dinghy because there was nothing on deck onto which we could tie it. Eventually a huge wave swamped it and the towline broke. We turned around and battled our way back to retrieve it, but we ran over it, jamming it between the hull and one of the floats, with a furious sea determined to push it in still further. Something had to give, and unfortunately it was *Highlight*'s hull. The dinghy poked a hole into Graham's locker, and by the end of the day we had one disgruntled crew member with a locker full of soaking clothes.

We abandoned our salvage attempts and pressed on for Wellington, but the winds were too much, even for our brand-new sails. Before long the jib blew out and, as *Highlight* wouldn't sail without a headsail, we were helpless. We radioed for help, and a fisherman from Island Bay, at the mouth of Wellington Harbor, came out and towed us in. Once the weather calmed, we sailed into the harbor and beached *Highlight* to repair the fin. As we worked, a

Rolls-Royce cruised past on the coast road above and we waved at the four Beatles, arriving from the airport for their tour of New Zealand.

A couple of days later a member of the Royal Port Nicholson Yacht Club kindly came out with us on *Highlight* to teach us some of the finer points of sailing, where to sheet the genoa to and where to place the cleats. We bought wet-weather gear, flares, and life jackets before sailing back across Cook Strait to Picton so that we could restock the boat ready for the trip to Tokyo.

When we left the second time, on our way to Japan, David was on the wheel. Fully recovered, he was determined to learn how to sail and to catch up with Graham and me in terms of experience. Not far into Cook Strait we hit something in the water that we later suspected was a whale. With David still at the helm, we spent several hours drifting around with the tide, going nowhere. He could not understand how we had managed to sail *Highlight* to Wellington and back, and now he didn't seem to be able to steer in a straight line. Finally it occurred to us to check the rudder. It had snapped off below the waterline.

Feeling rather foolish, we called up on the radio for help as we drifted toward rocks off Wellington Heads. Fortunately we raised the local whale-station owner, Gilbert Perano, who came to the rescue in a whale chaser just before we hit the rocks. We made another rudder and left again. I think our friends and families wondered if they would ever see the back of us.

We didn't know much about navigation in those days, and I can remember sailing up the Wairarapa coast on four-hour watches. We were steering with a tiny compass out of an old plane; the helmsman was lucky if he could steer within 15° of accuracy. The compass had no light, so once we had peered at it with a torch we would set a course and steer by the moon and stars. David and I couldn't understand why we kept heading in toward the coast. Then it dawned on us that over a four-hour watch the moon and the stars had moved considerably.

Bad weather off East Cape slowed our progress, but we eventually arrived in Auckland. We realized we were not going to make the Tokyo Olympics in time, so instead we sailed up north to the Bay of Islands for Christmas. It was in Russell that we met Penny Whiting, the daughter of Auckland's legendary sailing couple, D'Arcy and Molly Whiting. Penny was a blond teenager, the oldest of five children, mad keen on sailing and full of fun. She was staying on board *En Avant*, a catamaran owned by Mark Williams, one of the best sailors around in Auckland at the time. We rafted *Highlight* up next to *En Avant* and became good friends with the Williams family and the ever-bubbly Penny.

After taking *Highlight* on a quick trip to Norfolk Island and back to Auckland, we finally left on the long-dreamed-of cruise of the South Pacific. A few days out of Auckland we hit a whale and decided to head for Rarotonga to make permanent repairs to the damaged float. Rudders were something else that we were continually having to repair. During our time on *Highlight*, David and I made eight rudders and broke six of them.

My first sighting of a Polynesian island is something I will never forget. The surge of excitement and anticipation can never quite be recaptured, although when we sighted land after drifting on *Rose-Noëlle* for nearly four months, the feeling came close.

David and I loved the Polynesian people, and as two young men living a carefree life on a yacht, we had no trouble meeting the local young women. They were so beautiful with their long black hair and shy smiles.

We left Rarotonga with fresh crew and headed for Tahiti, arriving in Papeete in time for the Bastille Day celebrations in 1965. I grew to love Tahiti; it has such a romantic, magical feel about it. It was in Papeete that we met Mike Swift, a twenty-six-year-old British art student who was trying to find a yacht that would take him to the deserted coral atoll of Suwarrow in the Cook Islands. He wanted to live the life of a hermit like the legendary Tom Neale, the New

Zealander who wrote *An Island to Oneself* after living twice on Anchorage Island at Suwarrow in the 1950s and 1960s. Mike couldn't find anyone to take him, probably because of the nightmare of bureaucratic reaction should he be discovered. David and I had planned to return to Rarotonga, but when we heard of Mike's scheme we thought a trip to Suwarrow sounded a much better idea.

Mike and I became good friends while we were in Papeete. We used to spend our days wandering round the shops, fossicking for items that he might need to survive—a speargun, a coconut grater, butane lighters. Dad arrived in Papeete by ship to join us, and when we left Tahiti we had seven on board *Highlight*, including Mike Swift and all the gear intended for his hermit existence. Lashed to one of the floats was an outrigger canoe from which Mike planned to fish.

We sailed to Raiatea in French Polynesia, where I got to know a young woman, Tiare, quite well. The morning we left, she came down to the shore to see us off and I asked her if she would like to come to Bora Bora with us. She said yes and jumped on board then and there, without telling anyone where she was going. That is typical of the Tahitian—carefree and impulsive.

We spent an idyllic week on Bora Bora, but Dad fretted about Tiare because no one knew where she was. Tiare wasn't bothered at all, but we managed to arrange a passage home for her on a yacht going back to Raiatea. I wrote to her for years after that and gradually learned to read and write Tahitian.

After Tiare left, we sailed to Suwarrow and spent a few days exploring the atoll and helping Mike to settle in. Someone had left a copy of American adventurer Dwight Long's book *Seven Seas on a Shoestring* in Tom Neale's deserted cabin. I read about his cruising adventures in the ten-meter ketch *Idle Hour* and loved every word. Dwight Long became a man I admired from afar and would eventually meet during my cruise of the Pacific. I kept that book and one day found it, soaked through, in the upturned and flooded cabin of *Rose-Noëlle*. I dried it out, read it again while we were adrift and enjoyed it just as much.

We left Mike-the-hermit on Anchorage and headed for Pago Pago in American Samoa. When we came alongside the dock an official was waiting.

"Did you or did you not drop Mike Swift off at Suwarrow?" he demanded.

Somehow our discreet delivery trip had become common gossip through the Islands. We owned up, and the Cook Islands government threatened to fine us £1000 to cover the cost of sending a warship to collect Mike unless we went back to pick him up. We sailed to Apia in Western Samoa and the officials there were more reasonable. We explained that we could not go back to Suwarrow because it was dead to windward and we might damage *Highlight* and ourselves. In the end we were fined £100. I heard later that a boat had called in at Suwarrow, but Mike wouldn't leave. He was eventually picked up by a second boat. David fixed all the broken-down refrigerators on the island until we had enough money to pay the fine and leave.

The day Dad left to return to Blenheim, we took a Tongan woman, Kalolaine Siutaka, aboard as crew. Kalo was a professional dancer and danced the night away at Aggie Grey's Hotel in Apia.

Kalo was great to have on *Highlight*, and soon she became my girlfriend. She loved entertaining people, singing, dancing, and playing the guitar. She used to cook up great Island meals for whomever we had on board. We sailed to Fiji then to Noumea, where David and I got work building chicken farms. We stayed there for eight months, and eventually Kalo left after meeting one of the local policemen.

One day a friend in Noumea took me home and introduced me to his girlfriend, Noeline Harehoe. I knew instantly who she was. "Not *the* Noeline," I laughed. I had often dreamed about this beautiful Tahitian girl after seeing her photograph in Eric Hiscock's book *Beyond the West Horizon*, the epic story that had inspired me to build a boat and sail to the Pacific. Noeline and I became good friends; she used to call me her brother. She would sing and play her guitar at parties or on *Highlight*, and gradually I, too, learned to sing the Island songs.

David got a job as a guitarist at a local nightclub. My brother is very bright and always picked things up quickly, be it schoolwork, his trade, or learning to play musical instruments. Sometimes I used to dance the tamure with the Tahitian girls in the floorshow. As with cycling, if there was an audience, I would perform.

Finally we left the South Pacific and headed for Brisbane, vowing we would be back. When we reached the Brisbane River, I was thrilled to discover that Noeline had arrived on an American yacht. She joined us on *Highlight*, and we sailed to Surfers' Paradise, where she sang and danced in the hotels.

We then sailed to Lord Howe Island, where David and I managed to get work with the local Island board, lightering the ships, repairing the roads, and maintaining equipment. Noeline found a job cleaning the local guest houses. After a brief trip to Sydney, from where Noeline flew back to Noumea, we returned to Lord Howe and our old jobs. We spent eight months there and came to know the locals quite well before moving on to Norfolk Island. There was no safe anchorage on the island, so we hired a truck owned by Snipe's Delicate Deliveries to haul the boat from the wharf to the old salt-house, part of the ruins of the old convict settlement. After three months we were told to leave Norfolk because the locals were upset at us taking jobs from them, so David and I and two crew members sailed back to Picton at the end of 1967.

While it was good to be home after three years' cruising, we were soon anxious to be off again. We decided to sail to Rapa, south of the Austral Islands in French Polynesia. We left New Zealand in May 1968 with Pat, a young Canadian, on board as the third crew member. Somewhat naively, we decided to go through the Roaring Forties for a quick trip to Rapa. The storms on that voyage were like none we had experienced before. Once again I was so frightened, I forgot to be seasick. That was the first time I heard the roar of a rogue wave, similar to the one that capsized *Rose-Noëlle*, except this one was louder and we heard it coming from a long way off.

We were lying ahull with the sails down when the wave hit. It tipped *Highlight* over more than 90°, but somehow she righted herself. David was tossed from his bunk and gear from the lockers hurtled from one side of the cabin to the other. We had a small Honda motorbike on one of the bunks, but fortunately it was on the leeward side so it didn't join the flying debris.

After that we decided to sail through the storm, under a storm jib and a small reefed main. Once the sails were set we could steer from a second wheel in the cabin below to keep dry. Whoever was on the helm sat with a rug wrapped around his legs to ward off the cold, while the two others lay huddled in blankets. We were so far south we had to keep battling north, otherwise we would have ended up in the South Pole with the penguins rather than basking in the sun at Rapa.

The waves were massive rollers—ten meters high and half a mile apart. The helmsman would talk his way through, "Going up, going up, GOING UP, HANG ON!" as *Highlight* turned to face the crest of the wave then ploughed her way through. We thought every wave was our last, and afterward all three of us admitted we had silently prayed.

The constant pounding of water broke the deck below the wingdeck and flooded one of the floats. David and I carried out running repairs beneath the darkest sky I have seen during the day—an ominous sign of yet another storm.

When we got to Rapa our stomachs kept churning long after the boat had stopped moving. We were the first yacht to have called in ten years, and the locals made a real fuss of us.

We were at Tubuai in the Austral Islands when the French exploded a nuclear bomb at Mururoa Atoll, seven hundred miles to the east, on 6 July 1968. It was a Sunday, and we were getting ready to leave; the islanders were outside on their way to church. The winds changed, and it rained that day. The little children started to vomit, and the adults suffered headaches and a sick feeling in the stomach. Hours later, when we heard of the bomb explosion on Tahiti Radio, we suspected that we had suffered mild radiation sickness.

We left Tubuai the next day with one black and one white chicken aboard that an islander had given us to eat. In the end we couldn't bring ourselves to kill them, and they became pets. They used to sit out on deck underneath a big washing bucket, and in port they would perch on the boom with a cord around their claws. Sometimes they fell off and we would find them dangling upside down by their feet.

We arrived in Tahiti in time for the Bastille Day celebrations, and that is where I first saw a pretty teenager named Rose-Noëlle Coguiec. She was Miss July, and I thought her young, smiling face was the loveliest I had ever seen. I took her photograph but was not introduced to her until two years later on a return visit to Tahiti. Eventually my newly designed yacht would become her namesake.

We spent the next year wandering the Pacific. When we reached Hawaii a mutual friend introduced me to Dwight Long. By coincidence, his old yacht *Idle Hour*, now cherished by a new owner, was berthed out in Ala Wai Harbor. David and I took Dwight out sailing on *Highlight* a couple of times during our stay, and I told him about finding his book in Tom Neale's cabin.

We stayed in Hawaii for eight months and watched the first moon landing on television aboard another New Zealand yacht in Ala Wai in July 1969. Watching Neil Armstrong take that first step seemed so alien, so high-tech and remote compared with our simple way of life.

Throughout those cruising years I had always appreciated having David with me. He and I had always been close, and we both wanted the same thing. We yearned for adventure, and *Highlight* was our key to that dream. When I sailed with David we rarely needed to communicate on deck. We both knew what needed doing and got on with it. There was no need to issue instructions, no drama, no fights.

But even brothers eventually need to go their separate ways. We had sailed thirty-five thousand nautical miles together following our dreams, earning ourselves a reputation as playboys of the South Pacific. But I was sick of the ever-changing crews; I was tired of courting young women then sailing off to the next island, the next conquest. I wanted to share the next stage of my life with one special woman. I was knocking thirty and I needed more space, my own boat. So did David.

We decided to sell *Highlight* in the United States and settle in Australia to build a new boat each. I already had ideas for the new trimaran I wanted to design. The Piver Lodestar was a very forgiving sort of boat. It was one of the very early multihulls and still experimental, a little like comparing a Model T Ford with a Lamborghini. We had pushed *Highlight* to extremes, and she had borne the strain well. Now it was time for David and I to build our Lamborghinis.

We took *Highlight* to Vancouver, San Francisco, and on to Los Angeles, delivering yachts to earn money along the way. We moored *Highlight* at Marina del Rey, the huge marina next to Los Angeles Airport. Right through our cruising life we seemed to get into hot water over not having the right visa or overstaying our welcome with immigration authorities. The United States was no exception. However, we managed to stay there a year, and it was a life I grew to love. Marina del Rey was a community in itself. If you wanted to learn anything about boats, this was the place to be. Dwight Long lived nearby in Venice, and we soon renewed our friendship.

David and I earned just enough money to live on, doing odd jobs or taking sailing lessons. David taught Robert Wagner to sail, and another great actor, Peter Fonda, gave us the old deck box off his yacht—which was berthed next to *Highlight*—ready to pack our belongings in when we finally left. I began to draw the design of my new trimaran in the evenings, sitting at a drawing board of a friend's house in Los Angeles. I became completely absorbed in the work and would happily work until the early hours of the morning. Each time I completed some lines, I would make a wooden model using the bread-and-butter technique taught to me by Jack Morgan.

We didn't need much money to survive at the marina in Los Angeles, and I would spend any spare cash on buying stainless-steel galley equipment, which I continually hunted for in the local shops. My next boat would have only the very best gear.

I discovered that most yachts stored their batteries loose, so I would charge $25 to make fiberglass battery boxes. I usually averaged one job a week, and that was enough to pay my share of the marina charge, food, and $5 for a tank of gas for the car. I bought an old Volvo for $100 but never realized I had to put oil in strange places—it blew up after three weeks. Then I spotted a beaten-up Cadillac convertible on a car yard. I just had to own it. I paid $150 and knocked all the dents out, ready for a repaint. I took it into a paint shop, paid over my $29.95, and by the end of the day it was gleaming white. We had a lot of fun in that Cadillac. Christabel arrived with a group of girlfriends on a passenger liner, and we took them to Disneyland for the day.

Eventually we pushed our luck as overstayers. One time I raced on a yacht down to Mexico, and the authorities nearly didn't let me back into the United States. David was in Seattle at the time, and I was about to cable him and suggest that he bring *Highlight* down the coast and pick me up. But some fast talking with a sympathetic American consulate official got me the necessary stamp, and I made my way back to Los Angeles. However, I knew our days were numbered.

We eventually sold *Highlight* for $11,000, packed our gear into Peter Fonda's deck box, and shipped it home. David and I flew to Hawaii and on to Tahiti, where I finally met the beautiful, shy Rose-Noëlle Coguiec. She was a friend of a family we had gotten to know during our Pacific travels. We spent our days in Tahiti zooming round the island on little mopeds, and when I left for New Zealand, Rose-Noëlle and I decided to keep in touch.

FIVE

Water

For the first forty days and nights, we relied on food and equipment salvaged from the waterlogged lockers of *Rose-Noëlle*. We still could not accept that rescue was not just over the horizon, behind the next cloud, arriving the next day.

Rick, Phil, and Jim wanted to erect a jury rig and try to sail *Rose-Noëlle* upside down back to land. We had several arguments on this subject because I was convinced our priority was to remain safe and well, and to concentrate on survival, using the resources aboard the boat until we were spotted by a ship or found land. That meant building a reliable water-catchment system and establishing a regular supply of fish, something at which we had been unsuccessful so far.

I knew that even if we did manage to erect a jury rig, the trimaran was not designed to sail upside down three-quarters full of water and would be near impossible to steer. To make any progress against our drift, which I calculated to be between twelve and fifteen miles a day away from New Zealand, we would have to work long and hard at a time when we were rapidly losing weight and strength. Our time would be taken up with trying to sail the boat rather than catching fish and water, our only chance of long-term survival.

I suspected by now that we could be well on our way to South America, and unless we were lucky enough to bump into something like the Maria Theresa Reef, we could be in for a long wait. To me the water-catchment system was our top priority as our precious supply of soft drink dwindled and we struggled to survive on three ounces of fluid a day.

A few weeks after we capsized, I pulled out some technical books that had been stored in a cupboard by the fridge. They were soaked through, but there was one in particular I thought would be worth drying out and trying to read. It was the *Small Ships Manual*, published by the Marine Board of Queensland. When I pried apart its sodden pages, it opened at the chapter on survival. What I read encouraged me that we were at least on the right track in terms of our survival decisions. The manual recommended eight ounces of water a day, but added that survival was possible on two to eight ounces a day, depending on the climate and the water available. We were not adrift in a hot climate and we had only a limited supply of liquid, so we had no choice but to ration ourselves to the minimum.

Although we were extremely thirsty, we never got desperate enough to consider drinking seawater. The manual instructed survivors not to drink seawater because it contains more salt than the body can excrete, thus causing dehydration. (Nonetheless, Dr. Alain Bombard concluded in his book *The Bombard Story*, written after his epic survival experiment, that humans can survive by drinking seawater, at least for short periods, without affecting their health.)

Three weeks after we capsized, it began to drizzle one night. Phil, who was particularly worried about his fluid intake, grabbed a plastic sheet and scrambled up on deck, calling for me to give him a hand. The drizzle had turned to a heavy downpour, and he sat on top of the main hull with his face turned upward, as though he were being showered with gold.

I grabbed the bottom of the sheet from where I was standing straddled above the galley and funnelled the water into a pot in the cockpit. We were both fully clothed, and we got soaked, but we had water. I handed the pot carefully down to Rick, and he and Jim filled the empty plastic soft-drink bottles and stored them away in our larder. The rain was torrential, and we managed to fill several bottles, but it never rained that heavily again during our whole time adrift. However, this downpour gave us hope that we could collect water and so survive a little longer.

Dreaming up ways to collect rainwater became a priority. We tried deflecting water off the plastic sheet again, but we never gathered more than a cup at a time. I thought we could somehow rig up the cockpit suncover Rose had made on her sewing machine the night before we left. I had stowed it in the big locker where I kept the radios, and once again I dived to see if it was still there. The water was dark but clear, and I soon found the fingerhole in the door. I tugged at it, but it would not budge; it was jammed tight. Something stopped me from demolishing the offending door. I had spent years building my beautiful boat, and I wanted to damage it as little as possible. I still hoped that somehow *Rose-Noëlle*, Rick, Jim, Phil, and I would land safely. So I left the door jammed shut, and the next few times I dived for something I could use to pry it open.

Eventually I got desperate. Catching water was more important than a locker door. I picked up a large screwdriver, put on my snorkel and mask, and dived down to do battle. The fridge had moved slightly from its compartment when we capsized, and I had to push it back into place with my feet before I could get my screwdriver in place to lever open the cupboard.

Inside I found the suncover, another box of tools, and a little brass kerosene lamp. The lamp had no glass or wick, but I saved it, knowing that I had kerosene on board in one of the lockers. The batteries in our flashlights were getting weaker, and I thought that with a little ingenuity we might be able to use it as a light.

Up on deck we found that the suncover fitted almost exactly between the stays holding up our mast, but it would take all four of us to stop the edges from flapping in the wind and funnel rainwater into the bucket. There was no sign of rain, so I folded it up again and jammed it tightly in the back of the pots-and-pans cupboard in the galley. We had already learned the hard way how important it was to secure everything against the surge in the cabin.

When I next went to get the suncover during a rain shower, the pots and pans were still in the cupboard but the cover was gone. Someone had left the cupboard door open after clambering from the aft cabin and up through our new cockpit.

In a way it was a blessing that the suncover had disappeared. That water-collection system would have been cumbersome, and all four of us would have been drenched through holding the suncover down. If it rained in the middle of the night, we would have been groping around on the slippery hulls in the darkness. There had to be a better way.

I started to lie awake thinking about the problem, trying to remember what materials I had on board and how I could design a system that would catch water without our having to leap up on deck every time it rained. I remembered noticing lengths of plastic conduit pipe while diving to get something out of one of the floats. The pipes were strengthened with narrow lengths of timber to make supporting battens for a huge yellow suncover, which nearly covered the entire deck area when in port. I decided to lash these together like a sheaf of corn. If I spread the pipes out in the middle and tied them in a taper at the bottom, rainwater would drain down them into a bucket below. It would not matter which way the wind was blowing the rain; the water would still hit the pipe and dribble down, the conduit acting like a cluster of little masts. I drew a diagram on the wall of the aft cabin to explain to the others what I intended.

Phil, Rick, and Jim were still agitating for a jury rig, and we had lengthy arguments about it. Eventually we came to a compromise. I would dive down and climb into the port float to get the conduit pipe and then check the starboard float to see if I could salvage any of the sail bags. The two tramping packs belonging to Rick and Jim were also stored in that float and had all sorts of handy gear inside, including a tent, which we thought might help to keep us dry in the aft cabin.

The first blow was to find that much of the conduit pipe had been washed away; there were just a few lengths left. I was disappointed, but I saved them anyway. I would just have to think again. Phil was keen on building a guttering system to catch water trickling off the hull, so I retrieved some lengths of ash I used as spare battens for the main-sail. There were also lengths of western red cedar, used to strengthen the conduit battens. I tied a line round the conduit and pushed it down into the water to Rick, who pulled it as it appeared in the water off the wingdeck.

I swam across to the starboard float to look for the sails and the tramping packs, but when I checked inside I found it was almost completely empty. The capsize had been so fast and forceful, the hatch cover had been ripped clean off, and as the float thumped down, the contents had been emptied right out. In a way I was relieved the sails had gone; I no longer had to appear the bad guy by arguing against a plan I knew was foolhardy.

Tucked at the back of the float were two buckets that had managed to stay put. I passed one, full of containers of epoxy resin, up to Jim, and the other, full of sandpaper, up to Phil. Although I didn't realize it at the time, there was some sort of dispute going on between Rick and Phil up on deck.

Arguments and bickering were not uncommon between us; living in such close quarters and in such trying conditions caused tempers to flare quite regularly. We were all guilty of it, although Jim managed to remain the most even-tempered of the four of us. I learned later that Phil, still in a temper over his dispute with Rick, threw the bucket at the escape hole he and I had cut that first day. The bucket bounced off the side of the hull and toppled into the water near Rick. Phil reckoned that Rick should go after it and so left it to float away; both men were too stubborn to give in and retrieve it.

In the meantime I got out of the water shaking with cold and went down to the aft cabin to get dressed. I had stayed in the water a little too long, and my fingers and limbs would not work properly. I asked Phil to help me get dressed and to make me a cold drink of Milo to help warm me up. We didn't have much water, but I was sure that with the materials I had salvaged, the situation would improve.

Phil spotted a new packet of powdered fruit drink that I had retrieved from the cabin that day and asked if he could have some. I shrugged my shoulders and said, "Yes, sure. Go ahead." Had I known at that stage about his childish behavior and the subsequent loss of a precious bucket, I might not have been so amenable to the idea.

The weather was fine and calm on days thirty-nine and forty, so the four of us spent the time up on deck building the water-catchment systems. Overnight I had been pondering on how best to use the remaining lengths of plastic pipe. I imagined a rural New Zealand or Australian house and how rainwater trickled down the grooves of a sloping corrugated-iron roof into the guttering and was siphoned into a water tank for storage. That was it: I would design a corrugated framework by splitting the pipes up the middle and lashing them side by side with nylon fishing line to lengths of timber. We could secure the frame in an upright position to the mast and gather the pipes in at the bottom to drain into a bucket.

While Phil and I worked on the guttering, Rick and Jim concentrated on the conduit system. Once I start a job, I like to get it over and done with. I energetically sawed lengths of timber on an angle so that we could secure them to both sides of the hull with epoxy glue and nails. Phil kept warning me, "Take it easy, slow down." By the time I had finished cutting up the timber with a blunt and rusty saw, I was so dehydrated I had cramp in my hands and jaw. The worst part was that I could only dream of brewing up a kettle and having a long, hot cup of tea. The next drink I had would be my three-ounce ration that night.

Phil and I were pleased with our handiwork once we had finished. The water would collect in the guttering and trickle through the pipes, one leading down through the roof of the main cabin and the other into our cockpit area. That way, when it rained, the person nearest the aft cabin entrance could reach through and put a bottle under the pipes to collect water without getting drenched.

The corrugated conduit frame was about two and a half meters long and half a meter wide. Rick and Jim lashed it vertically up the spinnaker-pole mast and tied the bucket underneath about a meter off the hull. Now all we needed was rain.

The next day it rained for us. I began to believe in our ability to manifest miracles. When we desperately needed a sign that someone was watching over us, we got it. Jim came to believe that, too, in time.

The bucket beneath the conduit pipe slowly filled, and water trickled through the pipes from the guttering system along both sides of the hull. From that day on life was just that little more bearable. We were able to make cold drinks of Milo and coffee and mix water with orange powder to make juice. It was a luxury after our forty days of strictly rationed liquid.

Jim and I each had a one-liter plastic feeding bottle with a nozzle top that we had used while cycling. These proved invaluable, and I made a mental note to include one on the survival list I planned to write. We used them to siphon water from a bucket and squeeze it into a bottle, to mix milk powder or juice. But the feeding bottles had an even more important use. When a commodity is scarce in a survival ordeal, it is vitally important that no one feels he is being done out of his fair share. Food and liquid must be measured out as exactly as possible. After voting whether or not we would have a drink, Phil and I would mix up cold Milo, and Rick and Jim would make cold coffee. Because our cups were different sizes, we would count out four or five squeezes of the feeder bottle into each mug to make sure the amounts were identical.

Although pleased with our new water-catchment systems, we had to be constantly alert to the possibility of seawater contaminating our freshwater supply. Calm weather was ideal. When it rained we simply waited a few minutes to allow the salt to wash off the hulls before connecting the water hoses up to the bottles inside.

But it was still wintertime, and calm rainy days were rare. More often than not, a storm blew up, sending waves of seawater sloshing across the deck, into the guttering, and down through our water pipes to contaminate the precious supply we had just collected. During a storm we would lie in the aft cabin, and when we heard a big wave hit the hull, we would quickly pull the pipe out of the bottle. A few minutes later we would taste the water trickling through the pipe and, once the saltiness cleared, we would reconnect it to the bottle. As time went on and salt levels built up in our bodies, we didn't notice the briny taste so much and often needed a second opinion as to whether the water was too contaminated to drink.

The conduit system was less likely to be affected by seawater because the catchment bucket up the mast was about three meters above sea level, and the conduit gathered water efficiently unless we were lying ahull in light winds. The guttering system worked well in calm weather, but sometimes the wind would be so strong that it blew the rain off the hull before it could collect in the guttering. The only drawback with the conduit system was that someone had to brave the elements and crawl along the hull in a storm to empty the bucket. If we left the freshwater in the bucket too long, it would eventually get sprayed by saltwater. Retrieving it meant getting wet and cold at a time when staying warm and dry was a top priority.

Shortly after we rigged up the water catchments, a violent storm brought with it rain in the middle of the night. We knew that the bucket up by the mast would be full, so I took the first turn. I stripped off my clothes, put on a wet-weather jacket, and climbed up through the cockpit to face freezing rain and wind whipping at my thin frame. I dropped on all fours and crawled forward on the slippery surface, two empty soft-drink bottles slung around my neck on a cord. The whole boat was shuddering as huge waves hit one after the other, phosphorescence lighting up the water as it rolled like surf across the hull and across my lightly clad body. Apart from very calm weather, when *Rose-Noëlle* faced side-on

Gale winds and waves threatened to contaminate our fresh-water supply unless we emptied the bucket beneath the conduit system.

to the waves, the boat usually sat stern on, and the waves hit from behind and rolled forward across the deck. Tonight was particularly frightening. It was pitch-black, with bolts of lightning flashing across the horizon, followed by the boom of thunder.

The reality of what had happened to us hit me for the first time. Here I was crawling across the keel of my beautiful, perfect boat, which was upside down in a howling gale heading to nowhere. And here I was, risking my life, feeling miserable and scared, to fill up two water bottles.

Another wave nearly took me with it, and a feeling of anger replaced the sorrowful regrets of a moment before. I looked ahead at the mast and kept crawling. The bucket was overflowing, and I reached in to get the cup we kept tied inside. I took a gulp of water to check for contamination. Pure and fresh. I quickly filled the two bottles, replaced the caps, and crawled back with my load.

Rick, Jim, and Phil were waiting below in the cockpit to take the full bottles and hand me two more empty ones. On my third trip back I slung the full bottles around my neck, but one slipped out of the knotted cord and bounced over the side before I could catch it. I cursed my bad luck. Not only had we lost precious water, we had lost a very useful bottle. Later we tied a length of plastic tube into the bucket to use as a siphon. We put one end of the pipe in the water, sucked on the other end, and siphoned it into a bottle, which made the whole job a lot easier.

Once the guttering system was in use I began to worry about the toxic antifoul paint on the hull. When I brushed my hand across it I ended up with a layer of white dust on my skin. How much of it were we drinking in our water supply? On the next fine day Phil and I sat up on deck with a chisel each and began scraping the paint off round the water-catchment area. It was ironic that Phil and I had spent hours a couple of months ago painting on the antifoul, and now we were spending hours chiselling it off.

It was a terrible job, and once we had started, I wondered whether I had made the right decision. The dust and paint flakes blew everywhere and, although we tried to wash the hull down as we worked, it still seemed to get over everything. Rick and Jim would walk around in their socks, picking up bits of paint and spreading it still further. We finished one side of the hull that day, and three weeks later I got up on deck with a chisel and finished the other side on my own.

Around the time I dived into the float to retrieve the plastic piping and timber for the water systems, I spotted several planks still wedged in there. I had used them to drop down as buffers when coming alongside a wharf, to protect the pontoons.

I used one length of timber as a cutting board for filleting fish. Each time I finished using it I would tie the board onto the mast, looping a line through a hole in the wood, but one day it disappeared, the rope broken by the fury of a storm.

I thought that we could wedge another of the planks between the opening of our cabin, over the water in the galley and across to the cupboard opposite, thus making it a lot easier to get in and out of our new cockpit above. Jim had found it particularly difficult to haul himself up through the hole while balanced on the cupboard shelf below.

By this stage we were down to about three or four teaspoonfuls of food a day, so any physical effort like lugging a heavy plank into place left us exhausted. But each time we achieved something to make life a little more comfortable or easier, we felt immense satisfaction. And it gave us something to do, diverting our attention even for an hour from our predicament.

We used to store freshwater in a foam chiller bin at the foot of the cabin, a practice that irritated Rick because it was constantly getting in the way of his feet. The chiller bin caused a lot of arguments, and finally we balanced it on the plank leading into the aft cabin. However, during stormy weather the surging waves would sometimes slosh over the bin, contaminating our precious water supply.

Water that was just a little briny we used either to soak the cold rice, water down the vinegar, or to make homemade chili and garlic water. I used to grow chilies when I lived in Broadwater, northern New South Wales, and from them I made my own chili powder. I had a few jars left on the boat, and Jim would mix the briny water with powder to add flavor to our meals. He called it "spiced water." I had found a jar of cooked and pickled garlic during one of my salvage trips, and as its contents diminished, Jim added briny water and a few cloves of raw garlic. This lasted us almost to the end and always tasted just as good.

Sometimes our rainwater became so contaminated with salt that it was not fit to drink, and we could only use so much of it with meals. We were loath to pour it away, because it had taken us so much time and effort to collect in the first place. On a fine day I would use the briny water to wash out my clothes, particularly my two black woollen bush singlets, and hang them up in the rigging to dry. I used to alternate between wearing different items of clothing to try to make them last. We would often tear our trousers as we were climbing in and out of the cockpit, and Phil and I used to wear a pair of shorts on top of them as protection.

We had plenty of detergent, clothes-washing liquid, shampoo, and saltwater soap on board. But as time went on, we got out of the habit of wanting to wash or of keeping up those daily ablutions that you would normally not dream of leaving for the office without attending to. For the first few weeks I was quite clean because I was diving in the main cabin regularly. Sometimes, if I wasn't shivering too much, I would wade over to my little locker of personal belongings to lather myself with a tube of saltwater shampoo. When we capsized, we had taken a drawer out from beneath the dinette to use as packing in the aft cabin. The space it left was just above the waterline and became a sort of dressing table for me, complete with a collection of personal items I had come across while diving.

As we gradually lost condition, we became more concerned about keeping warm than keeping clean. Rick, Jim, and Phil rarely washed, and all three stayed in the same set of clothes the whole time unless they got something wet and had to hang it out to dry. We had one toothbrush and a tube of toothpaste on board, and I would brush my teeth once every week or so, when I thought of it. The others didn't seem to bother as much; while on land we would not feel right without brushing our teeth after breakfast; out there it just did not occur to us. Personal hygiene was something we had to remind ourselves to attend to, rather than feel the need of it.

The strange thing about all this was the lack of body odor. I am sure that with the four of us not washing and being cooped up for days on end in the tiny, airless aft cabin, we probably smelled to high heaven. We sweated and we slept within centimeters of each others' mouths and bodies, but we were never aware of any smell.

After about forty days adrift I began to keep my log. I had wanted to write one from the start, but Rick seemed upset by the idea, saying it was bad karma. I had tried to write significant events on the cabin walls, but he was against that, too—he did not want to accept that we would be adrift long enough to make writing a log worthwhile. Eventually, however, I decided to go ahead and write one anyway. I knew there were exercise books and stationery stored beneath the dinette seat. When we capsized, the seat had fallen off, but some of the contents were still jammed inside, just above the waterline. I reached in and carefully pulled out the paper and books, together with some of my eight-year-old son's drawings.

From then on I began to write down what we did each day, what we ate and how much, how we organized ourselves, and descriptions of our various inventions. To keep myself occupied during the long hours spent in the aft cabin, I began to write articles on capsize intended for multihull magazines. I wrote about how we tipped up, what I would do differently next time, survival hints, the mistakes we made and the lessons we learned, which equipment we found useful, and ways in which we improvised. I also began writing letters to family and friends; it was such a comfort to absorb myself in communicating silently with those close to me. And I began to design a catamaran I called a Sounds Cruiser, ideal for exploring the Marlborough Sounds.

After a few weeks, Rick decided that keeping a record wasn't such a bad idea after all. He used the other exercise book to write letters to Heather in the form of a diary; it was his way of letting her know that we were all right, his comfort.

Our loved ones would never see the various letters we wrote.

SIX

Fish—Our Favorite Dish

I have never grown tired of eating fish. I can eat them until the cows come home. In days past I have had to, but for some reason the fish were not keen on the luscious bits of bait we dangled alluringly from hooks over the side. In the early days we weren't too worried, because we had plenty of food and we thought rescue was imminent.

I had salvaged a box of fishing tackle from one of the lockers but stored it away up for'ard. From my years of sailing *Highlight* I knew not to expect to see fish unless near the coast, a reef, or an island—in the South Pacific at least. However, two days after we capsized, a big grouper swam lazily through the companionway into the main cabin. We watched it poke curiously into open cupboards before it slowly swam away. On day five we saw a grouper, perhaps the same one, swimming off the wingdeck when we emerged from the cabin for the first time. I had always assumed grouper were bottom-feeding fish and found it strange to see one on the surface 140 miles off the coast.

Jim was a keen freshwater fisherman in the United States and now he occasionally dangled a hook but without success. About a month after the capsize a fish swam into the main cabin, and Jim baited up a hook with several pieces of tinned sweetcorn. We lay quietly and watched. Suddenly Jim jerked the line and the fish was hooked. He lifted it straight out of the water and landed it on our bed while we whooped with delight. Jim's face lit up; I had never before seen him so delighted. We were so excited and eager for the taste of fresh fish that we attacked it on the spot. Jim cleaned it and I took over, filleting it in the cabin. Blood, fish scales, and bones went everywhere, and we stopped just short of eating the flesh raw. Fortunately I had ten liters of vinegar stored up for'ard, and I marinated the fish for twenty minutes before we stuffed the delicious morsels in our mouths.

Encouraged by Jim's success, we increased our efforts to hook fish to supplement our meager spoonfuls of tinned food. I dived into one of the floats and salvaged a fishing rod and reel, the only one I had on board. We used the head of Jim's fish to try to catch more, but our prey stayed well clear. The nosy grouper, whom we had named Harry, continued to visit regularly but stayed shy of any bait.

After a month drifting upturned, *Rose-Noëlle*'s topsides and wingdeck and cabin beneath the water became covered with a layer of brown slime. Tiny molluscs and goose barnacles began to form; slowly we were turning into a floating island—12.3 meters long by 8 meters wide. The more marine growth we grew, the more the fish—mostly yellowtail kingfish—became interested in our existence. They came to feed on us, and we planned to feed on them. The trouble was, we got the raw end of the deal.

We tried everything but to no avail. When they didn't seem interested in our lures, Phil and I sat up on deck and made colorful new ones. I strung two fish-hooks together and attached two stainless-steel nuts on the top shank to make it shiny. I cut two strips of red spinnaker cloth from the sail repair kit and dangled those from the end. The first time I used my homemade lure I caught a small kingfish, but I think it was more by accident than skill, because I never caught anything with it again.

We spent hours with baited hooks and lures, but the fish refused to be tempted. Occasionally we would fluke a catch, but our fish meals were frustratingly sporadic, and we grew thinner and more hungry. We needed to rethink how we fished and develop methods that were more efficient and productive.

Phil helped to speed up that process by losing the fishing rod one day. By now we were careful to tie every item on a line, both inside the hull and out on deck. At mealtimes pots, knives, cups, even an old teatowel were tied down. Once they slipped overboard they went three miles down, and there was no popping out to the local shop for a replacement. We had already lost so much gear either overboard or in the surge in the main cabin that we looked after a simple item as if it were gold. All except Phil. Either he was naturally clumsy or he just didn't care. He seemed to be always losing things, and the three of us were constantly admonishing him about his carelessness.

One day I was up on deck when I heard Phil curse. He had decided to read a book and left the fishing rod wedged in the cockpit without tying it on. Something tugged at the line, and it had disappeared over the side. Even though we weren't having much success fishing, that rod represented a food source and was therefore one of the most precious items on the boat.

"How did that happen?" I demanded. "Didn't you have it tied on?" Enraged at my scolding, Phil stormed down to the aft cabin to tell Rick and Jim what had happened, apologizing for his carelessness. He didn't meet with much more sympathy there and soon came back up on deck, stalked past me, and sat brooding up for'ard.

Rick and Jim made up a fishing gaff from a ten-centimeter hook lashed to an ash sail batten cut down to size. The first version didn't work too well because the hook was positioned at right angles, so that the flat side of the batten had to be dragged through the water. The fish were just too quick. I suggested we turn the hook so that the thin edge of the batten cut through the water. Although the gaff was weaker that way, the increased speed meant we began catching fish.

However, without a landing net, the gaff was next to useless, so Rick and Jim set about making one up with a timber frame and the prawn netting I had strung along the for'ard cabin to use as storage racks. One of the first times Rick used the net the fish were boiling in a frenzy on the surface of the water off the wingdeck. He lunged and scooped and caught four kingfish in one go, a record that was never beaten. We were sometimes lucky enough to catch the fish massing in this way, always just before sunrise or just before sunset. We assumed they were in a feeding frenzy, but we didn't really care what they were doing as long as one or two of them ended up on the gaff or in the net.

Harry the Grouper had become complacent by now, and one morning—shortly after the first net was made—Jim spotted him swimming into the main cabin as he leaned out through the aft cabin entrance. Slowly he positioned the net and swooped. Harry was history. He thrashed and flopped all over our bed, but I soon had him cut into large fillets.

I remembered the Tahitian raw fish dish *ei'a oto*, or *poisson cru*, which I used to eat constantly while cruising the South Pacific. I had the ingredients I needed; it was time for a feast. I marinated small pieces of the grouper in vinegar, drained it, and opened one of our precious cans of coconut milk. I added lemon pepper seasoning, onion flakes, and dried parsley. It tasted like heaven, better than I remembered. Harry fed us like kings for several meals. We discovered that fish prepared in this way would keep up to a week as long as the vinegar was not too diluted.

The first version of the net was somewhat crude and heavy, but Rick and Jim kept persevering and improving the design. I salvaged a collapsible square crab pot from one of the floats, and Rick used the steel frame from that to replace the original wooden frame of the net. He spent days up on deck perfecting it until the final version worked really well.

The best fishing spots were off the starboard wingdeck up for'ard and in the wingdeck opening where the trampoline had been. Here the water lapped level, and we could get close to our prey. There was a second spinnaker pole secured to the cabinside beneath the water, and I salvaged it to make a railing to lean on while we were fishing. We suspended it horizontally at chest height between the rigging lines that supported the mast up above on the main hull. Although the railing wobbled, it gave us support while reaching out over the wingdeck during the hours we spent

On fine days we fished off the wingdeck. The illustration shows
the conduit water-catchment system attached to the mast and the
guttering running down the main hull.

poised with the gaff and net. We felt like Eskimos fishing from a hole cut in the ice.

I began to lie awake at night and mull over how we could use a large gill-net I had salvaged from one of the floats around the time I had retrieved the materials to make the water-catchment systems. The net was packed in a bucket, and Phil had stowed it up for'ard, but when we next went to get it we discovered the bucket had washed away during a storm, leaving the net in a hopeless tangled mess. With the bucket had gone two long strings of plaited garlic, an ingredient we were to miss sorely later on.

Rick and Jim sat up on deck one day trying to untangle the gill-net, but after a couple of hours the wind came up and the fine netting was blowing everywhere. They stowed it back down in the main cabin, where the next storm twisted it into a tangled heap. Rick and Jim lost heart, and we ignored the net for a few weeks.

As our food supplies ran low and the pressure to develop a reliable method of catching fish grew, I thought again about the gill-net. On the next fine day I dragged it up on deck and sat for a couple of hours with Phil, slowly straightening it out. It was difficult to get a chance to do this sort of task, because fine days were so rare; when they did occur, we spent the time fishing and drying out our bedding from our soaking aft cabin.

Phil and I got half the net done and gradually finished the rest whenever we struck a fine, windless day. In my mind I had designed a foolproof way of catching fish using the net, and I was hell-bent on getting it untangled. I explained the concept to Phil, Jim, and Rick, and the four of us worked for hours and hours on the design. We cut the net to length and framed the four sides with heavy rope by tying the fine netting onto the rope every fifteen centimeters. Along the bottom we hung a row of heavy items—my kerosene iron, spare tools, anything that we didn't need.

The idea was to launch the net down over the hull and into the water by the wingdeck, where we could see the fish feeding off the marine life attached to the hull. I designed a way to launch and retrieve the net without getting it tangled and without anyone getting wet. I shackled some blocks into the starboard float, rigged up an endless line, and attached it to the net. Once in the water and under the fish, the net could be easily pulled up over the spinnaker railing suspended from the rigging and laid flat on the hull. Even when we were not using it, the weighted net could be lashed flat to the hull so that it would not tangle again. Phil, Rick, and Jim were impressed once they saw it working.

The design itself worked brilliantly. I had used only the best gear and had even attached cleats to the hull to fasten the ropes once the net was pulled up. The only trouble was, we never caught a single fish with that confounded net. Once it was lowered into the water, the fish disappeared. It actually scared them away, and they refused to come back until the net was pulled clear of the water.

We persevered with the net for a couple of weeks. After the hours we had spent rigging it up, we just could not accept that it would not work; we deserved to get at least one fish. But we still had lessons to learn. I admitted defeat and packed it away in the bucket. I consoled myself by reasoning that the design of the net had given me something to grapple with during the long, dark hours in the aft cabin when sleep would not come. Moreover, it had kept the four of us busy and hopeful, although the fact remained we were still hungry, and we still had no fish.

We began to rely more and more on the gaff as a method of catching fish. It served a double purpose: not only did it eventually become the main fish-catching tool, it changed Phil's pessimistic attitude toward our chances of survival. Jim, Rick, and I fluctuated between feeling sorry and concerned for Phil and being annoyed and at times enraged by him. Right from that first day, when he kicked open the companionway doors and caused the loss of valuable gear, he had been a liability. He was continually losing irreplaceable items, and he just did not seem to care. His mind was elsewhere.

We couldn't convince Phil that we had a fighting chance. He would sit for hours looking out at the sea, thinking about his family, thinking about dying. At one stage he considered tying his wedding ring round his neck and writing a final letter to Karen in case he was just a skeleton when he was found.

Dr. Alain Bombard concludes in *The Bombard Story* that terror and despair are greater threats than a lack of food or water. "If drink is more important than food, instilling confidence is more important than drink," he wrote. "Thirst kills more quickly than hunger, but despair is a greater danger than thirst. The survivor of a shipwreck, deprived of everything, must never lose hope. The simple and brutal problem confronting him is that of death or survival. He will need to bolster his courage with all his resources and all his faith in life to fight off despair."

What was to stop Phil slipping into the water while the rest of us were below and swimming away, ending his private agony? Rick, Jim, and I confronted him, told him he had to change his attitude and become part of a team effort to survive. We were constantly at him those first three months. Mind you, he never did tie his wedding ring around his neck. It was in fact his greenstone dress ring that left his finger. As his fingers grew thinner, this heavy ring kept slipping off, but someone would always find it up on deck before it was washed away.

The new Phil did not emerge until he discovered that he was a dab hand with the gaff. Right from the start he caught more fish than any of us using this method. We seized on this success to bolster his ego, to convince him that he had a valuable part to play in our survival. We had nicknamed the gaff "The Wand," and now we began calling Phil "The Wand" and "The Hook." You could almost see his chest puff out with pride. Suddenly he had a purpose on the boat; he was the provider. The more fish he caught, the more fuss we made. He used to put more hours into fishing than any of us; he became obsessed with catching fish. As he strutted off holding his gaff, Jim would grin and say, "Phil's showing off again."

*   *   *

Around day eighty, the main fishing-tackle box disappeared, plucked away by a breaking wave in the cockpit. We had kept the box in the cockpit, tied with a line from its handle to the taps on the water tank above. But after one storm all that was left was the line with the handle still attached. I was not too worried about the sinkers, because I had plenty of nuts and bolts in my tool box that would do, but gone were several big, strong hooks which, if we had broken the hook on our gaff, would have been invaluable.

As time went on, the kingfish were getting bigger and we were worried that our single hook would not cope. Ideally we needed a second gaff to make the most of the times when the fish boiled in a frenzy on the surface. I began to consider how I could make a replacement hook should the need arise. The thin stainless-steel safety rail around the stove would do nicely, I thought, but when I knelt on the plank and felt down below the oven, I discovered that the stainless steel had corroded against its aluminum housing and the rail had dropped off and disappeared. Next I thought of the stainless-steel pump shaft on the toilet we had demolished, but it was too difficult to get out. Finally I made a spear from a piece of scrap metal that I filed into a point and fashioned a barb at one end.

I jammed my new spear down the centerboard well, a handy space for storing odds and ends when we were on deck. On an average day you would find a couple of pairs of socks, books, fishing lines, and the odd tool in that space. The next time I checked for the spear it had gone, carried off, I suppose, by a storm. I had neglected to tie it on, a lesson I should have learned early on after Phil lost the fishing rod, and I cursed myself for the lapse.

We noticed that if we dropped a lure about six meters below the surface and drew it back up, the kingfish would follow it but never bite. Eventually we gave up trying to hook fish in this way, instead using the lures only to encourage our prey to the top ready to be gaffed or netted.

Gradually, as we improved our skill, the four of us developed into an efficient team. Jim would deftly dangle a lure

Phil "The Wand" Hofman in action with the gaff while Rick deftly positions the net.

from a line and entice the kingfish to the surface. Phil would be poised ready with the gaff, his eyes wide and intent on the task. When he struck, Rick was ready with the landing net. If our prey somehow wriggled off the gaff before it was in Rick's net, we would have no show of catching the slithering, flapping kingfish. We would desperately lunge at our vanishing prey, grabbing at it, kicking it, anything to stop it from disappearing over the side.

I had spent days sorting out two sail bags full of gear and special utensils from the galley that I particularly wanted to save. I thought that perhaps we might be rescued by a big ship or strike land, and then I would be able to hop off with my sackfuls of precious booty. But as the fishing became more successful, it was obvious that we needed a sail bag in which to transfer the catch from Rick's net. As I put the salvaged items back where I had found them, I thought optimistically that we might not need to abandon ship after all. Perhaps a ship would spot us and use its cranes to hoist the boat aboard; or perhaps we would just glide ashore on a calm, sandy beach and tie the upside-down *Rose-Noëlle* to a palm tree until she could be properly salvaged.

With the empty sail bag at the ready, I stood behind Rick, who would quickly transfer the catch into it, leaving the net free for the next swoop. I would then gut and fillet the fish and stand it in vinegar. The bones would marinate in another plastic container, and the internal organs in a screw-top coffee jar.

Years ago in the South Pacific I had followed the ways of the Tahitians and eaten parts of the fish raw. Now as I filleted our catch I would pick out the white roe peculiar to the male kingfish, and Jim and I would share the delicacy. We tried eating the stomach, but that wasn't too palatable. Rick and Phil refused to have anything to do with it, preferring to wait until the white flesh of the fillets was well marinated in vinegar.

One day we caught a big kingfish and found some smaller, half-digested fish inside. They were like herrings; the skin had been stripped off, and the flesh had turned white. We ate them raw, and they were delicious.

*   *   *

When there were fish around, we worked up on the wingdeck for twelve hours at a stretch without going below. On a good day we caught six fish with the odd one up to half a meter long. On a bad day we fished for hours without a single catch. There was no point in fishing if there were no fish to be seen; the water was clear, and we could see to at least sixteen meters down. Fragments of the mast and rigging dangled well below us, still attached to the stays.

The fish were always off the starboard float to leeward. Even though the marine growth was as thick on the port side, we never saw fish there. We assumed there was something dangling beneath the hull in the water that frightened them off, much as the gill-net had done.

In the final month we began to get a lot of good weather, and the fishing got better and better. On good fishing days we forgot to look for ships, we didn't argue, we stopped dwelling on our loved ones and wondering if we would ever see them again; all we thought about was catching fish . . . and more fish.

If we caught just one fish, I would cut the fillets into eight pieces, saving half in a plastic container for the following days in case the weather meant we could not get out on deck. Sometimes on fine, clear nights we kept working, and I would fillet the catch up on deck in the dark by feel. Then we would vote on whether we would save the fish for the following day or treat ourselves to a second dinner, a delicious morsel of fish each. The meat up by the gills was firm and sweet and became a favorite with the four of us.

Toward the end of our voyage the weather began to improve and we were able to fish from dawn until dusk. By this time our teamwork was well rehearsed, our artificial reef was working well, and we were catching plenty. Fortunately fish, the odd seabird, and seaweed were all that we attracted. During our entire drift we saw only one shark, and late one night we heard a whale blow near the boat.

Jim and I used to harvest the goose barnacles growing on stalks attached to the hull and eat them raw or add them to our meals. The barnacles exposed to the sun had short,

Collecting molluscs for dinner off the wingdeck.

black stalks that tasted strongly of iodine. Phil refused to eat any food if we had added in these, so Jim and I would shell the barnacles and discard the stalks. We also harvested the barnacles attached to the hull beneath the water; these grew opaque stalks fifteen to twenty centimeters long. Eventually a green, slimy grass began to grow on the stalks of the molluscs and on the wingdeck in the sun. I used to eat it, reasoning that anything green and growing had to be good for me.

When the weather closed in, we stowed away our fishing gear and went below. Sometimes we were confined for four or five days in the aft cabin while gale winds lashed and buffeted the boat. It was a time to catch up on the hours of lost sleep, for in fine weather we fished during the day and kept watch at night.

When we emerged from these days below, our limbs were stiff and cramped and we felt weak and depressed. Lying so close to one another, unable to get up and walk away when things got too much, our moods plunged. We prayed for fine weather . . . and for more fish.

SEVEN

If Only We Had Some Heat

Jim naturally became the chief cook on board. We all admired his skill; with a few ingredients he could make us think we had just eaten a sumptuous meal. We were restricted to just a few spoonfuls of food a day, but Jim prepared and served it as though it were a work of art. He soaked rice in cold water for twenty-four hours to add a teaspoon or two of carbohydrate to our rations, working hard to make sure whatever went with the rice was varied and interesting. He experimented with flavors, combining seasonings and spices from the galley cupboard with all the flair and imagination his training could muster. We lay for ages at mealtimes, savoring every mouthful.

A month after we capsized, I pulled a cabbage out from beneath the packing in the aft cabin. It had been in seawater all that time, but Jim chopped it up and pickled it in a mixture of vinegar and water. He called it *kapousta* and would add a little to the cold rice to give it flavor. When I found a pumpkin in a locker up for'ard, Jim cut it up into small pieces and marinated it in a vinaigrette dressing made from vinegar, oil, wholegrain mustard, pepper, and garlic. After a week or so it tasted great, and we would have a little with our meal each day.

The Granny Smith apples lasted fifty days, and even then we would occasionally spot the odd one floating about the cabin. By that stage the apple had become saturated with seawater, so Jim would grate it and pickle it in vinegar and sugar to add to our array of condiments.

After a while the supply of rice began to go moldy, and we were rationed to about three teaspoons a day. As a treat we might add a tiny dab of Marmite or jam to the side of our plates, or Jim would use a spoonful of his homemade pickle to enhance the flavor. Sometimes he would serve six different courses, all in minute amounts. Mealtimes were without a doubt the highlight of the day.

I consider it was Jim's culinary expertise that contributed more than anything to keeping up morale during those 119 days. But no matter how hard you try to dress it up, cold food is cold food. And in the middle of winter in a soaking-wet cabin, that can be depressing. Every so often Jim would mutter to me, "If we only had some heat."

When I first dived to the port float to retrieve the conduit pipe for the water system, I noticed my stainless-steel barbecue still wedged in there. A couple of days later I went back to get it. We had timber, kerosene, and matches. There was no reason why we could not cook a hot meal, at least once in a while.

Once the thought of hot food had taken root, there was no stopping us. We decided to light the barbecue right away and treat ourselves to fried bread. Up until then Jim had made rolls of raw dough filled with a layer of jam as a treat, and now we were about to taste the cooked version. He mixed up some dough and left it to rise while Phil, Rick, and I chopped up some scrap timber. It was too windy on deck for a match to stay alight, so we took the barbecue below, and Jim balanced it on the plank just outside the entrance to the aft cabin. As the rest of us crouched in the cabin and watched Jim pour oil into a big frypan, our saliva glands were drooling in anticipation of what was to come.

The oil spat as it heated, and the smell sent more signals to four sets of nostrils starved of that welcome odor. When Jim dropped the first of the dough lumps into the pan, the loud sizzling was one of the most delicious sounds I had ever heard. As fast as Jim could cook them, the four of us tore the hot bread into pieces with our fingers and wolfed it down. The dough filled our mouths and burned our throats. We concentrated on nothing but the taste and when the next piece of fried dough was coming out of the pan.

The fat got hotter and the smoke thickened. There was no way we could control the heat coming off the barbecue. The aft cabin filled with black smoke, choking us and stinging our eyes. In a panic, Phil pulled back the mattress so that he could gulp some air in the space between the sleeping platform and the water.

We could have done ourselves some serious damage. That would have been just great, I thought later. In the previous six weeks we had survived the capsize and the storms and were now eking out a reasonable existence— only to die from smoke inhalation or third-degree burns from an out-of-control barbecue. And all to satisfy a greedy, uncontrollable urge for hot food.

After that we only ever lit the barbecue up on deck on a very calm day. We tied it to our mast and kept a supply of chopped wood ready in case we should see a ship and need to light a signal fire in a hurry.

Then I remembered the kerosene lamp I had salvaged from the jammed locker and wondered if we could use it as a little burner to heat food. I found the kerosene in a for'ard bilge locker, now above our heads, where I had stored soft drinks, detergents, in fact anything in bottles. Rick cut a wick from the tie straps off a life jacket and, after a lot of fiddling around, he got the lamp working.

The four of us lay on our stomachs in the aft cabin concentrating on this minute source of heat. While Phil and I held the lamp and kept it going, Rick would hold an old baked-bean can half full of water over the flame. As it heated, Jim would concoct one of his wonderful sauces, using gravy or custard powder as thickener and maybe adding chili powder or tandoori mix to pour over a little cold rice or fish. But it didn't really matter what it was poured over; it could have been cardboard. I was such a fan of those thick, hot sauces, the others used to call me Captain Gravox. Sometimes Jim would make sweet custard and pour it over rice. It reminded me of the wonderful rice puddings with sultanas my mother used to make in a vain attempt to fill her three lanky children.

A few times when the weather was still we sat up on the main
hull and lit the barbecue, shielding it from the wind with a blanket
draped over our shoulders. The hot food tasted heavenly.

The kerosene burner gave us something to do during those long periods when we were cooped up in the aft cabin for days on end during a storm. We were uncomfortable, cold, cramped, sick of the sight of each other, and sick of existing in a cave with little headroom. We would bicker over nothing, over everything. Then we would vote on whether to use a little of our precious supply of kerosene to make a little hot sauce. Immediately morale lifted. The flame warmed the cabin and our hands. In fact, Rick warmed his hands a little too well the first time we used the lamp, so from then on we wrapped a piece of foam around the can to protect him from the heat.

The burner was constantly sooting up, and Rick was always cutting a fresh wick and topping up the fuel to get it to work. Jim's face would end up covered in soot and our tiny cabin would gradually turn black. That might have bothered us under normal conditions; in fact I would have been aghast two months earlier to see the gleaming paintwork on my beautiful *Rose-Noëlle* begin to look like the inside of a chimney. But all we thought about was savouring the warm mouthfuls of food smothered in sauce or custard.

We never made hot drinks over the burner because they took too long, and we were conscious of saving our supply of kerosene, which would be invaluable should we need to light the barbecue signal fire in a hurry. We sometimes used to make "sun tea" on a really fine day by filling a bottle with water, adding tea leaves, and hanging it up in the sun. The idea sounded better than it tasted; the result was an insipid beverage that looked like tea but was barely lukewarm. About every three weeks the weather would be still enough to light the barbecue. We would jam it in a hole on the hull where the speedo impeller used to be and sit in a row holding a blanket around us to shield the flames from the breeze. Jim would make up a batch of four dozen little buns to last us, with careful rationing, until the next time we could use the barbecue. He would leave some water in a bottle on deck to warm, add yeast, flour, oil, and sugar and cover the mixture with a pillow in the aft cabin to rise. Then he would thump and knead the dough while we stoked up the barbecue and heated the frypan. To preserve our supply of sugar, he used as a sweetener a little honey or lemonade essence I had on board for the soda siphon. We would eat two or three hot buns off the pan, then with great discipline put the rest away in a plastic container and ration them out—usually one a day with dinner.

While the barbecue was on, we usually made up a pot of gravy and poured it over a little fish or rice. The final luxury was a cup of hot tea. We had a dozen packets of tea on board, and Rick was good at making billy tea on the barbecue, a skill he had perfected from his years in the bush. He would bring a pot of water to a rolling boil then add the tea leaves and remove from the heat after two or three seconds; the leaves would slowly infuse and sink to the bottom. Jim would eat the tea leaves left in the bottom of the pot, and toward the end I joined him in the habit. We wasted nothing.

Around day fifty Jim hooked a big seabird. It settled on the water nearby, and Jim decided dinner had arrived. He stood on the stern, whirling a fishing line and baited hook around his head in large, slow circles, enticing the bird to take flight and swoop on the flying morsel. It was great to watch; he made it look so easy.

The bird struggled and flapped as Jim dragged it in and I grabbed it, planning to break its neck as I had done with countless chickens while growing up in the country. But it was too strong and I had to cut its throat with a knife.

Jim wanted to leave the skin on so that there would be more to eat and to preserve the juices while it was cooking. Normally I would pour boiling water over the bird to loosen the feathers, but, since we couldn't afford that extravagance, Jim and I sat down and began laboriously pulling out every feather, one at a time. Eventually we decided that this was going to take too long. Either the bird would have gone off or we would have starved to death. So I skinned and boned it, something I was used to doing with rabbits and chickens. Jim watched me, fascinated, wanting to learn the technique.

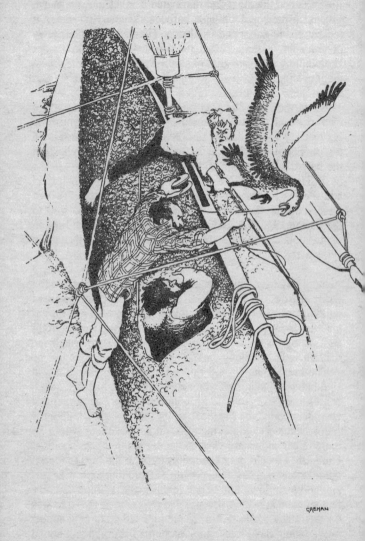

Hooking a seabird. Once marinated and sautéed, the meat was tender and delicious.

Jim cubed the meat and marinated it in a little soy sauce, vinegar, water, and Chinese barbecue sauce. He sautéed it lightly, made gravy and fried rice. The meat wasn't sinewy or fishy as we had thought. It was beautiful—like tender beef. I had also discovered an unexpected treasure—a tin of pineapple pieces wedged in behind the color radar. Part of the top had rusted away, and the sweet juice had been replaced with seawater, making the fruit horribly salty. Jim drained it and lightly cooked the pineapple with lemonade essence. It made a very passable dessert. We finished with a hot cup of tea, and I still think it was one of the best meals we had.

Jim used to ask me about the gas bottles every now and then. He'd usually throw in a wistful "if we only had some heat," and it would set me thinking. But I kept stalling on making a decision. The gas bottles were tucked up under the cockpit coamings, now upside down and underwater. I knew that gas regulators could be difficult to work at the best of times, even when new, and I suspected they may have corroded during their time underwater. My main fear was blowing the four of us and *Rose-Noëlle* clean away. Even if we survived the explosion, we might well be left floating in the water surrounded by bits of foam-sandwich flotsam. Better to eat cold food and at least stay in one piece, I reasoned.

But eventually I relented and, around day ninety, Jim went for'ard to where I had disconnected the boat's catalytic gas heater, while I turned on one of the gas taps beneath the stove in the galley. (One of the taps controlled a gas line leading to the heater; the other fed gas to the stove.)

"Yeah, there's gas coming through, all right," called a delighted Jim. Fortunately the gas bottle had been turned on out in the cockpit when we capsized. I waded for'ard and dismantled the heater, salvaging some copper pipe and fittings I would need to create our makeshift gas cooker. I took the flexible gas line from the heater, connected it to the stove tap in the galley, and ran the other end into the aft cabin. I made up a burner from a piece of copper pipe almost flattened at one end over a feeler gauge and attached that to the flexible hose. Later I used the feeler gauge to clean the burner each time it sooted up or needed adjusting.

The original system of cooking with the burner was crude to say the least. One of us would have to kneel on the plank in the galley to regulate the gas flow from the tap beneath the stove; if we misjudged the flow, the flame would go out, and we would have to use two or three more of our precious matches to light it again. The rest of us would lie on our stomachs in the cabin, Phil and I holding the burner and the pot, and Jim doing the cooking.

As soon as we got the heat, life became like paradise. I used to dream about being able to wake up and have a hot cup of tea in the morning. A full billy of tea gave us about a cup and a half each. Strangely, we had to have our tea boiling hot, and we would put it back on the heat to serve the second cup. (Once I was back on land the heat of tea was not nearly so important; in fact, I used to let it cool a little before drinking it.)

After about ten days the gas suddenly stopped working, an alarming development just as we were getting used to the indulgence of a hot meal each night. I couldn't tell if there was a fault or if we had run out of gas, so the next day I hacked a hole in the wingdeck above the gas bottle. As I knelt on the wingdeck, sawing through the fiberglass with waves breaking over the top of me, I thought that if it had not been for the lure of a hot meal that night I might have abandoned the task until a calmer day. The gas tank we had been using was empty; I must have used more gas than I thought before we left. But we still had three full bottles on board, enough to last us up to a year if used sparingly.

It was a calculation I dare not repeat to Rick, Jim, and Phil for fear of an angry reaction. They would not face up to the possibility that we could be in a for a long wait and resented my attitude of acceptance over our plight. No one liked to think that we might still be floating around the Pacific Ocean on day one hundred—but we were.

After three months eating mostly cold food, cooking hot meals with the gas burner in the entrance to the aft cabin was close to luxury.

I salvaged the gas line from the empty tank, got the second gas bottle out of the hole, and put it in our new cockpit. I took one of the gas taps from beneath the stove and fitted it near the end of the gas line by the burner, so that wc could regulate the flow without leaving the cabin. I joined the two flexible lines together and ran that from the gas bottle in the cockpit through to the aft cabin. When we had finished with the gas for the night, we could turn it off at the bottle in the new cockpit.

For a while we stood the pot or frypan on three empty upturned cans, a somewhat precarious arrangement. Again I mulled over the problem and came up with a design in my head, using the crab pot with metal mesh fold-down sides. I talked it over with Jim, but he couldn't understand what I meant until I made a model from a piece of paper. He then went off and made a thoroughly professional job of it. Now we had a stand a little like a metal cage to fit any size of pot.

Once we were able to cook regularly, the four of us discovered that the tastiest parts of the fish were those that we would normally throw away—the head and the guts. Jim would lightly sauté the guts in a little oil, sometimes adding Chinese barbecue sauce or some shelled molluscs for extra flavor. We would eat sautéed fish guts for breakfast or as a special entrée before a fish dinner. They had a strong, rich flavor like nothing I had ever tasted. Perhaps if we had caught the fish in a polluted area the guts would not have tasted so good, but out there they were like caviar.

We boiled up the fish heads for just a few minutes and ate everything—the eyes, bones, even the gills, which we discovered were one of the tastiest parts. Seafood chowder made from the heads and tails was another delicacy. Jim would add shelled molluscs gathered from the hull, spices, chili, and sometimes a little dried seaweed. The seaweed had caught round the bow of the boat and stayed there for weeks before it occurred to us to harvest it. Once dried, it took on a tasty, chewy texture and became a favorite to add to soup.

We talked about how it would be a treat to catch two fish the same size so that we could have a whole fillet each, and there was great discussion on how each of us wanted our fish cooked. The next day we caught the fish we had been waiting for, and again I wondered at our ability to make such things manifest. Jim would patiently fill the orders—pan-fried thoroughly for one person; half cooked for another. A couple of times we were lucky enough to catch four fish the same size so that we could have a fish head each. Such a treat.

One day I remembered our container of burley—the saturated cocoa and biscuits. It smelled well and truly off when we inspected the contents, but we refused to throw it out. We drained off the seawater and added freshwater, but it did nothing to improve the sight or smell of the mixture. In the end Jim mixed it with flour and made burley biscuits glazed with jam in the frypan. Cautiously we bit into the first piping-hot sample . . . they tasted wonderful! "Exquisite," as Rick used to say. (My expression was "Lovely!")

We were like kids sitting round a campfire eating pikelets late at night. We lay there in the aft cabin, eating burley biscuits until the whole mixture had gone.

Gradually the walls and roof of our little cabin turned black as we used the gas burner every day. The soot got over everything—our clothes, hands and feet, the pots and utensils. Jim's face seemed to be permanently black, as he did most of the cooking. One day I decided to have a real spring-clean and washed everything in the aft cabin with seawater and detergent. I cleaned the walls, the battery boxes, our cooking utensils, even the herb bottles in the galley. But I was fighting a losing battle; before long everything had once again turned black.

We were continually running out of places to put precious items where they would not get wet or be swept away. Most of the shelves and cupboards were underwater. I ran a line above the water in the main cabin within reach of the plank leading aft. When we had finished washing up, we would tie pots and pans, utensils, and Jim's cooking stand to the line, where they would slowly swing as the boat dipped in the swell.

One by one we had conquered our problems to survive and make life reasonably comfortable. We had a healthy water supply, we were catching fish, we had a dry cabin, and we could cook. We felt all our dreams had come true and that we had everything we wanted . . . almost.

EIGHT

Search and Rescue

About the time we capsized, my friend Rose Young from Picton decided to bake a batch of butter cookies and send some to me at my forwarding address in Tonga. In an empty chocolate box she packed a dozen of the freshly baked butter cookies and some chocolate bars (my weakness) and posted the package off. It cost her $9.10 in postage, an amount that far exceeded the worth of the contents, but this was typical of Rose's warm and giving nature.

During the following week Rose dropped in every now and then to see Jim Bramwell on *Argonauta* to ask if he had heard from *Rose-Noëlle*. On 9 June she visited *Argonauta* and was disappointed to hear that Jim had still not made contact, despite listening in every night on the agreed channel.

That night Jim turned his radio to 6128.6 kHz at 8:30 P.M. and once again called repeatedly: "*Rose-Noëlle, Rose-Noëlle*, do you copy? Over." After calling and listening for about ten minutes, Jim heard a faint voice. The signal was weak, as though the channel was slightly off frequency, and the message was garbled. Straining to hear, he jotted down a latitude and longitude position of 34°S, 179° 45'E and plotted the position on a chart.

The person speaking did not identify himself, give a call-sign, or name the vessel. Jim Bramwell was not certain the faint voice could hear him respond, but he assumed it was a message from *Rose-Noëlle* because the frequency and time were right. Jim's conviction that he had heard from *Rose-Noëlle* was to throw Search and Rescue officials completely off track three weeks later.

The coordinates put the vessel three hundred nautical miles northeast of Auckland, a position Jim Bramwell thought reasonable. It might have been reasonable had the *Rose-Noëlle* been a slow-moving monohull, but in a trimaran that averaged at least six knots, or 150 miles a day, 50 miles a day was extremely slow progress. The position was in fact 360 nautical miles north of where we capsized.

The day after Jim Bramwell made contact with a voice he assumed to be coming from *Rose-Noëlle*, Rose Young heard about the radio message and rang Christabel to tell her the news. Two days later Jim Bramwell picked up another faint signal on the six-meg frequency; this time all he heard was a latitude of 28°S, in line with the Kermadec Islands and what would have been on our fourth way-point. Jim had plotted both positions on his chart in pencil, but three weeks later, when Search and Rescue requested details, he had rubbed them out and was working from memory. Consequently the dates of the radio calls and the positions changed two or three times, throwing the issue into more confusion.

But a week later Heather Hellreigel, alone at home with her baby son, began to become concerned. Surely she should have heard something by now? Eventually she rang the National Rescue Co-ordination Center in Wellington to express her fears, but officials there told her it was too early to start worrying.

A close family friend and business partner of the Hellreigels, Peter Brady, was also anxious. He, too, knew that Rick would contact Heather the moment he reached land. He realized that there were several good reasons why the yacht could have been delayed, but he was sufficiently worried to ring Rose Young and ask if she was concerned about the lack of contact from *Rose-Noëlle*.

Rose was not sure how long a trip to Tonga should take, and Malcolm and Christabel were always so bright and breezy whenever they discussed *Rose-Noëlle*. They knew me, and they knew the boat, and they had every confidence in my ability to get around the Pacific safely.

I had given 15 June as our expected date of arrival in Tonga when I filled in the Ministry of Transport Marine

Division "ten-minute form" at Picton on the day we left, 1 June. To family and friends I hadn't been too specific about a date. Giving an optimistic arrival date causes those back home to start worrying prematurely if the yacht is becalmed or delayed for some reason.

"Two to three weeks," I said vaguely, if anyone asked. Realistically I thought the journey would take us ten days at the most.

Peter Brady's call stuck in Rose's mind. On the night of 18 June she tried several times to ring the Royal Sunset Island Resort Hotel in Tonga but could not get through. The next morning she had more success and spoke to New Zealander Terry Hunt, who, with her husband David, runs the resort. Terry had not heard of *Rose-Noëlle* before Rose's phone call. We were not listed as part of the fleet expected in with the South Seas Regatta, because I had never registered as a participant. I knew I would miss the start and wasn't quite sure when I would catch up.

The hotel is eleven kilometers from Nukualofa, but the Hunts were at the harbor every day and in constant contact with Customs officials clearing the yachts. Terry Hunt told Rose that she had not seen or heard of a trimaran answering that description but said she would watch out for it. She reassured Rose that the winds had not been favorable for a fast trip, and there could well be a simple explanation for the delay. Rose was to ring the resort several more times, but each time Terry Hunt had to say there had been no sign of *Rose-Noëlle*.

Rose kept in regular contact with Christabel and Malcolm in Blenheim, who were consistently confident and calm about our lateness. "We know John, we know his capabilities, we know the boat," they told Rose and any friends or family of the crew who called.

Meanwhile, the organizers of the South Seas Cruising Club Regatta had become concerned over the fact *Rose-Noëlle* had not appeared in Nukualofa Harbor. Through general chatter over the radio, they learned that we had left Picton on 1 June. Even though we were not officially part of the regatta, the escort vessel sent a message to ZLD

Auckland Radio on 20 June to register its concern.

Finally, after another call from Heather Hellreigel, Search and Rescue acknowledged that *Rose-Noëlle* did in fact appear to be overdue. The delay was not helped by false rumors—one that Heather had received a postcard from Rick from Norfolk Island and another that *Rose-Noëlle* had been sighted in Tonga.

Officials studied the "ten-minute form" I had filled out before leaving. This showed that I planned to head 450 miles east of the Kermadecs to compensate for the northerly winds experienced recently by cruising yachts. However, the first position received by the *Argonauta*, and passed on to Search and Rescue by Kerikeri Radio in the Bay of Islands, suggested that we had taken a direct track to Tonga.

On 30 June an air force Orion was sent up to search an area from the Kermadecs to the southern tip of Tongatapu and to the west to Minerva Reef. The following day the Orion went up again, this time searching a dogleg track to the east of the Kermadecs, an area that would have been our fourth way-point had we reached that far. In fact around this date we were drifting three hundred nautical miles due east of East Cape—six hundred miles south of the search area. In all, the aircraft spent sixteen hours in the air at a cost of $15,000 an hour, searching twenty thousand square miles; the Orion crew saw nothing, and on 1 July the search was abandoned. *Rose-Noëlle* was declared officially missing. Search and Rescue officials asked ham radio operators to listen out for *Rose-Noëlle*, but other than that there was little more they could do.

Our families and friends were stunned, refusing to believe that we were gone and that nothing more could be done. Malcolm rang my brother David in Australia, with whom I had sailed thousands of miles, and told him the news. David was initially so distressed that he was unable to absorb the details. His wife, Erica, phoned back the next day asking Malcolm to repeat what he had told David.

In Minnesota Jim's sister, Cathy Moynihan, tried her best to lobby support for another search, approaching the

A copy of the photograph of *Highlight*, taken by me in Moorea, which I had hung above the dinette on *Rose-Noëlle*.

Highlight en route from Vancouver to San Francisco.

Laying up the main hull of *Rose-Noëlle,* West Pennant Hills, Sydney, 1973.

Lauching *Rose-Noëlle,* Parramatta River, Sydney, 1979.

With Geordie and his
young friend Tammie,
Gold Coast, Queensland,
1985.

Rose-Noëlle Coguiec,
Miss July, 1968.

Cherry blossoms from Glenrose adorn the main cabin of *Rose-Noëlle*.

Fishing with friends on *Rose-Noëlle* at Great Barrier Reef, 1987.

In cruising rig, passing through the Whitsundays, 1987. Danielle Cordeau

My brother-in-law, Malcolm Tomes, at the helm of a speeding *Rose-Noëlle*, sailing from Abel Tasman National Park to Nelson, 1988.

Inside *Rose-Noëlle,* showing part of the dinette and galley, and the entrance to the aft cabin, where the four of us lived for four months.

Rose-Noëlle beached at Abel Tasman National Park, ready to have her hulls scrubbed. Clare Appleby

The last photograph taken of *Rose-Noëlle* as we set sail from Picton on 1 June 1989. Rose Young

Reunited with Malcolm and Christabel - and flowers from Glenrose.
Rob Tucker

Aerial view showing the flat-topped outer reef that *Rose-Noëlle* first struck while coming ashore at Great Barrier Island on 30 September 1989.

Almost there — the final climb up to the Scrimgeour house on Windy Hill, Great Barrier Island.

The cove next to Little Waterfall Bay on Great Barrier Island – *Rose-Noëlle*'s final resting place. We came ashore at the far right of the picture and made our way round to Little Waterfall Bay, past the point on the far left. *NZ Herald*

The Scrimgeour house at Windy Hill, Great Barrier Island.

Reunited with Pat Hanning on Great Barrier Island. At last I had a friend with me. Mark Mitchell/*NZ Herald*

Jim greeted by long-time friend Bob McKerrow, editor of *Adventure* magazine, at Mechanics Bay. *NZ Herald*

A clean-shaven Jim calls home. Bob McKerrow

Phil, Rick and Jim about to leave Great Barrier Island by helicopter.
Mark Mitchell/*NZ Herald*

Looking up at the cliff we scaled. Plenty of assorted wreckage on the shore, but no sign of the log-book. Mark Mitchell *NZ Herald*

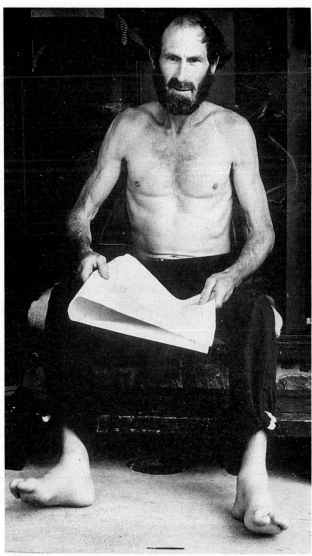

Trying to piece together where we had drifted. This photograph was taken the day after our arrival in Auckland. Note my swollen feet. *NZ Herald*

With part of the stern section of *Rose-Noëlle* at Little Waterfall Bay.

Mel Bowen with part of *Rose-Noëlle*'s main bulkhead which showed the registration numbers and tonnage.

Shane Godinet with one of *Rose-Noëlle*'s anchors at the wreck site.
Nigel Marple/*NZ Herald*

Shane and Mel Bowen retrieve my bicycle. Mark Mitchell/*NZ Herald*

Jim, Martha, Heather and Rick on the waterfront at Devonport. Bob McKerrow

Sharing crumbs with Christabel and Malcolm's labrador, Rhody, at Glenrose.
Jane Phare

United States Air Force, the Pentagon, the Coast Guard, and a Minnesota senator.

At Anakiwa, Heather Hellreigel and Jim's partner, Martha Bell, closed ranks, cheering each other up when either felt their faith and hope slipping away. Heather and Rick's friends and business partners, Peter Brady and Jenny Jones, enveloped her in love and friendship, offering practical help and advice wherever they could.

Although Malcolm and Christabel still had every confidence that we would turn up, they, too, could not accept that nothing more could be done to speed up the process. Malcolm rang Peter Brady and suggested an informal get-together of friends and families of the missing crew. Peter was already thinking along similar lines, but on a bigger scale.

The result was a highly organized and well-attended meeting, coordinated by Peter with Malcolm's help, on the night of 6 July. The meeting was originally to be held at the Picton police station, but when numbers swelled, the venue was shifted to the Waikawa Boating Club nearby. By the end of the night the organizers hoped to have formulated a proposal that would persuade Search and Rescue to authorize another Orion search. Those who knew me well told me later they were well aware I would be hopping mad had I known about the meeting's intention. They knew I was a firm believer in yachtsmen getting themselves out of trouble at sea.

The turnout was a mixture of friends and family of the four of us, a selection of the live-aboard yachties from Picton, and complete strangers who felt they might have some sort of expertise or knowledge to contribute. Rose Young was struck by the tremendous care and concern of all those present, whether or not they had a personal connection with a crew member.

Among my sailing colleagues were Rod and Karol Lovatt, who were neighboring live-aboards at Picton on their 12.3-meter trimaran *Afternoon Delight*, also painted yellow and white. The Lovatts had first heard of me through reading multihull magazines while living in Australia in the 1980s, but we did not meet until 1988, when both our boats were moored in Nelson. Rod and Karol were having trouble with Customs in Nelson after bringing *Afternoon Delight* over from Brisbane, and I intervened on their behalf. Ever since then we had been firm friends.

Rod Lovatt was puzzled by *Rose-Noëlle*'s disappearance. He knew the boat well and he knew me. The weather faxes showed bad weather in the first week, but nothing severe enough to upset a 6.5-ton boat. He was convinced a squall would not blow us over even if an inexperienced crew member was at the wheel, but he wondered about a massive wave. Rod knew that I would have sailed through any storm, and besides, the reported radio position picked up by *Argonauta* indicated that we had got safely through that patch of bad weather. Looking at the weather patterns and owning a similar-size trimaran, he knew that *Rose-Noëlle* should have reached Tonga on about 9 or 10 June.

The positions reported by Jim Bramwell meant we were averaging a speed of three knots; he thought we could have paddled faster. At that stage the meeting was not aware that Jim Bramwell could not confirm if the message he heard was from *Rose-Noëlle*, and that we had already been adrift for several days when he heard it.

Also at the meeting were Russell and Maureen Foley, who lived at Picton aboard their 16.9-meter ketch *Quintessa*, built by Russell years before for his family to cruise through the South Pacific. Russell, Maureen, David, and I were all at school together, and we were old friends. We shared the same ideology and the same views about seamanship; they, too, believed in getting themselves out of trouble once at sea. But the Foleys, like the families and friends of the four of us, could not just sit and do nothing, waiting for news.

Peter Brady and Malcolm Tomes spoke to the group gathered at the yacht club, outlining the situation to date and suggesting that everyone pool their knowledge. They asked friends and family to write anything they thought might be useful on a large blackboard at the front of the room.

Anything, Malcolm said, no matter how silly it might seem. Christabel began writing an extensive list of equipment and safety gear she knew was on the boat and others gradually added to it. People wanted to know more about the message Jim Bramwell had heard . . . "Was it John's voice?" "Did he sound distressed?" But Jim Bramwell was up in Auckland, and the meeting could not contact him.

Heather Hellreigel and Martha Bell listened intently as the meeting progressed, constantly taking notes. Karen Hofman sat calmly listening and at one stage surprised everybody by saying in a quiet, level voice, "Don't you think the men have gone out there knowing the risks? Even though I'm concerned about Phil being out there, the boat is well equipped and the skipper is experienced. Don't you think that it is too much to ask the government to send up another Orion to search for them at great expense?"

Peter Brady had with him four copies of weather faxes covering the conditions dating back to 1 June, and the meeting broke up into four groups, each one headed by an experienced yachtsman. At the end of the evening those men took a copy of the weather faxes back to their boats and, armed with what they had learned at the meeting, spread out their charts and spent the rest of the night working out where we might be.

Each came up with a suggested search area, three of which overlapped and covered an area west of the Kermadecs. Heather Hellreigel and Peter Brady collated the information gleaned at the meeting and included the suggested search patterns in a letter to the Member of Parliament for Marlborough, Doug Kidd, asking for his help in instigating another search. They also suggested approaching the American Embassy for assistance on behalf of Jim Nalepka. Kidd forwarded the letter to Search and Rescue coordinator Terry Knight in Wellington, who studied the information closely and plotted out the four suggested search patterns. They covered a total of 66,000 square miles, an area Knight knew was beyond the resources of Search and Rescue to investigate. In addition there was no concrete evidence to suggest *Rose-Noëlle* would be there anyway; by now the

Argonauta radio call was in doubt. A decision was made not to send an Orion up again, a decision I feel was quite correct. Even if Search and Rescue had guessed correctly the position and date we capsized, by the time the Orion searched, twenty-six days later, we would have drifted 650 miles; it would have been like looking for a needle in a haystack.

At Glenrose Malcolm tried to shield Christabel from the stress of coping with the constant ringing of the phone—friends and well-wishers calling with messages of sympathy or the news media wanting yet another statement. Strangers rang to express their thoughts and prayers. Sometimes they would ring back another day to ask if there had been any news. For the first ten days after we were declared missing, the phone at their normally peaceful country home rang from first thing in the morning until last thing at night.

A friend arrived with a huge fruit cake, and for a week Christabel and Malcolm lived off cake and cups of hot, milky chocolate drinks when they did feel like eating. Christabel spent those long, cold winter nights wrapped in a blanket, staring at the fire in a daze. A feeling of dread crept over her as she thought of the four gas bottles she and Malcolm had taken to Nelson. Had they been incorrectly filled? She dismissed the possibility, unable to accept or believe that anything had gone wrong. Her brother, she thought to herself, hadn't even said good-bye. But during the day, if she did happen to answer the phone, she was the usual Christabel—strong, no-nonsense and practical, constantly reassuring worried callers that the crew of *Rose-Noëlle* would return.

Family and friends talked of raising money to fund a private search, but in the end the enormity of such a project proved too much. Every now and then Malcolm would telephone Heather Hellreigel to make sure she was keeping her spirits up and to reassure her that he and Christabel were still confident that we would return. "Trust John, trust the boat. He is a survivor," he would say. "Obviously something has happened out there, but they will come home. It may take weeks, it may take months, but they will come back."

Heather told Malcolm that Rick's mother, Helen, would benefit from his calm reassurance and asked him to phone her in Auckland. Malcolm did so, repeating to Helen Hellreigel what he had told Heather. Later that night Rick's father, Peter, phoned Malcolm back; he, too, needed to hear the words. Toward the end of our drift, Peter Hellreigel had almost given up hope and wondered whether to hold a memorial service for Rick.

By August even the New Zealand Water Safety Council had given us up for dead. In its August/September 1989 bulletin, John Glennie, Rick Hellreigel, Phil Hofman, and Jim Nalepka are listed as drowned in the vicinity of the Kermadec Islands.

NINE

Rose-Noëlle

Sometimes when I was sitting alone up on deck in the early morning, my mind would drift and I would sink into a melancholy mood. All those suppressed emotions and regrets over the capsize and what was happening to my once proud and beautiful boat would flow over me. As the sun rose, it would reflect on the highly polished yellow paintwork on the inverted floats on either side. The gleam of her hulls took me back three years earlier to Broadwater, when I had spent hours and hours sanding *Rose-Noëlle*'s fine lines. I spent months perfecting the hull; I would peer at every square centimeter, searching for flaws and filling them the moment I spotted one.

My wife, Danielle, would follow behind me with wet-and-dry sandpaper. I was a perfectionist; I wanted that paint to gleam like a new automobile. Near enough wasn't good enough. I bought expensive marine paint that I couldn't really afford. For *Rose-Noëlle*, only the best.

The dreaded ferment flies used to congregate around the banana trees in our backyard, and they seemed to be attracted to the paint. They weren't happy just to hit the paint and make a dent; they swam around doing the breast-stroke, leaving circular trails of destruction on my near-perfect finish.

When the time came to apply the final coat it was a still, windless day, but just as we were ready to commence, a gusting southerly hit Broadwater, and *Rose-Noëlle* was covered with a layer of dust and grit. There was nothing for it but to sand her back and start again. Finally she was ready. Danielle and I stood back to admire the result, and to our dismay decided the color looked awful. How could we have gone so wrong? What had happened to the pretty yellow I had chosen? However, we decided to leave it alone, and once we launched Rose-Noëlle, she looked as pretty as a picture on the water. The green grass of our back lawn had been reflecting against the hulls while the boat was up on blocks, distorting the color.

Now, as I sat gazing down at the upturned hull, all I could see was the brown slime clinging to the wingdecks, the molluscs and marine plants that had quickly made *Rose-Noëlle* their floating island home, the mass of wrecked rigging dangling below. I thought of my new portable color television, the color radar Danielle's father had given us, the stereo system, in fact everything I owned—underwater and ruined.

But I knew I could not let my mood dip for long. I would shake off the depression, concentrate on writing my log or designing another multihull, think about how to catch more fish, or wonder what delicious concoction Jim would invent for dinner that night. I would turn my mind to what I would do when we returned home. I wanted to go back to Glenrose, to put my feet up and smell the roses. It was never a matter of *if* I returned; it was *when*.

Nineteen years of designing, planning, building, earning money had been poured into my dream of returning to the islands. My mind drifted back to when David and I sold *Highlight*, and all I could think of was the plans for my new floating home.

I kept in touch with my young Tahitian friend, Rose-Noëlle Coguiec, after David and I settled in Australia and began to build our twin 12.3-meter trimarans. We wrote regularly, she in faltering English, me in even worse Tahitian.

Rose-Noëlle planned to travel overseas, and in 1973 she wrote to say she hoped to visit me in Australia. At that stage David and I were on a peach orchard in the West Pennant Hills, near Sydney, building boats and living like bachelors in two run-down rented rooms joined onto a barn.

"By the time I arrive you will look like a peach," Rose-Noëlle wrote.

I replied saying how much I was looking forward to her visit, but the letter was returned the following month with "*décédé*" stamped on the envelope. I knew what the word meant, but I took the letter to a French-speaking friend, who confirmed my fears. It said "deceased." I wrote to a friend of Rose-Noëlle's in Tahiti to find out what had happened.

On 23 July 1973, a Pan American Boeing 707 airliner crashed shortly after takeoff from Papeete, Tahiti, on its way to Los Angeles. Of the sixty-nine passengers and ten crew, there was just one survivor, a twenty-eight-year-old Canadian. Rose-Noëlle was on board that flight. Twenty of the passengers were New Zealanders who had boarded the plane from Auckland, some of them from my hometown, Blenheim.

I decided to call my new boat, my new love, *Rose-Noëlle*. I knew she would always look over me.

One night I attended a meeting of the New South Wales Multihull Yacht Club to show slides of our adventures on *Highlight* while cruising the South Pacific. There I met Pat Hanning, a journalist working for *The Australian* in Sydney. He was interested in building a catamaran but lacked the technical skills or experience in boatbuilding. I had decided back in Los Angeles when we sold *Highlight* that I wanted to write a book about our adventures.

Pat and I spent hundreds of hours together, and Pat produced an eighty-thousand-word manuscript, yet to be published, entitled *Playboys of the South Pacific*. We worked either at his flat near Bondi Beach, or he would visit David and me at the peach orchard.

David and I had persuaded the orchard owner to allow us to build a shed so that we could build our boats under shelter. We went to an auction and bought some old aluminum army huts, which we pulled apart and erected on the orchard. In those days we were building high-performance catamarans and trimarans for top multihull designer Lock Crowther, and gradually my ideas on multihull design changed. Once again I redrew the lines of the new trimarans for David and myself.

At one stage there were seven of us living in these two tiny rooms. We used to wash outside under a cold-water hose next to the long-drop toilet. One day we decided to cut up the floorboards in what was our kitchen, dining room, and bathroom, and sink a bath in the hole next to the fireplace. We thought it made a great improvement, but the landlord went berserk.

The place was a wreck, and the inside walls were covered with *Playboy* pinups. We were visited regularly by two young Mormon men and became locked in an unspoken battle over who was converting whom. Finally I couldn't resist it any longer and asked them about their church services. They were eager to tell me when and where these were held until I said, "You must have a lot of nice girls going to your church."

"Sure," they said, warily.

"Would you mind terribly if we came along this Sunday?" I asked in all apparent innocence. We never saw the Mormons again after that.

By 1976 I was fed up with boatbuilding. We were being paid $2.50 an hour, and then only in fine weather, and we were using our own tools and our own shed. I got a night-shift job printing glossy magazines and comics so that I could work on *Rose-Noëlle* during the day. It was at the printery that I injured my back one night, the result of which was three months spent lying on it. At times I wondered if I would ever be well enough to go sailing again. But eventually my back healed, and I rode myself into shape again. After a year and a half I was on scratch and winning veteran races.

All this time progress on *Rose-Noëlle* and David's boat, *Janzsia*, was slow but steady. David had married his first wife, Moira, and they came to live with me in the little hut with their newborn baby. David finished off *Janzsia* in 1978 while I was still working on *Rose-Noëlle*, and

Christabel and Malcolm flew across for the launching in the Parramatta River.

At the end of that year David decided to take his family to New Zealand for the maiden ocean voyage. Malcolm flew across to Sydney to join *Janzsia* there for the Tasman crossing. Apart from Moira and their two young daughters, Hayley and Erin, David had on board Pat Hanning's brother Vince, and an Australian woman, Jill Taylor.

Janzsia set sail in fine weather, but halfway across the Tasman she was struck by Cyclone Paul, which caused conditions so rugged that two New Zealand yachts returning from the Sydney to Hobart race disappeared without a trace. Sadly, David and I learned that among those missing was Penny Whiting's younger brother, the top sailor and designer Paul Whiting, who was on board his yacht *Smackwater Jack*. The Whiting family would never know exactly what happened.

The storm hit *Janzsia* suddenly, and the men took turns steering under reduced sail. Malcolm was on the wheel, doing eighteen to twenty knots, when the yacht was hit by a rogue wave that he still talks about. As *Janzsia* lurched up on her side, Malcolm clung to the wheel, fortunately turning it in the right direction. Next to him in the cockpit, David clung to a winch to stop himself from being swept overboard. Down below in the cabin, David's children were flung from their bunks, and the remains of a meal spread themselves across the galley. David took down all sail, lashed the wheel, and the crew went below to ride out the storm.

Days later, as they were approaching Farewell Spit at the tip of the west coast of the South Island, *Janzsia* took another beating, lurching off steep waves which had built up in the shallow water. Hour after hour her hulls pounded as she fell off the waves, and Malcolm wondered if the boat could stand the strain. He remembered visiting the University of New South Wales with David to have a section of the material we were using for *Janzsia* and *Rose-Noëlle* stress tested. They stood wearing earmuffs behind a Perspex screen watching as the eighty strands of fiberglass filament windings extruded through to twenty-millimeter diameter were put under immense pressure and finally gave way with a loud explosion. Afterward they were told the material had the strength of thirteen tons in tension.

The trip across the Tasman should have taken them seven days, but they finally arrived in the Marlborough Sounds after thirteen days at sea. As they approached, David insisted on anchoring for a while and trying their luck at fishing. It was typical of my brother: *Janzsia* was a week overdue and had no radio on board, the crew had weathered a cyclone and a rough passage and some of them had been seasick, but he had taken it all in his stride, and he wasn't going to miss out on an opportunity to do a spot of fishing.

When *Janzsia* sailed through the Marlborough Sounds to Picton, David got out his bagpipes and gave a stirring recital to announce their arrival. Malcolm turned to him and thanked him for bringing them all home safely and for putting the time, effort, and experience into building such a strong boat.

That same strength in *Rose-Noëlle* was what made me confident, once I launched her, that she was indestructible and that while we were adrift she would not break up. But I had also convinced myself during her design and construction that she would never turn over, so much so that when David built escape hatches in the under-wingdeck of *Janzsia* I decided not to do the same on *Rose-Noëlle*.

The following year I made a determined effort to launch *Rose-Noëlle*. Over the years, I had enjoyed building her. I had designed the boat myself, and I had worked hard toward her completion. It seemed to me that I was creating a work of art, a piece of sculpture, and I gained much satisfaction from that.

Building a boat can also be boring; the process can stretch out to what seems like a lifetime of drudgery. You need the discipline to go and work on it for a few more hours even when you are sick of it. You have to make financial sacrifices in terms of life-style, because all spare money seems to be absorbed by the boat. And you need to do it when you are young, still have the energy and determination to see it through and then actually go sailing in the end.

Christabel and Malcolm flew over to help me finish *Rose-Noëlle*, and while they were visiting, I met an attractive blond woman named Elizabeth Ross. I had become a bit of a recluse by this stage; I was sick of chasing women and had no inclination to visit pubs or wine bars in search of the opposite sex. Elizabeth and I became good friends, and she would often visit me on weekends, bringing with her exotic home-cooked food for dinner and sewing the curtains and seat covers for the boat.

Finally, in April of that year, I launched *Rose-Noëlle* in the Parramatta River. However, she was without a mast and sails, and it would be another year before I sailed her.

Shortly after I launched *Rose-Noëlle*, Elizabeth started a catering business, but her partner let her down, and I stepped in to help out. I quickly became adept at boning chickens, a skill I later found handy when operating on the seabirds we caught while adrift. We ran the business together for about six months, and we started living together in Elizabeth's rented house, visiting the boat on the weekends. I don't think we ever fell in love. We were just very good friends and still are.

We made enough money to buy a little house in Broadwater, near Ballina in northern New South Wales, for $6,000. Elizabeth wanted to live in the country, and I wanted to live somewhere near water where I could moor the boat. This house, in sugarcane country between the Pacific Highway and the Richmond River, fitted our requirements perfectly. It was in a terrible state and was under threat of demolition. There was grass growing inside, and it had an outdoor toilet, but I knew that with hard work we could make it into a waterfront hideaway. We worked on it for three months to make it liveable before moving in, just Elizabeth and me and our two Siamese cats.

* * *

In 1980 I went down to Sydney to prepare *Rose-Noëlle* for the trip up the coast to Broadwater. Elizabeth was by this time pregnant, and she joined me, living on the boat in Sydney Harbor until our son, Geordie, was born in January 1981. Geordie spent the first year of his life aboard *Rose-Noëlle* and brought us both a lot of joy. During the day he and our Siamese cat, Puss, would sleep together on the double berth in the main cabin.

I got a job boatbuilding and earned enough to have sails made for *Rose-Noëlle* and get her ready to sail up the coast to Ballina. The day we got home, Geordie started to crawl; he had never needed to before. He was such a good baby, and on the boat he was always up where he could see everything anyway.

Over the next two years Geordie and I formed a very close bond. I spent a lot of time at home, finishing the house, landscaping the grounds, and joining forces with a friend, John Hitch, to redesign his Hitchiker catamarans.

Elizabeth and I parted when Geordie was three. She met and married Ken Conley, another multihull sailor, moved to Brisbane and later to Mooloolaba. Now Geordie has a young brother, Freeman.

It was hard losing Geordie, particularly as we had become so close. I missed him terribly and had to reconcile myself to the fact that he had a new life and that I could no longer be there to bring him up. Elizabeth and I remained friends, and she has always acknowledged the special relationship Geordie and I have.

For the first six months after our parting I could not even bear to go out and work on the boat. It represented too many memories, and everywhere I looked, Geordie was there. I started cycling again and took my hurt and frustration out on the bike.

By 1985 I decided I should make an effort to find a woman companion, someone to love, someone who wanted to come sailing with me. I saw an advertisement in a singles magazine placed by a woman who was looking for adventure, a woman who sounded like she knew what she wanted. She wanted to sail around the world with the right partner. I kept the advertisement for a while, pondered over it, and finally wrote to her.

Danielle Cordeau had received plenty of replies from that advertisement, but she contacted me from her home in Sydney. We fell in love over the phone. I used to adore listening to her voice. We had similar goals; we thought the same way; we wanted the same things out of life; we had a lot in common. She eventually sold her belongings in Sydney and moved into the house at Broadwater, buying Elizabeth out of her half-share. We lived together for a year and worked hard on the property, building a two-story shed on the waterfront, landscaping the garden with rock walls, paths, and a barbecue, and planting tropical plants and trees.

We decided to get married and set 16 April 1986 as the day—strangely enough, the same date as Elizabeth's birthday. The weather was perfect, and we stood on our front lawn by the river with John Hitch as my best man and my brother David playing the bagpipes. Coming from Sydney, Danielle had been used to shopping in all the best boutiques, but we didn't have much money after we had finished restoring the house. I acknowledged the special day by wearing a new pair of rubber thongs, and Danielle bought a top from a secondhand shop. There she was, dressed in secondhand clothes, and she still looked beautiful.

We had a party which went on into the night. Danielle had done all the catering, and for once the mosquitoes left us alone. It was a perfect day.

Danielle and I then turned our attention to *Rose-Noëlle* and made a determined effort to ready her for ocean cruising. We sanded her right back and painted her bright yellow and white. Gradually we fitted more and more equipment— wind and speed instruments, an electric windlass for the anchor, a satellite navigation system, depth sounder, VHF radio. I already had more gadgetry than I knew what to do with. *Rose-Noëlle* had a hydraulic backstay, thirteen winches, a pressure water supply, and even a full-size gas oven, which I thought would be ideal to use in those idle hours when becalmed, for baking or cooking a roast. In the end I never got to use that oven out at sea.

Looking back, I realize I got carried away with delusions of grandeur. *Rose-Noëlle* became too expensive, too elaborate, and too much to lose.

We relaunched *Rose-Noëlle* in 1987, and she was keen to get back in the water. She slid off her supports before we could secure lines to her and glided free into the river; I had to jump in the dinghy to rescue her.

Just after my birthday that year we decided to rent the house out and cruise to Australia's Great Barrier Reef. It was a chance for Danielle to get used to the boat and the sailing life. She had already done a course in coastal navigation, and we had both sat for our Australian radio license.

We set sail with John Hitch on board, and on our way up the coast to Brunswick Heads we suddenly remembered the soap opera *The Young and the Restless*. One of the things we always used to do when working on the house or boat was to take a break around lunchtime to watch our favorite soap. Well, there was no need to miss the next episode, we thought. We set up the autopilot, went below, and switched on the television. Once we got to Queensland we found they were behind in the episodes, so we lost the urge to watch.

We stopped in at Surfer's Paradise where John Hitch left us, and then continued on to Brisbane, staying three weeks while I fixed one or two things on the boat. While we were there Geordie came to stay for a few days, and it was wonderful to have him around.

We set sail again to explore the beautiful coves and islands of the Great Barrier Reef; Elizabeth and Ken planned a trip a little later on their catamaran with Geordie and Freeman, so we hoped to be able to meet up. When this occurred, Geordie came aboard *Rose-Noëlle* for a few days. We used to go fishing for whiting together and dip our catch in corn flour and curry before frying. They were delicious.

By the time we had finished our cruise of the Barrier Reef, Danielle was pregnant, news that was a shock to us both. We had talked about children, but I had wanted to cruise for a couple of years first before starting a family. Toward the end of 1987 we took on crew and sailed to Lord Howe Island, planning to reach New Zealand by Christmas.

Even though I had not been back to Lord Howe in twenty years, to me it was like coming home. The friends that David and I had made during our months working on the island in 1967 were still there. Young people who had been little children during our stay still remembered me. Danielle, however, was not having such a good time. She was suffering from morning sickness and could not be as enthusiastic about the island as I was. She decided to fly to Sydney while I sailed on to New Zealand, and we planned to meet in Blenheim for Christmas.

I arrived back in New Zealand on Christmas Eve 1987, an appropriate time for a boat named *Rose-Noëlle* (Christmas Rose). Danielle flew over to join me for a cruise around the Marlborough Sounds. The boat was stacked full of food and supplies, and I thought we could explore the coves and bays I remembered so well. I had worked hard for the past eighteen years to get to this point, and now this was my reward.

After about six weeks Danielle flew home; already I could sense that our relationship had changed. With the baby on the way, she wanted me to give up my plans to cruise the islands; she wanted me to get sailing out of my system and come home with her. But I just could not abandon my dream. I had come too far, dreamed too long over this trip on *Rose-Noëlle* to give it all up. I liked the idea of bringing children up on a boat, having seen it work successfully for other cruising couples, and I did not see why Danielle and I could not do the same.

I stayed on in New Zealand and flew over to Sydney for the birth of our daughter, Alexandra, on 28 July 1988. I wanted to be with Danielle for the birth, but I realized I could never allow myself to get as close to Alexandra as I had to Geordie, knowing the hurt of separation that never quite healed. I realized then that Danielle would not join me on the trip to Tonga; she was scared something was going to happen to the boat. It was almost as if she had a premonition. Finally, shortly before I left, I returned to Australia to arrange a legal separation and sort out our affairs. Alexandra had turned into a bonny little baby and looked very much like her mother.

All I wanted was to have a permanent relationship with a woman, someone to share the cruising life, the adventures. I used to look at other cruising couples with envy. There is something about sailing offshore together, facing the dangers and the everyday challenges of life at sea. It seems to draw two people closer together; they form a bond that is like no other relationship. There is no going off to work in a huff, or walking out and slamming a door when things get tough. You exist twenty-four hours a day on a yacht together, and you can't run away from any problems. You have to stick around and work them out.

While I was adrift I used to think back on the good times I spent with Elizabeth and Danielle. In a letter I wrote to Elizabeth, which was lost when we came ashore, I reminded her of all the food we used to cook up for the catering business, and of the two of us going out to eat fish and chips. I remembered driving along the Pacific Highway in our little van singing "Our house, is a very, very, very fine house . . . with two cats in the yard . . ." I used to lie in the aft cabin, picturing the gallons of fresh rainwater that would overflow the gutters on the roof during a downpour. It was a memory that became sharper as the weeks passed.

I wondered when I would next see the house at Broadwater.

TEN

Four Men in a Boat

My three crewmates resented the fact that I appeared to be enjoying myself. In a way I was. Apart from spasmodic flashes of regret about the ruin of my beautiful boat, I had accepted our situation more or less straightaway. There was nothing any of us could do about our predicament. There was no point in laying blame or regretting ever having stepped foot on *Rose-Noëlle*—although I am sure all three of them did.

To my way of thinking, the whole experience would be a total tragedy if we did not learn from it, and I don't mean safety procedures or survival techniques. I mean learn personally from our enforced time adrift, all those hours to think and reflect. No one was about to help us; our hope, our belief, had to come from within. We had to create our own good luck, our own future, drawing on faith that we generated ourselves.

In a strange sort of way I didn't really want to be rescued too soon. "If a thing is worth doing, it is worth doing well," my mother always used to say. If we had just capsized and then been picked up after a week, I really would have lost everything. *Rose-Noëlle* would be gone, we would have spent one uncomfortable week huddled together, and none of us would have learned a thing. As each day passed, we developed a new skill or invented something to make survival a little easier. We were undergoing an experience that no one could ever take away from us.

I even pondered about the longest record for being adrift. Would we beat it? Certainly we would have endured the longest journey in an upside-down yacht—although in 1942

132

Poon Lim of the British merchant navy survived for 133 days alone on a raft in the Atlantic after his ship, the SS *Ben Lomond*, was torpedoed.

Rick and Jim in particular fiercely resented the time they were wasting, drifting day after day while their life passed them by. By the end of our time adrift, Rick felt as though he had lost four months of his life. He wrote letters to Heather, a sort of diary, as a way of communicating with her in his mind. When he got back, he told us, he vowed to be a better husband and father. He wanted to buy Heather a washing machine so that she would no longer have to wash nappies by hand. Sometimes he would forget to write for a while, and he would look at my log to remember what had happened on the days he had missed. Although the confines of our tiny floating island were limited, each day was very different.

Jim was convinced that the drug habit developed during his days in the U.S. Army had severely affected his emotional development and his ability to cope with life's problems. He felt his life had really just begun in 1980— all the more reason to resent spending four months of it drifting around on an upturned trimaran.

It was hard to know exactly what Phil was thinking or feeling. He rarely talked about himself. We had to rely on body language to judge if he was pleased with himself or down in the dumps. He seemed to take the longest to accept what had happened and to convince himself that we would survive if we all worked as a team.

We began to say grace together before each meal, crammed together on our stomachs in the aft cabin with our little portions of precious food before us. Although I was brought up in the Methodist faith, religion has never had a great influence on my life. My mother was a strict Methodist and she sent David, Christabel, and me along to church and Sunday school regularly. However, I think she despaired that we would ever stop acting the fool long enough to actually absorb any of the religious education.

David and I and our friends were always getting into trouble. Something would strike us as funny and we would collapse in hysterical laughter in the middle of a church service, stuffing handkerchiefs in our mouths so as not to make a noise. I quite enjoyed singing the hymns, but there my appreciation of all things religious ended.

We were thrown out of Boys' Brigade because we were undesirable; we were always clowning around or doing something unChristianlike. I remember the cause of my finally leaving the church. I was working as an apprentice boatbuilder and not earning very much. A group of stewards from our local church tried to persuade me to pledge a tithe, a percentage of my wages. I didn't like the idea and so never returned.

Years later when we were sailing *Highlight* through the Pacific Islands, I became disillusioned by the influence of the Christian missions. It did not matter how poor or how remote the island, there was always a big white church there. In Rarotonga no work could be done on Sundays, the day of rest. The local people could not even cook. Polynesians love to dance and sing, but they had to refrain on Sundays. Some of the men used to go up in the bush and brew bush beer from oranges for something to do.

The religious and Western influence meant that the men dressed up in ridiculous-looking suits in the heat of the day to attend church. When one Rarotongan gentleman came to dinner on *Highlight*, David and I were amazed to discover he had never used a knife and fork before in his life, and yet here he was, sitting at the table dressed up in his best suit.

Over the years I have developed my own religion, my own code by which I live, taken from different cultures, philosophies, and religions. It is a little like visiting a foreign country and adopting what suits you, what appeals. When David and I first visited Tahiti, we discovered eau de Cologne—for men. Long before the average New Zealand bloke wore aftershave, we were in the habit of liberally sprinkling eau de Cologne, which we bought in the supermarket in half-gallon containers, on our shirts before we ironed them. Off we would go to a local dance, and in the early hours of the morning, when we were energetically dancing the tamure, the eau de Cologne would go to work.

I looked at boat designing the same way. I might not like the whole concept, but I would be struck by one aspect that I would borrow and adapt to include in my own design. The book *The Holy Blood and the Holy Grail* by Michael Baigent, Richard Leigh, and Henry Lincoln had become my Bible. The authors believed that of all the religions in the world, not one of them had the monopoly on the truth.

I had always considered the Bible should be taken as a guide, and I could not accept that, because I no longer went to church, I was a sinner. I do believe in God and I believe in myself. Cycling taught me to have faith in myself; it taught me physical and mental discipline. It taught me, as my father had always told me, that there is nothing I could not do if I set my mind to it. However, I do accept that there are those who need to believe in one religion and find comfort from that.

Having said all that, there is no doubt that at times of great stress and trauma, we return to that early religious conditioning and ask the Lord for help. I remember going through the atrocious storm in the Roaring Forties in *Highlight* and wondering in my terrified state if each massive wave was going to be our last. It wasn't until it was all over and the weather had calmed that we admitted to each other that we had prayed the whole way through.

Jim Nalepka was brought up a Catholic and still went to church regularly. When he was in the U.S. army he assisted the chaplain, a wise man who used to say that there are no atheists in foxholes. It became one of our favorite sayings aboard *Rose-Noëlle*.

Rick and Phil had had little to do with religion in the past, and neither were churchgoers. However, Rick found great comfort from praying and repeating grace together while we were adrift. Rick would say his grace aloud and then silently lie for a minute, with his eyes closed and his hand pressed to his brow, saying a private prayer. He and Jim used to talk about worshipping together at a little local church when they got back.

Jim was the best at saying grace. He would open up and the words would just flow. He would thank the Lord for the food we were about to eat, thank Him for the water if it had just rained. If the mood was a little tense on board, Jim and I would quite often ask for help in getting along better. He was always the diplomatic one; he always tried to keep the peace, and he was the least argumentative of the four of us.

Phil would often say the standard grace heard around so many family dinner tables: "For what we are about to receive may the Lord make us truly thankful." However, I would always substitute the word "Lord" with "God" when it was my turn.

Jim and I came to agree that someone was looking after us. When the food or fish supply ran dangerously low, I would privately ask for a sign to give us hope. The next day something significant would happen, such as sighting a ship. Jim would touch the St. Christopher medal he wore around his neck and ask for a sign if he was feeling particularly low about not being rescued.

Soon after we capsized, I became determined to make the most of each day. I would make an attempt at humor, but the others were not amused. They blamed me for the situation we were in, and they were not about to let me forget it. They wanted to be anywhere but floating around the South Pacific on an upturned trimaran. Rick in particular used to resent my attitude, and he would round on me and snap, "You're enjoying this, aren't you? This is the highlight of your life."

I told him, "I didn't plan to do this. I would sooner be up in the islands. But we're here, and we have to make the best of it."

Dougal Robertson says in his book *Survive the Savage Sea*: "If any single civilised factor in a castaway's character helps survival, it is a well-developed sense of the ridiculous. . . . A pompous adherence to precedence, an assertion of physical superiority, the inability to abandon prudish reserve, these and many other such traits are as deadly as thirst and starvation in the confines of a survival craft."

Rick used to say that I had a Peter Pan attitude toward life, and he and I would clash bitterly over many things. There were times when I thought we would come to blows, but then there were times when all of us could have come to blows with someone. But we never did. We never got to the stage where we lost that final thread of self-control and could not pull back. Sometimes I wondered if we argued for the sake of it, because we were bored and sick of the sight of each other.

Looking back, I wondered if I should not have been more forceful from the start, asserted my authority on the boat and made more of an attempt to be leader. But I did not believe in throwing my weight around. The four of us were all very different people; we each had opinions, our own way of doing things, our individual contributions and strengths. My hope was that we could work as a team. I wanted us to get along and, as far as possible, enjoy each day. I strongly believed we would make it, and I thought there were other ways of getting the others interested in surviving efficiently than issuing orders.

Again quoting Dougal Robertson: "In real terms, knowledge is leadership, common sense is duty, and the practical observance of survival laws is discipline. . . . There is usually plenty of time for discussion about policy decisions and if people know why they are doing a thing it helps them to do it."

Mike Greenwald writes in his book *Survivor* that in a nonmilitary survival craft, group survival always outweighs all other considerations. He also suggests giving everyone a chance to be the "captain" of something to increase their feeling of self-worth. I agree with the sentiment, but the concept works better if the person is not told to do something but is allowed to develop the idea himself.

* * *

When the weather was bad and we could not fish, we would lie for days cooped up in the cabin below. The arguments and depressed moods got worse. We lashed out at each other then apologized a few minutes later. Very soon we had read all the books we had salvaged and run out of conversation. We all dreaded spending a day in the position furthest away from the cabin entrance. It was dark and stuffy there and impossible to read or write.

Rick and Jim played chess constantly, oblivious to the presence of Phil and me. They would lie facing each other with the magnetic chessboard between them and play game after game. If it was their turn to lie on the dark side of the cabin, away from the opening, they would want Phil and me to change positions with them or move down from the doorway to let in the light. I used to say, "Hey, guys, why don't the four of us play a game together?"

I had a lot of games on board—backgammon, magnetic Chinese puzzles, draughts, and Scrabble—but we never did play together. Jim used to say it was his right to play chess with whom he chose. I guess he was correct, under normal circumstances. But these weren't normal circumstances, and I thought he and Rick could have made an effort to include Phil and me occasionally so that the four of us could become closer.

The only time Jim and Rick did not play chess regularly was toward the end, when we were so busy fishing in the spell of fine weather there was no time to relax. Rick would suddenly realize he hadn't played chess in ages and suggest a game. But it wasn't just a chess game, it was a chess game with Jim. I think it made them both feel close and separated off from Phil and me at the same time.

Although I usually have an aversion to games of any sort, I considered them important for our morale and team spirit while we were adrift. Phil was pretty low much of the time; whether up on deck sitting staring out to sea, or down in the aft cabin where he would lie stroking his beard over and over again. Occasionally I would suggest a game of draughts to distract him, and the few times we played he always won.

Every now and then I would just want to get away from them all. While I would have dreaded surviving out there on my own, simply because I like company, there were occasions when all of us needed time to ourselves. Even Rick and Jim would lose patience with each other and, because they were so close, their arguments seemed worse. They would say bitter, personal things and then a few minutes later would apologize and hug. Rick would sometimes break down and get quite emotional about it all.

The worst arguments happened at night. We always seemed to strike bad storms at night, when the hours of darkness dragged on and on. Most of the complaints were over the single blanket, which never seemed to quite cover the four of us, or over not having enough room.

We had to piece ourselves together like a jigsaw puzzle, and in the early weeks that was how we kept warm. We would move up or down until we fitted, so that our hips weren't banging together and our shoulders weren't jammed. One of us would only need to move a fraction and it would upset the whole cabin and someone would yell, "Hey, give me some space. I don't have any room over here!"

It would take us ages to get settled again. In the cold weather I often mused about how lucky we were to have four on board. If there had been five of us, we could not have all sheltered in the aft cabin at the same time; if there had been three, we would have been considerably colder.

But as the weather grew warmer in the last few weeks everyone became very sensitive about being touched. I think it was a combination of getting overheated and the fact that the strain of living together in such cramped quarters was starting to tell. Now that we no longer needed each other for body heat we would not tolerate an arm or a knee pressing against our thin bodies.

Little habits and mannerisms began to irritate. Sometimes I would clean the bowls with my finger, and that irritated

Rick. I know that my cheerful attitude toward our predicament irritated everybody. In the early days Phil used to have
a variety of habits that grated, from belching to sighing
loudly after he had drunk his ration of liquid. Phil was
bald, but he grew long, wispy hair down the back of his
head. When we were nestled together at night, he could
never keep still. He had a habit of jerking his head up
and the long hairs would tickle the face of whoever was
lying directly behind him, usually me. Eventually I got so
impatient I used to pull his hair to make him lie still.

I would often rise earlier than the others and sit quietly up
on the keel watching the sun appear. It was my favorite time
of the day. Sometimes I would take my logbook with me to
write it up. Away on the distant horizon a thin scattering
of clouds would catch the sun's first rays, turning them
pale pink like a decoration in a child's bedroom. The sun
surfaced in a large, blazing ball, and I would write about
its power, its brilliance and its color in my log. I had never
before seen anything like it.

We did have some special, enjoyable days while we were
adrift; days when the weather was fine, we caught fish, Jim
cooked an excellent meal, and we were full of hope. I liked
to have something to look forward to, perhaps marking day
fifty or day seventy-five with a special meal. But I had
to be careful voicing my thoughts, because the others did
not want to face the thought of still being out there after
seventy-five days. However, we realized that Phil's and
Rick's birthdays fell on days seventy-six and seventy-seven
anyway, so we decided to combine the celebration.
    As it turned out, Phil's birthday, 18 August, was cold and
the sea was rough. It was too windy to light the barbecue,
and we spent most of the day down in the cabin. However,
Phil did manage to hook a small mottled seabird, like a
cape pigeon, which I skinned and boned ready for Jim to
marinate in vinegar, pepper, garlic, and brown sugar.
    That day Rick presented Phil with a half a sweet biscuit,
his ration for the day, as a birthday present to have with his

cold Milo. The look on Phil's face was testimony that Rick couldn't have given him a better gift if he had shopped at Harrods.

On the morning of Rick's birthday, 19 August, I was up early watching a magnificent sunrise. It was going to be a clear, fine day, ideal for a celebration. When the weather was like this we used to say, "It's a good day to see ships." Rick, Phil, and Jim were below, and I thought they should share in the beauty. "Hey, isn't anyone going to come up and watch the sunrise?" I called. There was no response. I tried again, "What about Rick's birthday. Isn't anyone going to celebrate his birthday?" Still no response, not even from Rick.

Suddenly my eyes riveted on a white shape on the horizon. A sail! There was a yacht out there. This would make them move, I thought. Casually I called down through the cockpit, "Does anyone want to see this yacht sail by?"

There was a flurry of bodies and bedding as Rick, Phil, and Jim struggled to clamber out of the cabin at the same time. Eagerly they peered at the horizon.

"Quick, get the barbecue lit!" Rick yelled.

Like others who have been adrift at sea for a long time, I soon came to the conclusion that a passing yacht or ship would have to be close enough to see us easily rather than the other way round. We had already seen two ships in the distance, both at night, but they sailed on, oblivious to our frantic signalling with a tiny strobe light. In this case the barbecue was worth a try. Anything was worth a try.

We loaded the barbecue with kindling and added a little petrol that Phil had siphoned from the Honda generator. Once the fire was alight we added a rubber flipper and some epoxy resin to create black smoke, hoping it would rise in the air like an Indian smoke signal. Today Rick turned thirty-two, and there was a chance that we would be rescued. But there was a tiny breeze, just enough to pull the smoke sideways and disperse it before it reached the top of the mast. The white sail got smaller and smaller until it disappeared. We sagged with disappointment.

Nevertheless, it was a beautiful, sunny day, and we had the barbecue going—an opportunity not to be wasted. The little seabird was nicely marinated, and Jim diced the meat, lightly sautéed it, and served it with a little rice and gravy as an appetizer. Next we had Mexican burritos, which Jim made from bread dough wrapped around baked beans flavored with cumin and chili powder. He pan-fried them and smothered them in hot chili sauce and made corn chips with the leftover dough. We opened one of our precious bottles of lemonade; we could not recall such a wonderful feast.

Phil had two heavy jackets on board, one of which we used to call "The Bear." It was leather, lined with sheepskin and, because of its size, took up a lot of room in the aft cabin. On the morning of Rick's birthday, Phil presented him with this; he had not forgotten the sweet-biscuit ration of the previous day.

Phil, Jim, and I sang "Happy Birthday" to Rick, who beamed with pleasure. Rick having a good day was a joy to witness. His whole face lit up with happiness, and we felt as though he truly wanted us to share in his good mood.

After Jim cooked the burritos, Phil was sold on Mexican food, even though he had never liked it before. He had never eaten anything spicier than black pepper. All our tastes changed. Rick never used to like fish, and he wasn't particularly fond of garlic. Jim didn't like the strong taste of Vegemite, and I had never been keen on shellfish before. But after we had been adrift for a few weeks we became avid fans of anything flavorsome. To us, nibbling on a whole peppercorn was sheer bliss.

On good days, when we were all getting along well and I was feeling happy, I used to sit up on deck and sing, mostly Tahitian songs I had learned from Noeline Harehoe while we were on *Highlight*. I kept a tape on board *Rose-Noëlle* of her singing, but it, too, was underwater. One of my favorites was a Tahitian song, "Beyond the Reef," which I sang in both Tahitian and English:

Beyond the reef where the sea is dark and cold,
my love has gone and our dreams grow old.
There'll be no tears, there'll be no regretting.
Will she remember me? Will she forget?
I'll send a thousand flowers where the tradewinds blow.
I'll spend my lonely hours, for I will love her so.
Someday I know she'll come back again to me.
'Til then my heart will be beyond the reef.

One of the best times of the day for me was after dinner. Before we rigged up the gas burner, we would have a cold Milo or coffee and lie on our backs for an hour before turning on our sides, ready to sleep. I used to lie back, close my eyes, and savor the feeling of the liquid in my stomach; I could feel it passing through my system, probably because there was not much food in there. It was bliss, until someone fidgeted or wanted to turn over, and the spell would be broken.

The weather was improving all the time, and the gales that used to cause the surge to soak us in the aft cabin were less frequent. We had repacked our sleeping platform a third time and had retrieved the two sodden sleeping bags below us to dry out on deck. I dived into one of the floats to see if I could find the tent and groundsheet I had tied in at the back. The tent had never been used, and I thought I could spread it over our sleeping platform as extra waterproofing. Fortunately the line had held, and I dragged the tent out and passed it up to Jim to dry out.

The big ten-centimeter foam squab from the double berth had been floating around in the main cabin since we capsized. We eventually hauled that up on deck and dried it out. While I repacked the cabin, Rick, Phil, and Jim cut it to size and shape so that I could lay it across our wooden sleeping platform as a much-welcomed buffer for our thin frames.

We laid one of the dried-out sleeping bags over the top and covered that with the tent and the sea parachute, which we had hauled on board, to keep us dry. The other sleeping

bag was shared by Rick and Jim as a cover, which left Phil
and me to share the single woollen blanket. Heavenly. No
more fights with the two on the outside tugging at the corner
of the blanket, complaining they were cold.

Finally I wedged a big plastic box beneath the roof by
our feet to hold the platform down and stop it rising with
the surge. We used to keep our jerseys and outside coats
in the box when we were not up on deck fishing.

We dried out pillows and cushions to replace the life
jackets and clothes on which we had rested our heads in
the early days. Rick and Jim used to blow up the plastic
interior of the three-liter orange-juice cask and share that as
a pillow, while Phil used a life jacket, and I used a rolled-up
jersey.

The four or five days we spent cooped up in the aft cabin
during gales began to drag even more because, as we lost
condition, our bony frames protested at the pressure of lying
in one position for too long. During fine weather we were
up and about during the day fishing, and we were able to
exercise by walking on the spot and doing kneebends, as
our strength and time permitted, on deck. During the night
someone would get up each hour to check for ships, and we
would all change positions down below so that we moved
regularly. But when the weather was rough we just lay there
for days without moving, except to turn over.

If there was a chance that a wave might wash across the
boat and completely drench the cockpit, that was a good
enough reason not to venture outside. Sometimes if we had
to go up on deck to collect rainwater or go to the toilet, Jim
would say, "Roll the dice," as the person cautiously climbed
out the cockpit. We would wait for a big wave to wash over
the boat; chances were that there would not be another big
one for a while.

It seemed at one stage that whenever I went up on deck
I would get drenched . . . BOOM! The wave would dump
itself on me, and I would have to crawl below, dripping wet,
and share my misery with three disgruntled crewmates in
what had been a dry cabin. After a while I began to look up

and plead in a comical fashion, "Why me, Lord, why me?"
A fortnight later it was Jim's turn. I would escape without
so much as a splash, but he would get drenched. It seemed
to run in cycles. By the time the weather improved and we
crawled outside, blinking in the bright sun, we were weak,
our limbs seemingly useless.

On fine days we used to take photographs up on deck,
posing and smiling like a group of friends on a day's
outing. My good camera was long gone, plucked away in
the capsize, but I had an automatic Olympus Trip tucked in
a drawer above the water under the dinette. I felt around and
found a few packets of film; why not record our life-style
with photographs? The camera's aperture was jammed on
f22, but we hoped that wouldn't matter.

We took photographs of the fish we caught, having bar-
becues on the hull, the water-catchment area, the opening
for our cockpit. I took some beautiful shots of sunrises with
the still-gleaming pontoon and main hull framing the scene.
We kept the camera and film up in the battery box in the
aft cabin where it was dry and only ever used it on fine
days.

Phil eventually began to get possessive about his "share" of
the remaining food. He was convinced he was being cheated
out of his fair share, and he no longer thought it was safe
in the ship's larder. He kept insisting that we divide up the
remaining supplies and take charge of our own share. Rick,
Jim, and I knew full well that Phil's decision-making was
dictated by his stomach, and that if rationing had been left
up to him, we would have starved weeks ago. We knew,
too, that if we gave Phil a supply of food today it would be
gone within a week. It was yet another subject we argued
over for hours.

The trouble was that we had "rats in the cupboard," as
Rick used to say. Little bits of food went missing, and I am
sure we were all guilty of snacking on the side. It would
start with a few fingers in the peanut butter, until suddenly
the jar was empty. After food began to go missing, no one
was allowed down in the aft cabin on his own.

We decided to store a cache of provisions—rice, muesli, bread crumbs, honey, jam, and Vegemite—in a locker, the door of which was blocked by the plank and the folded mattress by the entrance to the aft cabin, so that we could not easily get to it. That way we knew we always had a reserve when our main supply ran out . . . and "the rats" couldn't get in.

ELEVEN

One Hundred Days

Monday, 11 September, was a special day; it marked one hundred days since the capsize. We could hardly believe how quickly the time had gone. But there was no doubt about it; down in the aft cabin our calendar and daily marks clearly showed how long we had been drifting. We had run out of room in the two battery boxes and had drawn up August and September on the cabin wall.

As the day approached, we planned a special celebration meal. The last of the flour was starting to go off, so Jim decided to cook Danish pastries. He rolled out the dough and spread jam inside, cooked them in the frypan, and made a toffee sauce from jam and sugar. We opened peaches and a can of cream and shared the final kiwifruit. Life seemed pretty good right then.

By this stage our precious and vastly depleted supply of canned food was starting to deteriorate. We kept the cans in the cupboard above our heads in the aft cabin, an area that would drip with condensation after our combined body heat had warmed up the cabin overnight. We would regularly wipe out the cupboard and dry the cans, but they still gradually went rusty and a few bulged until they blew.

Jim remembered quite clearly being told to never, ever be tempted to eat the contents of a bulging can. But of course we were tempted, because we were hungry and the idea of throwing away a whole can of food was abhorrent. We would have long discussions and arguments over whether or not to eat the contents. We discovered two tins of apricots that had blown and decided to risk it. Jim mixed them with milk powder and water to make a sweet-and-sour topping

147

for our fish one morning. Delicious . . . and we lived to tell
the tale.

We had become adept at experimenting with odd com-
binations of food and flavors. We struck on the idea of
combining milk powder with powdered orange juice. Mixed
with water and shaken vigorously, it tasted very much like
Orange Julius, a specialty I remembered from our days in
Hawaii.

Toward the end I became less willing to dive into the cabin
to search for supplies, because it seemed to take me hours
to stop shaking from the cold. Either the water was getting
colder or I was losing condition fast. All four of us had lost
a lot of weight, and Rick and I were particularly thin. Lying
wedged on my side in the cabin, I found the pressure on my
hips and knees extremely uncomfortable at times. I used to
stuff my jersey or the edge of Rick and Jim's sleeping bag
between my knees to ease the discomfort.

Phil had lost his big paunch, and in its place were hand-
fuls of skin hanging down from his stomach. When he
stripped off to dry out his clothes, he was quite a sight,
with his long hair and beard, his sagging skin, and a tattoo
of his wife's name, Karen, on his shoulder.

Overall we had been blessed with good health during our
time adrift. Although we were cold and wet for much of the
time during those early days, none of us caught colds. Rick
had not suffered from asthma nor been even the slightest
bit wheezy. He was dismayed to find that within a week
of returning to land he once again needed his inhaler. In
the early days Phil used to need medication for his heart
condition, but he eventually stopped taking that. Perhaps
he'd taken it more from habit than anything else.

I was in good health when we left, although I used to
suffer from a dermatitis on my scalp. That cleared up and
only recurred once I got back and started washing my hair
regularly. However, toward the end I developed a boil on
my elbow, which made it painful for me to lie on my
stomach when eating, reading, or writing in the aft cabin.
I began to worry about the sore, because I did not know

what had caused it, and I knew that without the medical kit I had no way of healing it.

To ease the pressure on my elbow I would lie on my side in the cabin, with my back to the others, when eating or resting. Rick, Phil, and Jim thought I was becoming withdrawn, and the more worried I grew about my elbow, the more annoyed they became at my behavior.

Suddenly the boil cleared up and turned into a hard lump. I realized that I had probably suffered a complaint similar to housemaid's knee, from the constant pressure of leaning on my elbows. As the pain eased, my mood improved and so did the attitude of the others toward me.

The only other slight medical complication was entirely of my own making. I had salvaged a soaked packet of cotton wool buds from my locker beneath the dinette. I dried them out, but they were still fragile and the tips would fall off under the slightest pressure. One day I was cleaning out my ear, and the cotton bud came out with the end missing. I tried to fish it out with the remaining shaft, but succeeded only in pushing the tip further into the passage. Rick tried to get it out, and then Jim heated a little cooking oil by holding a match under a teaspoonful and poured that down my ear. I lay on my side and shook my head, but the cotton-bud tip stayed put.

Three days later my ear was painful, and I was having trouble hearing. The others were worried because they knew we had nothing on board with which to treat inflammation or infection. How wise the doctor's advice, I thought, of never putting anything smaller in your ear than an elbow.

Finally I bent the end of a piece of copper wire to form a little hook, and I lay down on my side on deck in the sun while Rick poked around and managed to flick the tip out. It wasn't until the operation was over that I realized how worried and depressed I had become at the thought of a serious health problem.

Our worst ailment during the four months was constipation. Way back on that sixth day, when we all emerged from the cabin, I had warned Rick, Phil, and Jim about the dangers of constipation. Rick in particular would be a prime candidate, I thought, because he had led a physically active life. A couple of years ago when I had injured my back and spent three weeks in hospital, a nurse had warned me of the same thing.

Every few days I would take off my trousers and crouch on the wingdeck and wait until I passed a motion, no matter whether I felt the urge or not. Our entire supply of toilet paper was stuffed in a sodden mass below our sleeping platform in the aft cabin, so I just used to wash myself in the seawater. Sometimes someone would complain about the lack of privacy, but I never used to worry.

As time went on the others gradually grew more and more constipated, until Rick became quite sick. He managed to pass a motion only five times during the four months, and the pain of forcing himself to go left him ashen-faced. He used to say that he now realized the agony women suffered in childbirth. Rick even drank cooking oil to try to solve the problem, and at one stage he became so constipated that Jim was about to administer an enema using the oil. The very thought of that unpleasant treatment seemed to do the trick.

When we first capsized it was Phil who suffered from claustrophobia and could not bear to be cooped up in the cabin during a gale. But in the last few weeks I was the one affected by it. I think it was the spicy food. Jim had become so adventurous with his spices and seasonings that he used to load everything in together—tandoori, chili, pepper, curry, the works. I would wake up in the night, my body on fire, panic-stricken that I was being smothered. I would have to clamber over the others and escape up on deck. I would tear all my clothes off until my body temperature dropped and I began to feel cold.

"Coming down!" I'd warn, and Rick, Jim, and Phil would roll over to let me back in. An hour later the same thing would happen, and I would need to clamber out once again. It must have been extremely irritating for the other three. Weeks after we eventually returned, I continued to wake in the night, drenched in sweat and feeling panicky.

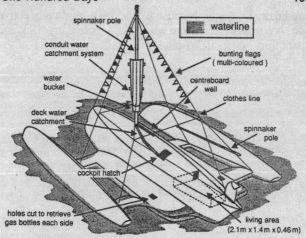

spinnaker pole

waterline

conduit water
catchment system

bunting flags
(multi-coloured)

water
bucket

centreboard
well

clothes line

deck water
catchment

spinnaker
pole

cockpit hatch

holes cut to retrieve
gas bottles each side

living area
(2.1m x 1.4m x 0.46m)

Our capsized home.

When we were getting too weak to climb easily from the
wingdeck up onto the hull, we discussed making a step from
a plywood shelf that was stowed in the port pontoon. By this
stage Phil was game to try anything, so successful was he as
"The Wand," and he ventured into the float to retrieve the
step. It was one of the few times that any of the other three
dived to get something that we needed. Once the step was
in place, it was a lot easier to get from the wingdeck and
up onto the keel after fishing or going to the toilet.

Our water-collection systems were working so efficiently
that when the rainfall increased toward the end of August
and through September, we began to build up a healthy
supply. Eventually all the water bottles and the chiller bin
were full, so I decided to transfer some to the sixty-liter
water tank above our heads in the aft cabin. I thought we
should build up reserves to prepare for the coming summer
months, when rain would be scarce.

By sucking on a length of plastic water pipe we were
able to siphon water from the chiller bin or a bucket into
the tank. I fitted a stainless-steel bolt and clamp on the

end of the breather pipe to act as a tap, and by the end
of our time adrift I estimated we had about one hundred
liters stored in the tank, bottles, and chiller bin.

As time went on, Jim watered down our supplies of Chinese
barbecue sauce, chili, and garlic water. The vinegar was
mixed with four parts of water, and any leftover fish took
longer and longer to marinate. Eventually we saved one lot
of fish too long, and we could smell it starting to go off, but
we were reluctant to throw it away. We decided to have a
big cook-up of fish heads, bones, and fillets, and the four of
us demolished the lot. However, I kept eating long after the
others had stopped, and that night I was violently sick up on
deck until I had rid myself of the last piece of rotten fish.

Toward the end the weather began to improve, and we were
catching so much fish that I was able to dry some of our
catch, literally to save for a rainy day. We kept worrying
about what would happen if the weather packed up and
we were once again confined to the aft cabin, unable to
fish. Our supply of cans was starting to run out, and we
were loath to return to the days of just a few teaspoonfuls
of food.

I had experimented with drying fish before at home in
Broadwater, so whenever I filleted a good catch I would cut
off a few strips, thread them through a line, and hang them
up from the rigging on fine days. At night I took them down
into the aft cabin and laid them out on grills—the remainder
of the craypot and the mesh off the catalytic heater—which
I jammed up above our heads in the two holes where the
battery boxes had been. It was a little like putting them in
the chimney of a smokehouse, for when we cooked at night
the battery boxes would get very hot from the heat trapped
up there.

I experimented with cuts, thicknesses, and parts of the
fish, and the resulting tastes, textures, and colors were
vastly different. They ranged from a dark, chewy, and very
tasty stick, similar in texture to beef jerky, to a pale, oily
fish, delicious on its own as an appetizer. I became quite

absorbed with the experiment and used to call the fingers of fish "my babies."

We relied heavily on dried fish to sustain us during the spells of bad weather that would hit us for days at a time. One of us would choose a fish stick to be cut into four pieces as an entrée. Then it would be someone else's turn to choose, and so on. Sometimes we got a little carried away with our democratic system and ended up eating more than we really needed to, only to make sure all four of us had a turn at choosing.

It seemed that the more fish we caught, the more we wanted. We stopped dreaming about childhood treats— white bread, roast dinners, and New Zealand's traditional dessert, pavlova. We were catching plenty and had more than enough to eat, yet we would want to catch more.

It was as though we were panning for gold. Fish was the most valuable commodity, and we had to have more of it. Jim and I began to notice bizarre behavior on the part of Rick and Phil at mealtimes. Jim called it "fish fever." It became a source of amusement to the two of us, and we began to monitor it. Jim was fascinated by the state of mind that was causing the classic symptoms of gold fever. It was strange witnessing the behavior and being aware of the change in Rick and Phil but remaining detached from it.

Jim and I would just want to get on with preparing a meal, but the other two were adamant that the fish had to be divided out exactly, to the last scrap. I am sure that if I had been able to weigh the fillets they would have been exactly the same, but each one had to be carefully examined for size. Rick and Phil insisted that we each take our turn choosing which piece of fish we wanted to eat. We decided to take turns in order of age, and even then Rick and Phil insisted that we draw straws— or in this case fish sticks—to see who was going to start the whole procedure. Phil would cut a dried fish stick into different lengths and we would each solemnly pick one from his clenched hand. The whole performance became quite ridiculous.

Rick and Phil would constantly check to see who had the biggest fillet or the most rice, their eyes wide and intense and constantly darting from plate to plate. By the time we had gone through the process the food was cold, but that didn't seem to matter to them.

I used to stir Rick and Phil by copying their behavior, but they never twigged, although Jim knew what I was up to. We would have a plateful of fish fillets in front of us, more than we needed to satisfy our appetites, but I would pick up each fillet and turn it over and over, examining it carefully for size. Rick and Phil would watch me intently.

One night I thought it would be great to cube the fish, fry it lightly with our last packet of nasi goreng rice, mix it with onion flakes, and cover it with a thick sauce. We could eat a civilized meal together as though we were at home. But Rick and Phil wouldn't have it. They still wanted to choose their own fillet of fish and, they pointed out, someone might end up with more if we mixed it all together. So once again Jim cooked each piece of fish individually and prepared the nasi goreng separately. By this time the fish had gone cold.

Rick was particularly worried about our supply of matches. We had about 150 left, which Phil and I kept in the pockets of our woollen Swanndri shirts to keep dry. Every time we cooked, we used two or three matches to get the burner going, and we would talk about how we could make a spark once the matches ran out. (I had a manual flint lighter for the stove, but it was washed away once we capsized.)

I suddenly remembered a water heater I had bought for the shower. It was still new and in its box. Fitting the water heater was one of those jobs I had not got round to before we left, and I figured cold showers in the tropics weren't so bad anyway. The trouble was that the heater was right underneath our sleeping platform. It had been one of the things I had pulled from the aft lazaret cupboard to use as packing the day we capsized.

Jim and I lay propped on our elbows for a couple of hours, pulling the platform apart. The packing was a sodden, heavy mess, and the work was tiring to do on empty stomachs. My elbow was still sore from the lump, and by the end of the exercise I was in considerable pain. That was the fourth and final time we repacked the aft cabin. We had become quite expert at the process, but it left us exhausted.

I took the shower heater up on deck and discovered it had a manual electronic flint. I dried it out, and there was no doubt it worked from the belt I got. I modified the wiring so that it sparked a little more reliably, and from that day on the mood on board lifted notably.

We also had a small butane torch to light the barbecue or gas burner. I had pulled it out of the water two months earlier and dried it out, but it would not work. I tried it again in our final month at sea, and it worked perfectly.

About ten days before we sighted land we decided we were sick of looking at each other's shaggy appearance. When we set sail, Rick and I were the only ones with beards, but now all four of us had long hair and long beards. Phil looked a character, with his bald pate and long, wispy hair flowing from his chin and the back of his head. When we licked our plates clean we ended up with bits of sauce clinging to our facial hair. It was time to visit the home barber.

I found a pair of hair-cutting scissors in my personal locker, and we sat up on deck one day to operate on one another. Rick and Jim cut each other's beards and mustaches, and then it was our turn. Phil wanted his hair cut really short, a relief to all of us who had suffered strands of it tickling our faces as he shuffled about in the cabin.

We had enjoyed the joint birthday for Rick and Phil so much back in August that the others decided that perhaps my birthday had passed a little unceremoniously in June, when we were huddled miserable and wet in the aft cabin waiting to be rescued. They said I was to pick a day and a special dish; it became known as "John's treat." Once we decided on this, Phil kept agitating about the actual day. "When are we going to have John's treat?" he kept asking. For Phil, there was no tomorrow as far as food was concerned.

I settled on rice pudding cooked with milk powder, water, raisins and sugar, and I waited until a really fine day so that we could all sit out on deck and enjoy it. I made up a big pot of pudding, and we opened one of our precious cans of peaches and a can of reduced cream. We ate half for lunch and the rest for dinner. What a feast! It almost made up for that miserable day when I turned forty-eight, the EPIRB had stopped working, and our main battery had gone flat. It all seemed such a long time ago.

TWELVE

Land

On our 116th day adrift I wrote in my log: "It's been 116 days today. Is that enough? Can I go home now?" I remembered the survival book by the Robinsons, *116 Days Adrift.*

I considered we had done well. We had coped with the initial shock of capsize, we had surmounted the problems as they arose, and we had learned to work as a team. Each one of us had done a great deal of thinking during our time adrift, and I knew I was a better person for the experience. None of us would ever be the same.

I had personally learned it was possible to manifest miracles; the saying "Where there is a will, there is a way," had never rung more true. I knew now to appreciate the simple things in life and to be happy with what I had rather than always looking toward some elusive dream at the end of a nonexistent rainbow.

We thought land couldn't be far away. We had spotted bluebottle jellyfish in the water, the fish were changing, and there were more land-based seabirds about; we began to see them flying in flocks. I sensed that our time was almost up.

The next day—28 September—we spotted land. I was lying in the aft cabin writing up my log, Jim was reading, and Phil was dozing. Rick had been sitting up on the keel for a while watching the horizon, his eyes focused on the hazy bank of clouds ahead. It was a misty, overcast day, and he was concentrating on a pale, gray form in the distance. Was that land or was it just another cloud that would lift and disperse in ten minutes like all the others? The four

of us had argued so often over shapes on the horizon, and
always it had ended in disappointment. So this time Rick
remained silent.

After a while Jim went up on deck and stood by the
mast, peering out to sea. He, too, noticed the gray form
in the cloud and stole a glance at Rick, who was staring
silently ahead and did not acknowledge his look. When I
came up on deck Rick called out to me, "Come over here,
John. Can you see anything out there?" He waved his hand
vaguely out to sea, but I spotted the shape instantly. It was
a darker image within the cloud, and I knew what Rick and
Jim were thinking.

"It certainly looks like land," I replied. "Let's have another look in ten minutes and see if it's changed shape."

It didn't move, and Rick and Jim told me they had been
watching it for a while. When Phil climbed up on deck he
stood up and looked around.

"Land!" he cried out. "That's land!"

You would have thought that once we had established
that terra firma lay dead ahead we would have whooped
and jumped for joy. Instead, our reactions were all very
matter-of-fact and calm. We kept fishing and looking ahead
at the dark, misty form, which gradually sharpened. Maybe
we didn't want to get our hopes up in case we were wrong
or in case the winds and currents played a cruel trick and
pushed us away.

My first reaction was to get my house in order, or what
was left of it. I would need to sort out the few things I really
wanted to save, and I needed to get my log up to date.

I wasn't really surprised when we spotted land. For days
we had seen a long, low bank of pale cloud on the horizon,
and I knew New Zealand must be out there somewhere. The
Maori named their land Aotearoa—land of the long white
cloud. There had been other signs in the past few weeks; we
had seen the lights of two ships at night and then the yacht
on Rick's birthday. Just a few days previously we had seen
another large yacht heading toward where I suspected land
lay, but it was too far away to signal.

However, it was the planes that gave me the strongest clue. Several weeks before we sighted land we were all up on deck early, watching the sunrise. It was a calm, clear Sunday, and as I watched the pink rays of the sun warm the sky I noticed a thin white line just above the sun itself—a jetstream. I pointed it out to the others, and we wondered where the plane had come from, where it was heading. . . . Auckland to Tahiti perhaps?

The following Sunday I was up early again, and there was another jetstream, and this time I could see from its position that we had drifted to the west. Both planes were flying northeast, which meant we were on an air route, but we still had no idea which airport they had come from. A week later the weather was overcast and cloudy, and though I searched as the sun rose, I saw nothing.

Then one day we saw a jetstream right overhead, and I was able to get a direction of magnetic north with the hand-held compass. That meant we were somewhere north of New Zealand. The international airports of Christchurch, Wellington, and Auckland are all roughly in line, and the plane was heading north.

On the afternoon of day 116 I was standing up, holding on to the rigging ropes supporting the mast and relieving myself over the side, when I noticed a humming noise vibrating through the rigging. About an hour later I heard the same noise. I looked up to see a plane flying overhead, low enough to see and hear clearly. We estimated that it was about fifteen thousand feet up and still climbing. It flew directly overhead, and I took a bearing. It was heading magnetic north.

We had a lengthy discussion about how long it takes big passenger planes to reach altitude and decided the one we had seen was about 80 miles from the airport. I knew the plane could not have come from Wellington or Christchurch, because that would have put our position somewhere inland; it had to have taken off from Auckland, which gave us the longitude of the airport.

Most of the charts in the bin below the chart table had been soaked for months and were ruined. But there was one—a small-scale chart covering the east coast of Australia, the Tasman Sea, and New Zealand—that I now spread out in the aft cabin. Although we could not see land, I was convinced we were close. The height of the northbound plane gave us the latitude from Auckland, assuming that was where it had recently taken off from.

We couldn't believe it. If our assumptions were correct, we were drifting toward the Hauraki Gulf, one of the most populated boating areas in the South Pacific. By rights we should have been well on our way to Chile.

It was like a script for a grade-B movie. A sense of the absurd took over, and I chuckled to myself as I imagined us floating up Auckland Harbor to step ashore before an astonished crowd of weekend shoppers. Or maybe a local fisherman would discover us and give us a tow, passing us cold drinks and taking our photograph.

This was the first real indication of our position during the entire trip. Although I had a sextant on board, I did not attempt to use it because the declination tables were long gone. The other tables were in the satellite navigation system, which was underwater. All the rest of my navigation gear was stored in the deep drawers that were pulled out, upside down, to use as packing in the aft cabin. The contents were lost.

I went below and did a lot of writing that day. There was my log to write, eighty pages of survival notes and articles for multihull magazines, and the letter to Geordie and Elizabeth. There was so much I wanted to say, and suddenly there seemed so little time. I knew once we hit land, things would change. Now was my chance to purge my thoughts and feelings, to get it all down. I wrote for hours.

On the morning of day 118 the outline of the land was quite clear, and the color had deepened to a dark green. We were all up on deck early, eagerly checking to make sure that our landmark was still there and that we were still drifting toward it. After so many days of scanning an empty horizon it was hard to believe that we were nearly home.

As the day progressed, Rick and Phil became convinced that the mountainous shape ahead was Great Barrier Island, which literally forms a barrier to the Hauraki Gulf at its northeastern boundary, 53 miles from Auckland. Both Rick and Phil had grown up in Auckland, and Rick had spent time tramping on the island as a youngster.

I vaguely remembered visiting Great Barrier just before Christmas 1964, when David, Graham, and I sailed *Highlight* over there and spent the day shooting rabbits. We had decided to cook our catch in the pressure cooker and succeeded in blowing rabbit stew all over the roof of the galley.

As we drifted closer I still hoped that someone would spot us and take *Rose-Noëlle* in tow. I began to collect a bundle of personal possessions in two airtight plastic containers ready to take ashore. The contents of these boxes would represent the most treasured and sentimental mementoes of my life to date, and I was determined they would not be claimed by the sea. In them I put the logbook, the pages of survival notes and articles for multihull magazines, sketch plans of the new catamaran, the letters I had written, my traveller's checks, passport, photographs, bank accounts, my boatbuilding apprenticeship papers from Morgan's boatyard, and a collection of cycling medals won by myself and my father. In a locker beneath the dinette I had discovered some drawings Geordie had done some years ago, when he stayed with Danielle and me on *Rose-Noëlle* in the Brisbane River. He had watched me updating the Hitchiker catamaran and had decided to draw his own boat. His design had an underwater observatory, which he made his bedroom. I tucked those drawings in one of the containers with a lock of his hair saved after his first haircut when he was a year old.

That night, the last we spent on *Rose-Noëlle*, I became so angry over an incident involving Phil that I wondered later how close I had come to losing control. Phil and I had been arguing a lot in the past fortnight. I felt he had become intolerably big-headed and suddenly thought he knew it all. He started challenging everything I said, and we seemed to be always bickering. All four of us were starting to lose patience with one another.

Late on the night of day 118 I crawled up through the cockpit to check for ships and noticed the mast lights of a big ship that had come from Auckland and was heading away from us out past the Barrier. It was several miles away, and I knew it would be pointless trying to signal it. The only light we could use at such short notice was a small, rapid-flashing strobe, which was not nearly powerful enough and could not be used for Morse code. Even if a crewman happened to be on deck and spotted the light, it would only look like a tiny light on a fishing buoy. It was better, I thought, to save the precious battery power for something closer.

I went below to tell the others what I had seen, and Phil disappeared up on deck to see for himself. A minute later he crawled back through the opening calling out for the strobe light.

"I don't want you to use the strobe, Phil," I told him. "The ship is too far away, and you'll just be wasting the battery." He took no notice, and once again we were arguing. His defiance was the culmination of four months of my opinion and knowledge being ignored or challenged. I felt the anger well up in me as Phil and Rick disappeared on deck with the strobe.

Jim, always the diplomat, sat quietly and listened as I vented my anger on him. Then curiosity overcame me, and I poked my head through the cockpit to see what was happening up on deck. The sight of Rick sitting on Phil's shoulders, hanging on to the mast and flashing this tiny light at a rapidly disappearing set of ship's lights in the distance, suddenly struck me as funny; the laughter bubbled out as uncontrollably as the anger. "If you want a good laugh, go up and look at those two," I said to Jim.

The incident was over as far as I was concerned. I knew we were near land; soon we would be back with our families and friends, no longer having to put up with one another's idiosyncrasies and irritating habits.

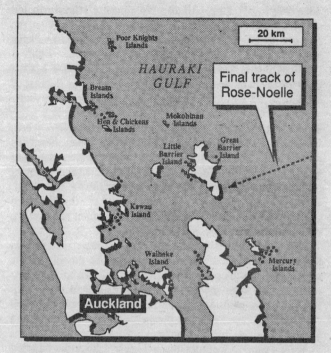

20 km

HAURAKI
GULF

Poor Knights
Islands

Bream
Islands

Hen & Chickens
Islands

Mokohinau
Islands

Little
Barrier
Island

Great
Barrier
Island

Final track of
Rose-Noelle

Kawau
Island

Waiheke
Island

Mercury
Islands

Auckland

Landfall: Great Barrier Island isn't very far from Auckland.

That night I needed to pass water and, not wanting to disturb the others while crawling out of the cabin, I searched around the darkness for the screw-top coffee jar we used as a miniature latrine. Before the jar, we used to kneel on the plank and urinate in the flooded main cabin if the weather was too rough outside. In the early days Jim and Rick were not keen on us urinating there, thinking we would pollute it, but as time passed, those sorts of shore-bound ideals became less important as practicality took over.

As I unscrewed the top of the coffee jar and began to relieve myself, I noticed a strong smell of garlic. I thought it strange to notice an odor in my urine, as we had become immune to such things. Then it dawned on me what I had done. "Oh no!" I exclaimed involuntarily. I had urinated in the remains of our pickled garlic! Rick couldn't let the opportunity pass. "That," he said with heavy sarcasm, "says it all."

It was just as well we were so close to land, for I don't think my crewmates would have forgiven me for the rest of the journey. I would have found it hard to forgive myself.

That night we slept fitfully, the atmosphere below tense, wondering what the morning would bring. Then there was the welcome sight of lush green bush, the white outline of breaking waves on Great Barrier's coastline, and a north-easterly wind that was steadily pushing us toward the island. It was obvious that we were going to hit land that day, and I scanned the horizon anxiously for fishermen or pleasure cruisers who might be in the area.

Phil, Rick, and Jim began to collect their possessions until we each had a separate bundle. Rick put his letters to Heather and his passport in a bag. I asked about the two rolls of film from my camera. He already had them with his things, he said. I took the white sail bag we had used for fishing and put my two plastic containers inside with a jersey and a pair of woollen socks.

We put four cans of food in a bucket with a yellow-handled diving knife Danielle had given me, and Phil retrieved the woollen blanket, the tent, and a cooking pot from the aft cabin in case we had to spend a night in the bush.

Knowing that there was no longer any need to conserve food and water, we ate well that day. Jim caught a fish in the landing net and bent the handle in the process, but it no longer mattered. I made up fish soup using leftovers, and we ate Jim's fresh fish, pan fried. The meal fortified us for what lay ahead.

Just after 12:30 P.M. on our final day at sea, an eighteen-year-old student pilot from Auckland Aero Club was flying over Great Barrier Island on a cross-country training exercise. Mark Hughston had just made a touch-and-go landing at Great Barrier's Claris airfield in his two-seater Grumman aircraft and headed out to sea, gradually climbing to two thousand feet.

As Hughston followed the coastline south toward Whitianga, on the east coast of the Coromandel Peninsula, he caught sight of what looked like a long, yellow life raft, the kind used by airliners in emergencies, about three nautical miles offshore. Curious, he altered course and began to circle around it. As he flew closer, Hughston decided the long life raft was in fact some sort of multihull yacht.

At this height he could just make out a mast of some kind and flags, but he didn't notice anyone on deck. Assuming the occupants were getting ready for an afternoon's fishing, Hughston continued banking in a counterclockwise circle and continued south to Whitianga.

I was below in the aft cabin writing my log when I heard a commotion on deck. "John!" I heard someone yell. "There's a plane coming. I think he's seen us!"

I scrambled up through the cockpit and saw a small red-and-white aircraft beginning to circle overhead. Jim was frantically waving a yellow quarantine flag attached to a piece of conduit pipe that we had rigged up that morning in readiness. Rick was waving a yellow raincoat, while Phil and I leapt up and down, waving and screaming ourselves hoarse. We were convinced we had been spotted and that the pilot would radio ahead for help.

The four of us sat up on the keel, clutching our bundles, waiting. Nervously I eyed the wild and rugged coastline looming before us and constantly scanned the horizon for any sign of a rescue boat. If help was on its way, they had better be quick.

I had often wondered what we looked like from the air or what rescuers would think should they stumble across us out at sea when we were all below in the aft cabin. On fine days we looked like a cross between a junkyard and a Chinese laundry, with clothing, the rug and sleeping bag, life jackets, and socks strung through the rigging to air. Toward the end I laid the charts out over the keel to dry; there was the Honda generator up on deck—which I gave

a decent burial at sea shortly before we struck land—coils
of rigging wire, cans of epoxy resin, the barbecue and crab
pot lashed to the mast.

An hour and a half after the plane circled, it became obvious
that once again we were on our own and that we were going
to hit Great Barrier, probably in an unfriendly spot. Further
out we had seen long, white beaches, but as *Rose-Noëlle*
drifted closer we could only see cliffs and rocks.

High above on a ridge across a valley I could make out
the pitched roof and television aerial of a well-built house,
the first sign of life. I decided that would be a good spot
to head once we got ashore.

Ahead of us lay a tiny cove with a strip of beach, and
we hoped we would be lucky enough to drift ashore there.
But the wind pushed us past to a neighboring but much
wilder cove, guarded by a reef about seventy-five meters
offshore.

While the sea had been relatively calm offshore, the
waves grew stronger and angrier as we approached land,
and now they picked *Rose-Noëlle* up and pushed her toward
those rocks. She hit with a sickening crunch; the waves
lifted her firmly onto the reef and abandoned her, leaving
the full weight of the upturned trimaran to grind itself over
the remains of the mast and rigging.

Phil looked at me and said quietly, "I'm sorry about your
boat, John." In the first few weeks after we capsized, Phil
had been vehemently outspoken against multihulls, but as
time went on, his attitude softened. Toward the end he had,
in fact, talked of the possibility of buying the remains of
Rose-Noëlle should she be salvaged.

I shook my head and told him it didn't matter. I had
designed and built *Rose-Noëlle* to the highest standards
of strength, and I had known all along she would hold
together for as long as it took for us to find land or be
rescued. She had carried us home safely, and that was
all I expected. If we escaped with our lives, the spirit
of Rose-Noëlle Coguiec would have guarded us to the
end.

*   *   *

We sat on the reef for an hour or more while the waves crashed around us, until *Rose-Noëlle* moved no further. The moment we hit the reef I had repeatedly said to Rick, Jim, and Phil that we should stay with the boat right to the end, as each wave carried us further over the reef. While the land looked agonizingly close, the stretch of water in between was turbulent and peppered with rocks. If we hung on until the last minute, we could hurl our bundles and clamber ashore, scarcely getting wet in the process. I knew the boat would float no matter how many pieces it broke into. All we had to do was sit tight and keep an eye out for rogue waves that might wash us off the hull. But as time wore on, the others became concerned that we should make a move soon, before the sun sank much lower. We judged it was getting toward late afternoon, and we did not want to risk coming ashore on the rocks in the dark.

I still thought it was foolish to abandon the boat and swim for it, but the others were adamant, so we decided to lash our bundles of possessions together to make a crude floating life raft. We added the blanket and the stainless-steel pot before wrapping everything up in the tent and attaching the orange buoy from the spinnaker mast to the rope lashing. We tied on old life jackets and empty plastic bottles for extra buoyancy, and each put on a life jacket.

I ducked through the first escape hatch we had cut up for'ard in the main cabin to see if I could find anything below we could use for flotation. The cabinside had broken away, and the waves were pouring through. The pole supporting the dinette table had been ripped away, and the foam/glass tabletop was floating about in the swirling water, so I knew the cabintop had been ground away. It was too dangerous for me to get in the water, so I balanced on the main bulkhead beam and tried to haul the tabletop out through the for'ard hole; but it was too large to fit. I pushed it away, hoping it would find its own way out of the cabin once the boat began to break up, and went back up on deck to join the others.

We clung to the upturned hull as *Rose-Noëlle* slowly ground her way over the rocks toward the shore of Great Barrier Island.

Rick was keen to make a move, so the four of us heaved our cumbersome bundle of belongings over the float, ready to push it into the water. However, before we could position it, the raft tumbled into the water in the space next to the wingdeck, where we had spent so many hours fishing. It was useless to us there, so we heaved and pulled until the sodden and by now very heavy mass came clear of the water. I climbed over the top of the float onto the reef to pull the bundle free.

The wave hit without warning. It smashed into *Rose-Noëlle*, lifting her off the rock and posing a new threat. Suddenly 6.5 tons of trimaran was moving, threatening to wash over me and trap me beneath. In that split second I wondered whether to dive off the rock, but the decision was made for me. The wave washed underneath *Rose-Noëlle* and carried me with it in a whirl of boiling seawater. Like an out-of-control roller coaster I flew across the rocks, waiting for the painful jar I remembered so many times when I had come off my racing bike. But suddenly I was clear of the rocks and floating in the swell not far away.

Rose-Noëlle had floated free after she was hit by two more large waves, and I could hear Phil, Rick, and Jim yelling at me to swim toward the boat. But I was having difficulty swimming; for a start I was fully clothed, and the life jacket was riding up over my face because Rick had cut the fastening straps off to make wicks for our kerosene lamp weeks before.

Rick grabbed the line of bunting flags and hurled them toward me. As they pulled me back toward the boat I felt a tangle of rope and rigging fold around my legs, and a new panic surged in me. I pushed myself away from the pitching hull and paddled toward the stern, where there was less debris beneath the water.

By the time I got to the wingdeck, which was level with the water, I did not have enough strength to pull myself horizontally out. It took the combined strength of Rick, Phil, and Jim to get me back on board. I was extremely annoyed with myself. I had been so insistent about staying with the boat and watching out for rogue waves—and who should end up being swept away?

I sat there shivering, weak and cold, while we waited for *Rose-Noëlle* to drift closer to shore. Finally we hit rocks near the foot of the cliff and waited until the wreck could go no further. It was time to leave. We stumbled and clawed our way through the water until we reached dry land. We had made it.

Behind me *Rose-Noëlle* was in her death throes, her gleaming yellow hull starting to break up. She had stayed with us until the end, having floated nineteen hundred miles around the ocean looking for somewhere to rest. I never even looked back at her.

I had long decided it was all meant to be for a reason, and losing the boat did not worry me. I had believed in our future. I had done what was expected of me, and *Rose-Noëlle* had done the same.

Rick and Jim had gone ahead, and Phil paused to wait for me. Our floating bundle had washed ashore and was lying on a ledge above the waterline at the headland we needed to walk around to reach the cove leading up to the bush. Phil cut the bucket of food free with the knife and followed the others.

I hesitated for just a moment. All I had in the pocket of my Swanndri was a little plastic folder holding a couple of business cards, an out-of-date credit card, and my Australian driver's license. There was no way I had the strength to lift the bundle to safety on my own. Should I call the others back to help me lift it high above the tidemark so that we could come back and retrieve its irreplaceable contents?

In the end I turned and followed Phil, too weak and tired to think straight. Maybe I hoped the sea would be kind and leave our sodden bundle behind. It is a decision I will probably regret for the rest of my life.

The four of us staggered round the rocky headland, only to be confronted by another obstacle—fifteen meters of deep water which we had to swim through to reach the beach.

The wave hit me without warning, washing me over rocks and
away from *Rose-Noëlle*.

Phil went first and Rick, Jim and I followed. By the time my feet touched the ground I was exhausted and the others again had to lift me from the water. I lay on the beach as the water drained from my heavy clothes, waiting for my strength to return.

We were in Little Waterfall Bay, although we did not know it at the time, and ahead we could see the waterfall tumbling down a bank from the bush. As we drifted into the mouth of the bay, I had noticed some fishing buoys marking craypots and thought the owner might well return to check his catch. I suggested we find a flat, sheltered spot in the bush to set up camp and hope that someone spotted the wreckage. But Rick was adamant that we should keep walking and, as he had more bush survival training than the rest of us put together, we followed along.

The trouble was, we discovered, that after four months adrift we had lost our balance and, seemingly, the skill of walking in a straight line. Anyone observing us from the bush might have assumed we were drunken revellers making our way home from a beach party. We were all soaked through, and I wanted to take my clothes off to wring the excess water out, but Rick told me not to. He was worried about hypothermia and thought we should just get moving.

We walked and walked up through the bush as the darkness closed in until we could no longer see where we were going and the whack of branches in our faces was the only indication we were still upright. We stumbled over rocks and fern roots, sometimes on our hands and knees, until eventually we had to stop. We had no idea where we were going and very little strength left to get there anyway. Were we going to die from exposure here in the bush after all we had been through? Where was the force, the being, the God who had watched over us so far?

It had started to rain, so we groped around in the dark until we found a thick tree fern over a reasonably flat piece of ground. The four of us crawled underneath and once again huddled together for warmth. We opened a can of corned beef and ate it cold, using our fingers. Beneath us the sharp volcanic rock jabbed at our thin frames as we tried to get comfortable. Suddenly the thought of our tiny aft cabin seemed almost alluring; toward the end it had become quite dry and comfortable.

Now we were back to being wet, cold, and miserable. My feet were freezing, and my woollen socks were down on the beach in the sail bag. Just as I was becoming quite distressed about the cold, I realized I was wearing another old pair of socks over my knees, under my trousers. I had cut the feet out of them to make a pair of woollen stockings. For some reason I used to get very cold knees, and the condition was accentuated as I lost weight. Gratefully I pulled the socks back down over my feet and huddled in my wet clothing against Phil.

We were so weak and exhausted, we wondered whether we would survive the night or if we would have the strength to get up and keep climbing. It was a frightening thought. We nestled together like spoons and tried not to move, knowing that a freezing jet of air would hit an exposed limb like a knife.

The problem was that nature forced me to move. I had drunk so much water and had so much fish soup during our final two days at sea that I had to get up three or four times in the night. No sooner would we have settled down again than the sharp rocks would jab mercilessly at our bones, and we would all need to change positions.

Surprisingly enough the night passed quickly. We assumed it was the middle of the night until we heard the stirring of the birds, the first songs of a new day and a new month—1 October. Jim was first up and found he was still having trouble with his balance; he fell straight over, and the four of us swayed about holding on to branches to stay upright. We ate another can of food and set off in the semidarkness, determined to find civilization. We knew we could not survive another night out in the open.

We tramped for hours, arguing about which way to go, which direction we were heading. It was classic lost-in-the-bush behavior. First Rick led the way, then Phil. In reality all four of us were lost, but we followed the person with the loudest and most persuasive argument. Phil was convinced that he knew the way to a clearing and houses he had seen from out at sea. From its description Rick was pretty certain Phil had seen signs of the settlement at Medlands Beach. I did not think we could make it that far and wanted to head for the house I had seen, but followed the others through the bush.

Phil was still badly constipated, and every so often he would call out, "Hang on, you guys, wait a minute." He would disappear down into the bush, and the minute would turn into a quarter of an hour. In the meantime we were getting cold and impatient to move on. This happened three or four times, and he ignored our loud teasing.

As the day wore on we seemed to be no closer to finding the settlement or, more importantly, our way out of the bush. After further arguments and a vote we decided to backtrack and head for the house up on the ridge beyond the valley. I led the way, and as we walked, the bush thinned and the afternoon sunlight filtered through, dancing like laser beams on the leaves and fronds.

For the first time since coming ashore I began to enjoy the bush, to hear its sounds, breathe its smells. It was truly beautiful, and it reminded me of home in the South Island. I began to notice signs that someone had walked through the bush before us. The undergrowth had been flattened, and a little further on small trees and roots had been cut back. I called excitedly to the others ahead, "Hey, I think we're on a track."

We stopped by a nikau palm, and Rick told us the clusters of fruit beneath the frond were edible. They looked like tiny white grapes but tasted floury and only slightly sweet. Still, it was food and it was fresh.

The further we went, the more formed the track became, until all of a sudden we emerged on a wide clay road. The four of us whooped and hollered. Our first real sign of civilization! There were tire marks from four-wheel-drive vehicles embedded in the wet clay, and we wondered when the next island resident would drive by.

In the meantime we kept walking. We turned left and headed up the road toward the top of a ridge, from which we could see houses across the valley in the distance. We found a caravan, but it was locked and appeared to be used as storage for a building site nearby. A little further up the road we came across a clearing and a new concrete foundation for a house.

The forward-thinking owners of the land had planted citrus trees, and we gorged ourselves on fresh grapefruit, the yellow juice streaming down our chins. Jim still talks about that grapefruit; it was the best thing he had ever tasted, he told us.

We passed another small house, but it looked abandoned, so we kept walking, determined to find either a human being or a supply of food. That final one hundred meters up the hill to reach the house that I had originally seen out at sea was the toughest of the whole two days. I climbed slowly, my hands supporting my knees, willing my legs to keep working as I fixed my gaze on the house above. We had climbed over three hundred meters and had tramped for miles, much of it in circles. Now we were spent.

There was nobody home and, judging from the pile of building equipment and materials stacked in the living room, the owner was away. We walked round the back, and I found a loose window, which I levered open. Phil wriggled inside and opened the front door for us. What a haven we had stumbled across! The place was amply stocked with food, and its multilevel design meant that for the first time in 119 days the four of us would not only have the novelty of a bed each but a whole room to ourselves. The only amenity it didn't have was a telephone.

The weather had closed in and the dirt road was awash, so we realized we would probably need to spend a night at the house to regain our strength before walking out in the morning. But first we had some serious eating to do, and we hoped the owner wouldn't mind under the circumstances.

In the kitchen we found a healthy supply of wonderful muesli full of grains, nuts, and fruit. We mixed it with powdered milk and water and ate for an hour, tucking into packets of sweet biscuits at the same time. Jim got the gas stove to work, and we drank freshly brewed coffee and tea. We were like greedy children at a tea party; we didn't know what to eat next even after our appetites were well satisfied.

That afternoon I heated water on the stove and treated myself to the first warm-water wash since 1 June, when I had showered for fifty cents at Picton wharf. The black soot that seemed to have ingrained itself in our skin poured onto the shower floor. I was surprised I cleaned up so well.

Phil had been exploring in one of the wardrobes upstairs and emerged looking a new man. The straggly beard was gone and, with his weight loss contributing to his healthy appearance, he looked like he had just come home from a country club rather than a shipwreck.

"Hey, man," Jim exclaimed with a grin. "You look a million dollars."

Rick, Jim, and I decided to follow suit and borrow some clothes, although the three of us ended up not quite so smartly dressed in what was left. While our old clothes were stiff with salt and dirt, to us they were precious remnants of the past four months. I washed my trousers, singlet, socks, and Swanndri out in freshwater and detergent and laid them out on the balcony to dry.

All the excitement, eating, and activity had worn us out, and we rested for a while, each in private corners of the house. I chose a little attic room tucked up under the eaves of the pitched roof. From the north window I could see the white surf and sand of Medlands Beach in the distance; the east window looked down across the bush-clad valley where we had climbed and beyond to the stretch of sea where we had drifted onto the reef. The site of the house was aptly named Windy Hill, for perched up here it was well exposed to the northeasterly blow that had deposited us on the Barrier.

I stretched out on the bed and began to write letters to friends and family in the peace and quiet of my own company. I wrote to Geordie, Elizabeth, Ken, and Freeman, briefly telling them what had happened and how we had survived. "I'm now a free man with a brand new life ahead of me," I wrote. "It will take time to recuperate. It's been quite a trip and a journey—also a journey within. Someone has been looking after me; but then I always knew that and my faith didn't let me down. It's been for a reason, to learn, to improve and appreciate many things. I prayed for you all every night and morning, and I trust that Geordie's faith in his dad coming back got through. . . ."

In my semi-exhausted and still-shocked state I rambled on, leaping from subject to subject, one minute asking for Elizabeth's famous almond torte recipe, which I had dreamed about on the boat, and the next talking about Jim catching a kingfish on the morning we landed.

"I've lost everything but as I always said if I come out of it with my life I will be happy. Well, love, I truly am a happy man. I learned that out there. The other crew couldn't understand that and resented it. But they learned also. I made the most of it. . . .

"It was a great experience, especially to have behind me. I would only have liked to have had a friend of mine with me—one I could relate to and like. But it wasn't to be."

To Christabel and Malcolm I wrote: "Back in the land of the living again. I missed you both terribly. Trust you knew I'd be back anyway. I didn't get to say good-bye, Christabel, so I had to come back. My time is not up yet. I had to manifest a miracle to do it though."

Again I talked about food, a subject that was to be a favorite for the four of us in the weeks to come. I was desperate to visit Glenrose and gave Christabel a garbled menu request, which included roast chicken, lamb, pork, peas, new potatoes, pavlova, chocolate, icc cream, and white bread . . . and a hot bath.

I wrote a letter to Danielle telling her and Alexandra of my adventures, adding that in hindsight it was probably wiser that they hadn't accompanied me.

Downstairs Phil had found a key to the generator house outside and discovered a motorbike in there, but the weather had closed in and the road was impassable. Rick planned to ride out to find help when it stopped raining.

Phil was agitating to start the generator so that we could use the radio, television, and water pump for the house water supply. I went outside to the shed with him and attempted to turn the generator over, but the more I thought about it, the more uneasy I became. The house looked like it was in the middle of being rewired; it had 12-volt and 240-volt power, and there were wires everywhere. We could quite easily blow the whole system up.

We had survived quite well for four months without electricity, television, or running water, and I told Phil that we could survive another day like that. We were quite comfortable in the house using the gas stove, candles, and spirit lamps for light and an outside tap on the tank for water. Once again Phil and I were at loggerheads, and he stormed off in a rage.

That night the four of us sat down at the table together and bowed our heads to say grace. This time we thanked God for guiding us to Great Barrier; we thanked Him for this house and this food. We no longer had to ask Him hopefully for rain or for a fish. Before us were steaming platefuls of spaghetti with a beautiful sauce Jim had made from canned tomatoes, asparagus, and herbs.

The four of us sat there, upright, with our washed faces and change of clothes, drinking wine from glasses, eating with cutlery by candlelight and dabbing our mouths on paper napkins as though we were at an exclusive dinner party. We ate spaghetti until we were bursting, and then we ate some more.

We all expected that after the past exhausting twenty-four hours, our hard physical climb through the bush and our terrible night out in the open, that sleep would come easily. But upstairs alone in my room I was wide awake, my heart pounding. I wrote more of my letters and began to relax. Shortly before midnight I heard the rain start to patter on the iron roof above and had to suppress the automatic urge to yell, "Hey, guys, it's raining," while fumbling for the water bottles.

I lay there in the dark for an hour feeling nauseated and knowing I had overindulged myself with the spaghetti. Finally I went downstairs and outside in the dark to be sick. I saw Jim come in and wash his mouth out with a glass of water and wondered if he had done the same thing. Then we both ate more spaghetti; it was like a Roman vomitorium.

Next to the bed in my room was a table equipped with three torches, batteries, a candle, and matches. As I blew out my candle and settled down to rest, I knew I was at last safe. I had the luxury of my own room, my own bed. I did not have to fight for space, for air, or for a corner of the blanket.

In the middle of the night I woke in a panic; my body was on fire and I was drenched in sweat. I didn't know where I was, I felt panicky and claustrophobic. I fumbled next to the bed and felt for the torches, desperately trying to fit the batteries and switch on a light. Later I wondered why I was so desperate for light. I had survived for four months in our tiny cabin without being able to turn a light on at night. The more I panicked, the more I fumbled, until finally I got a torch to work.

I had to get out of the room. Feeling my way down the stairs, I tripped over something and hurtled my way to the bottom. Downstairs I discovered Rick, Phil, and Jim were also up. We boiled up the kettle and had a cup of tea and a biscuit, as though we were kids having a midnight feast.

In the morning we talked about how long the night was and how isolated we felt. Jim made a big pot of rice pudding for breakfast, and for once the four of us could not finish it. I went back up to my room to finish writing my letter to Pat, grabbing a handful of the popcorn Jim had made the night before. "Four months is a long time, Pat. What's been happening in the world?"

It would be weeks before we had filled in the gaps, found out what our families and friends had been doing, heard about world news. The Ayatollah Khomeini had died (announced the day we capsized); the New Zealand prime minister, David Lange, had announced his retirement for health reasons, and Geoffrey Palmer had taken over in his place; Princess Anne and Captain Mark Phillips had officially separated; Poland had its first noncommunist prime minister in forty years. While we were away the world had changed, and so had the four of us.

Jim wandered into my room, and we sat talking for a while. He mentioned that Phil was outside having another go at starting the generator. I knew I had to stop him. How would I feel if someone had tampered with the electrics on *Rose-Noëlle* when it was unnecessary? Again Phil and I argued; and he walked angrily away up the hill. I returned to my room to finish my letter to Pat, wrung out by the strain of always being at odds with him.

A while later I heard Phil's voice downstairs, but it had changed from tight anger to one of sheer excitement. "Hey, guys, I can hear a phone ringing in a house up there!"

I clambered downstairs and began pulling off my socks, ready to join Phil and Jim, who planned to break into the house up the hill; I wanted to ring Pat to tell him we were back.

"Where do you think you're going?" Jim asked me crossly.

I told him I planned to go up to the house and use the phone.

"Oh, well, if you're going there's no need for me to go."

I shrugged, surprised at Jim's attitude, but decided that for the sake of peace I would stay behind with Rick. I retreated back to my little attic room and kept writing; the pen and paper were such a comfort to me. I was alone in the space, in touch with those people who really mattered to me.

Phil and Jim climbed up over the hill until they found the house with the telephone ringing. They broke a latch on a window and climbed in. The telephone was an old-fashioned black instrument with a turn handle. Stuck on the wall to which it was mounted was a list of the Morse codes used to reach various services on the island, including the police. Phil lifted the receiver and wound the handle vigorously.

Further down the hill a local horticulturalist, Peter Speck, was trying to make a toll call on his shared party line when he heard a voice on the other end asking him how to reach the exchange. The man introduced himself as Phil Hofman and said he had to contact the local police station to report a shipwreck. He briefly told Speck what had happened.

Peter Speck couldn't believe his ears. He was used to a quiet, hardworking life, having spent the past ten years establishing organically grown fruit and nut trees on his property. Born in New Zealand but raised in Switzerland, he spoke with a heavy Swiss accent. Had he misunderstood this man calling himself Phil Hofman?

Speck called to his wife Helga that he was going out for a while, pulled on his boots, and rode his three-wheeled farm trike up to the house he knew the caller was in. He shouted out and heard a voice say, "You'll have to get in through the window." Peter Speck became the first new face that Jim and Phil had set eyes on in four months. "Man, are we glad to see you," Jim said, shaking his hand and hugging him.

While listening to their story, Peter Speck rang through to the Tryphena telephone exchange, and Phil told the operator that he needed to contact the police station to report the fact that he had been shipwrecked and had broken into two small houses on Windy Hill. The operator said she would pass the message on and to wait where they were.

While they waited, Phil told Peter Speck a little more of the past four months. Peter remembered the *Rose-Noëlle* going missing, and he simply could not believe he was talking to two of its crew. With the hospitality typical of the Barrier, he offered the four of us showers and a bed for the night at his home in case we could not get off the island that day.

*   *   *

While they talked, Jim rang Ngaire Gibbs at the Tryphena exchange and asked her to put a collect call through to the Outward Bound School at Anakiwa. "Tell them it's Jim."

Ngaire Gibbs rang the number and asked the school's director, Jon D'Almeida, if he would accept a collect call from Jim at Great Barrier. "We don't have anyone called Jim," was D'Almeida's first reaction. Then it dawned on him. Ngaire Gibbs heard an ear-piercing shriek before the call was accepted.

"Jon," Jim drawled to his boss in his unmistakable American accent. "It's me. I'm back. Have I still got a job?"

THIRTEEN

Homecoming

We could not have wished for a more caring, considerate rescuer than Constable Shane Godinet, the Great Barrier Island policeman. A large, jovial man, he was warm and sensitive toward us, yet efficient and capable.

He went beyond the call of duty to help Rick, Phil, Jim, and me, and to make us welcome in his home. Later on he made several determined attempts to search for my logbook at Little Waterfall Bay, where we had landed, and when my coauthor and I revisited Great Barrier to do research for the book, he entered into the spirit of things in his usual generous and helpful manner.

He gave the impression that he felt honored to have been part of the *Rose-Noëlle* saga, and we certainly felt honored to have him as part of it. The man has a heart of gold, and I hope he will remain a friend for life.

On the morning of 2 October, Shane Godinet was driving his longwheel-base patrol wagon along one of Great Barrier's many unsealed roads toward Okiwi at the northern end of the island. A small house had burned to the ground, and he needed to make a report on the incident before the stranded family could claim insurance.

The radio mounted on the dashboard crackled, and he faintly heard his wife, calling him from their police home at Claris. Teresa was an important part of his job as sole policeman on the island, and he appreciated the work she did while bringing up their two young children. The Godinets had arrived on Great Barrier eighteen months earlier, with Shane sick of the stress of policing a city like Auckland for seventeen years.

Already Godinet loved the island. Slowly he had come to be accepted and liked by the permanent residents; he had bought a little boat and had been out fishing with a couple of the island's old-timers. While he loved his work, it meant he was on call twenty-four hours a day, and the only way to get a break was to leave the island altogether. He often mused that in order to explore and enjoy the island he would need to return one day when he was no longer the local policeman.

Shane Godinet turned the volume up on the radio, straining to hear Teresa's message over the noise of the engine. "Some guy has just rung me to say his boat has gone on the rocks." The man, she said, had broken into two houses up on Windy Hill.

Godinet rolled his eyes and thought to himself, "That's all I need. I'm on my way to a house fire, and now some yachtie from Auckland has put his boat on the bricks." He chuckled to himself as he thought it was not often he got a call from someone to say he had committed two burglaries and could the police come and get him. His first instinct was to let the caller wait; he was more concerned right now for the stranded local family. But something made him change his mind. He turned the wagon around and headed back to the Tryphena end to gas up his vehicle and call in at the local telephone exchange. Teresa had given him a party line 4X to ring, and he decided to call up the man himself to find out what the trouble was.

Inside the exchange, operator Ngaire Gibbs was getting cross. Whoever was placing calls from 4X kept picking up the phone every time it rang, not realizing it was a shared party line. Finally losing patience, she snapped at him down the receiver, "Will you please stop picking up the phone? This call is not for you."

"I'm sorry," Phil Hofman replied, "I'm not used to this."

Shane Godinet then placed a call to the 4X line, and Phil answered.

"This is Constable Godinet. What's the story?"

Ngaire Gibbs watched Godinet's face drop as he listened

to Phil Hofman say he was one of four survivors off the
shipwrecked *Rose-Noëlle*.

"The *Rose-Noëlle*! But that boat's been missing for
months," he exclaimed.

"I know, we've been on it," retorted Phil.

Godinet was certain it was one of the islanders pulling his
leg. It had happened before, and he was wary. He had heard
of the *Rose-Noëlle* and knew the yacht had been missing
for a long time, several months, he was sure. If this man
was telling the truth, he was about to witness a miracle, he
thought to himself.

Still suspicious, Godinet asked Phil for the full names of
the crew. He jotted them down as Phil spoke and hesitated
over the last one—Rick Hellreigel. It rang a bell, because
Rick had been a policeman in Auckland years ago, and the
name was unusual. The name of the skipper, John Glennie,
also sounded familiar, he thought.

"I'm on my way," Godinet said. Before he left he telephoned his senior officer in Auckland, Senior Sergeant
Graeme "Rocky" Rounthwaite, to report what he had been
told and to have the four names checked out.

Godinet began to wind up the steep clay roads toward
Windy Hill. After two days of rain the track was awash
with red sludge and holes filled with water. It was days
like today that he was thankful the police department had
provided him with a decent four-wheel-drive vehicle. The
wagon slid and struggled its way up the road, climbing to
three hundred meters above sea level.

Godinet pulled up outside a house that looked deserted,
and he still half expected to see a wise-guy local emerge
grinning from ear to ear, amused by this latest prank. Then
he noticed a three-wheeler farm trike belonging to Peter
Speck parked outside. Godinet knew Speck to be a serious
and hardworking resident; surely he would not pull this
sort of trick. Hearing voices inside the house, Godinet
called out.

"You'll have to get through the window," a voice replied.

Shane Godinet was a big man, born in New Zealand of

Samoan parents. "There's no way I'm going to get through there," he retorted.

After a few seconds' silence he heard a roller door round the other side open, and he saw two men standing with Peter Speck. "Man, are we glad to see you," an American voice called out from behind a bushy beard and a big smile. "Guys, we're outa here. We're outa here!"

Godinet could hear the overwhelming excitement and emotion in Jim Nalepka's voice. The other man was smartly dressed and clean shaven, a fact that puzzled the policeman briefly. Phil Hofman introduced himself and shook Shane Godinet's hand, briefly repeating the story of the past 119 days, which he had just been relating to Peter Speck.

I was up in my attic room writing my letter to Pat Hanning when I heard a stranger's voice, and I wasted no time in bolting down the stairs. Constable Godinet was standing there smiling, dressed in police overalls, a jersey, and boots, shaking his head while Jim kept calling to Rick and me, "We're outa here, guys."

Shane Godinet seemed as delighted to see us as we were to see him. "I never thought I'd see the day when I would meet four ghosts," he told us.

The house erupted in a flurry of activity. Phil and Jim wanted to drop everything and go, but Rick and I insisted on leaving the house as we had found it. We spent the next half hour cleaning up the mess we had made in the kitchen and nearly cried when we had to throw out the leftover rice pudding and the popcorn. "Are you sure you don't want some popcorn?" I kept asking our rescuer. It seemed such a waste, but there was no time to eat it.

We stored all the ladders and building materials back in the living room as we had found them and locked up, mentally thanking whomever owned the house for his unwitting hospitality. (It was in fact owned by John Scrimgeour, an Aucklander whom I was later able to thank personally.) Godinet and I carried a box containing our old clothes down the slope to his wagon and heaved it into the back. I think he wondered why we were saving our rather smelly, tatty rags, but we would not even consider leaving them behind.

We piled into the police wagon, taking five small bags of rubbish with us full of the empty wrappers from food we had devoured in the past twenty-four hours. We talked nonstop about what had happened and what sort of food we wanted to eat, as the wagon slid and ground its way back down the road. Near the bottom Godinet pulled up and leaned out the window to speak to a resident, Cora Van Der Oest, standing on the side of the road. "These guys have just broken a window latch in your house, Cora. They needed to use the telephone. They've just been shipwrecked."

Cora raised her eyebrows, grinned, and shrugged. "That's okay," she said.

After drifting at half a knot for four months, the speed of the wagon seemed breakneck to us. To calm our nerves Shane Godinet put on a tape of Gene Pitney's greatest hits, the first music we had heard since the early hours of 4 June, apart from my attempts at singing while we were adrift. While Gene Pitney crooned, the four of us gabbled at the policeman, mostly about what sort of food we wanted to eat.

I still wanted to get hold of Pat Hanning, and I could hear Teresa calling her husband on the radio, telling him that already the media were phoning. I suggested that Teresa could call Pat for me, but Rick, Phil, and Jim again talked me down. It was another of those times when I wished I had not saddled myself with such a woeful and overbearing crew. I was so sick of bowing to their demands and being overruled. Inside I was seething with anger.

Godinet stopped at the Claris store to stock up on our food fetishes. He bought more than a kilogram of bacon, two dozen eggs, two loaves of bread, a big block of chocolate, and ten ice creams and took it all home to serve up in one glorious hot and cold mixture of indescribably magnificent flavors that had our tastebuds screaming for more long after our stomachs were filled.

While Teresa admonished me for pinching bits of bacon out of the pan, Shane Godinet poured whiskies and rum for Rick, Jim, and Phil, while I drank milk. I had an idea what we were in for, and I wanted a clear head. I knew the media in New Zealand and overseas and in fact the world press would want our story and that we would face a barrage of attention and questioning over where we had been and what we had been doing for the past 119 days.

We lined up for showers, liberally plastering our hair with shampoo and our bodies with soap. The next hour was a relay between the lunch table, the bathroom, and the telephone, all the while trying to tell Shane and Teresa Godinet what had happened.

Phil did a lot of the talking. Rick, Jim, and I were quieter, still in a state of shock, still overwhelmed by the events of the past few hours. We were desperate to let our loved ones know we were safe, and the local exchange operator worked flat out putting calls through.

Even before we began making calls from the Godinet home, word that we were back was spreading quickly through Picton as a result of Jim's earlier call to the Outward Bound School. Just the day before D'Almeida had reluctantly peeled the name Jim Nalepka off one of the staff message pigeonholes after his colleagues told him it was time to be realistic and hire a replacement cook.

"Where are you?" D'Almeida had asked in amazement when Jim called.

"Great Barrier . . . Noo Zeeland," came the reply.

"No, you must mean Australia, Jim. You're on Great Barrier Reef in Australia." D'Almeida was convinced Jim was confused, and he did not think it possible that the trimaran could have ended up in Auckland.

When D'Almeida hung up the phone, staff at the Outward Bound School went wild. They were adventurers, people who pushed themselves to the limit of physical endurance and daring. Sometimes their expeditions ended with an injury or even death. But this time the story had a happy ending. The cook from Minnesota had outdone them all.

Jim had asked D'Almeida to ring his family in the United States to let them know he was alive. For the Outward

Bound director it was one of the greatest joys of his life, and when he spoke to Jim's sister, Cathy, he had to hold the phone away from his ear, the screaming, crying, and laughing was so loud.

In the meantime the Outward Bound staff had used the VHF to transmit their jubilant news to staff out in the field and to the yachting community. In the Float Air office at Picton, Rebecca Downes heard the message come over the VHF and immediately disbelieved it. The last time she had heard from *Rose-Noëlle* was on 1 June, when she passed on our forwarding address to Christabel for me. It couldn't possibly be *Rose-Noëlle* after all this time, she thought.

Elsewhere news spread quickly and was picked up by a visiting yachtsman moored at Picton wharf. He called out to a group of people standing chatting nearby. In that group was Rose Young. The disappearance of *Rose-Noëlle* had drawn her closer to the "live-aboards," particularly those who knew me or one of the other crew. She had made some good friends and had returned their support and reassurance by leaving gifts of freshly cooked meals and baking. When Phil's wife decided to have their yacht taken out of the water and repainted, Rose had Karen and their two teenage children stay in her home.

That morning Rose had rung Christabel to say she had a strange and vivid dream in the early hours of the morning. She clearly saw me standing in the cockpit of *Rose-Noëlle*, saying, "I'm back." The two women chatted, and once again Christabel said she still strongly believed that the four of us were alive and out there somewhere.

When Rose heard the visiting yachtsman call out about the *Rose-Noëlle*, she stopped talking and gave him her full attention. He had just heard over his VHF radio that the *Rose-Noëlle* had been washed up on Great Barrier and that there were three survivors. Minutes later came a message that there were just two survivors, and no one was quite sure if the place was Great Barrier Reef, Australia, or Great Barrier Island, Auckland. A minute later a new report. Four survivors.

Rose started to run, grabbed the phone in the local harbor

board office, and asked the police to confirm the message. Then she rang Glenrose.

Malcolm had just arrived back from picking asparagus up the road when he answered Rose's call. She was breathlessly trying to tell him what she had heard and kept saying, "They're back. I think they're back."

Out on the verandah, Christabel looked up from her task of squeezing a bucketful of oranges and searched Malcolm's face for confirmation of what she thought the conversation was about. Malcolm hung up the phone and immediately rang Picton police, who said they had heard the same story. They would ring back when they had confirmation. Ten minutes later a reporter from the *Dominion* newspaper in Wellington telephoned and told Malcolm that the wreckage of *Rose-Noëlle* had been washed up on Great Barrier; all four men had survived, but they had no details on their condition. A helicopter was on its way to interview and collect the survivors.

At Great Barrier it was Rick's turn to use the phone at the Godinet home. He tried his home number at Anakiwa but got no reply. He then rang his parents in Auckland. Shane Godinet gave him a chair, but he was shaking so much he had to sit on the floor. There was so much emotion on his face and in his voice as we heard him say, "Dad, it's Rick."

We were all sitting in this small living area, and the phone was right there on the wall. We felt we were eavesdropping on a very private and special moment. Shane Godinet told me later that he and Teresa had felt like intruders in their home, witnessing and hearing the tearful, emotional reunions by phone.

When it came to my turn to use the phone, I rang Christabel in Blenheim. She had been sitting, waiting tensely for confirmation of second-hand information that the crew of the *Rose-Noëlle* had been found.

"Hello, Christabel," I said. "I'm back."

Fighting back tears, my forever levelheaded sister said, "Where have you been?"

"I don't know," I laughed.

There was a pause before she said, "I'm not shocked or surprised really. I knew you would come back."

"I knew you would know," I told her. "I got through to you. I prayed for you every night and told you that I was okay."

Next I rang David Barnes in Auckland to tell him I was back and asked him to pass the news on to his brother Alan and father Bob in Picton. I tried to get through to Pat Hanning at the *Herald* office, but he was out, so I left a message.

After I spoke to Christabel, Malcolm rang my brother David and his wife at Swan Bay in northern New South Wales to tell him what they knew so far, and then he rang some close sailing friends in Blenheim. He just managed to say, "John's been found. . . ." when he broke down. The stress and emotion of the past four months, the endless telephone calls to reassure the family of the other crew and our friends that we would return, the months of supporting Christabel, had caught up. He was in tears, and Christabel had to take the phone to finish the conversation.

From that moment Malcolm and Christabel's phone went mad. Somehow the whole world had got to know. They took forty-five personal calls interspersed with interviews from television, radio, and newspapers from New Zealand and Australia, and the phone kept ringing until they left to visit me in Auckland a few days later.

Karen Hofman was taking dictation in a solicitor's office in Blenheim when her workmates heard snatches of news about the *Rose-Noëlle* over the radio. She emerged from the office just as the phone was ringing; it was a newspaper reporter in Wellington to say that her husband and the rest of the *Rose-Noëlle* crew had been washed up on Great Barrier and were alive and well.

Karen treated the information cautiously. She wanted to check it out herself before ringing the children at their school. She rang Outward Bound and spoke to Jon D'Almeida, who confirmed that he had spoken to Jim. Phil was alive and well.

Karen Hofman coped with the news with calm efficiency, as she had through the whole ordeal. She had never given up hope and had always talked to friends in terms of "When Phil gets back . . ." She had taken over the running and maintenance decisions of the Hofman yacht, practicing tying bowlines efficiently in the privacy of the main cabin in case anyone was watching when she next checked the mooring lines. She had begun to study navigation and planned to sit for her radio license.

During the time we were away, Karen made it her business to find out as much about *Rose-Noëlle*, me, Rick, and Jim as she could. She talked to our friends and family, and even to my boatbuilding teacher, Jack Morgan, until she had satisfied herself that *Rose-Noëlle* was well built and that I was a capable skipper. The day she heard we were back Karen returned to work at her office, privately elated but outwardly calm. She waited for the call from Phil that she always knew would come. It had just been a matter of when.

Heather Hellreigel and Jim's companion, Martha Bell, were having lunch together at Rarangi Beach with the Women Outdoors New Zealand group when a friend arrived and told them to sit down; he had some news to tell them.

The two women spent the next few minutes laughing, hugging, and crying. They had become very close in the past four months, spending hours talking, cheering each other up, jogging together, hoping, praying that they would not be on their own much longer. When others despaired that we would ever be found, Heather and Martha found courage and hope that they were unaware existed. Now that it was over, they were exhausted by the ordeal and had little to give Rick and Jim when they were reunited.

Back on Great Barrier we all heard the whirr of the helicopter blades as the machine put down neatly in the paddock next to the Godinets' home.

"Here they come," someone said, as *Dominion* newspaper reporter Philip Macalister and photographer John Selkirk scrambled out of the machine.

Shane Godinet had checked in with his boss, "Rocky" Rounthwaite, at the wharf police in Auckland. When we returned to the house we found that our names and the story stood up. "You're in for a hard time," Rounthwaite said, "because the media are on their way."

The *Dominion* had been quick off the mark upon hearing the news of our return direct from a contact working at the Outward Bound School after Jim phoned Jon D'Almeida from the house. When Philip Macalister walked into the small living room, he was struck by the bizarre yet warm scene before him. It was raining outside, and it had been touch-and-go for the helicopter pilot to find his way to Great Barrier.

Inside the Godinets' home it was hot and steamed up as Teresa tried to keep pace with food orders; their two children played with their toys, wondering who all these strange people in the house were; and the four of us shuffled around, eating and talking on the phone. Selkirk started taking pictures of us tucking into ice creams, standing smiling together, and a classic one of Phil puffing on his first cigarette since kicking the habit several years ago after his heart bypass surgery.

Macalister was having a hard job trying to get a cohesive story out of us. He knew that by reaching us first, he had had a lucky break. We were tired out, vague, and still in shock. I didn't help matters by clamming up because I still wanted to get hold of Pat. He had helped me so much in the past that I wanted him to have my story. I didn't want to talk to anyone else. If I had ignored the others and used the phone at Windy Hill, Pat would be there by now.

The phone was ringing constantly with media wanting interviews. It was time to go. The four of us thanked Shane and Teresa Godinet for their hospitality and kindness and ran out to the waiting helicopter.

Inside the Godinets' house the phone rang yet again. It was the *New Zealand Herald* team assigned to the story. Their helicopter had landed at Claris airfield in bad weather, and the reporter wanted to know how to get up to the house.

"You're too late," Shane told him, not realizing Pat Hanning was also on board the *Herald* helicopter. "They're just leaving."

A few minutes later one of the island taxis pulled to a halt outside the Godinets' house, and a man with a distressed expression ran up the path, calling to Shane Godinet, "Where are they?" Godinet waved Pat Hanning toward the paddock, suddenly realizing who he was.

It was a tight squeeze inside the helicopter with Rick, Phil, Jim, and me plus the pilot, the reporter, and the photographer. It had taken us some time to get seated comfortably and buckle ourselves in. I was sitting in the front seat, staring ahead and still brooding about Pat when Jim said suddenly, "There's your friend." He was pointing back toward the Godinet house where a man was running and waving. It was Pat! Weeks later I remembered the incident and wondered how Jim knew, for he and Pat had never met.

I struggled to get out of the front seat and clamber over the others. I thought for a minute that they would not let me out, because the helicopter was all set to go and the *Dominion* reporter wasn't keen to see me escape. But I struggled out of my harness and jumped clear, running to embrace Pat.

I grinned at him and said, "You should have come. You would have loved it." Anyone else would have wondered if I was being sarcastic, but Pat knew that I meant it. It was so wonderful to see him, a true friend, just the sort of person I needed to be with right now. Suddenly I felt safe and my head cleared. There was so much I wanted to tell him.

Shane Godinet stood and watched us embracing, chattering and laughing, and looked away. Again he seemed embarrassed at the intrusion. Weeks later he told me that his family still jokingly refer to the path as "John-and-Pat's Alley."

The helicopter carrying Rick, Phil, and Jim took off while

I went back to Claris to hitch a ride with Pat in the *Herald*'s helicopter. They had a mobile telephone on board, and I couldn't resist playing with it. Even though I had already telephoned Christabel, I rang her again. She said I sounded like an excited kid with a new toy. "There's nothing wrong with you," she said. "You're just the same."

Before we headed out to sea the helicopter pilot, under my direction, flew over Little Waterfall Bay so that the *Herald* photographer, Mark Mitchell, could take pictures of the wreck site. I was expecting to see *Rose-Noëlle*, or at least parts of her, below but there was nothing left, just tiny fragments scattered across the rocks. I couldn't believe it. The sight saddened me and to some extent tainted the joy of reaching land and being reunited with Pat.

For me *Rose-Noëlle* was far more than just a yacht. It had been my home; everything I owned had been on it. It had been a whole way of life, my passport to adventure, my ticket to the islands I loved so much. To build her I had to give up so much. My health had suffered from exposure to the polyesters, epoxies, PVC foam, and other indestructible materials that had gone into her. The power of the sea had destroyed her. My dreams had been shattered. And yet in a strange way I could feel the first signs of a new sort of freedom. There were new dreams to be fullfilled. But that was in the future.

The weather had by this stage closed in to the point where the pilot was having trouble getting his bearings without a compass and was concerned about his fuel level.

"Oh, no," I managed to joke. "You're not going to do it to me again, are you?"

About an hour after we left, Shane Godinet flew over the wreck site in a helicopter hired by a television crew to take aerial shots of Little Waterfall Bay. He wanted to see for himself the place we had described. As the helicopter hovered above the rugged coastline and heavy seas, Godinet looked down and saw the pieces of yellow-and-white debris scattered across Little Waterfall Bay and the adjacent cove.

There was nothing large enough left to give any clues as to the size or shape of the boat. The sea had slowly and mercilessly pounded *Rose-Noëlle* to death.

Godinet, too, felt a tinge of sadness as he looked down on the site; he and I had talked about *Rose-Noëlle* and what a big part of my life she had been. But as the helicopter rose higher over the coastline, he was struck with another thought—of our incredible good luck. Stretching for a couple of kilometers either side of Little Waterfall Bay was a line of sheer, rugged, and inhospitable coastline, impossible to penetrate from sea level. Our wreck site was in fact the only cove in the area where the bush ran down to the shore, offering a way out. He concluded that had *Rose-Noëlle* drifted a few hundred meters either side of the cove, he would now be filing a report concerning four bodies.

FOURTEEN

The Inquiry

Just after lunch on 2 October, Captain Mel Bowen was in his office high above the Auckland waterfront ready to start another full afternoon of appointments and phone calls. His job overseeing navigation safety for the Maritime Transport Division of the Ministry of Transport meant that he found himself handling everything from navigation examinations to major harbor obstructions in a territory covering the northern half of the North Island.

When Search and Rescue headquarters in Wellington rang, Mel Bowen raised his eyebrows as he listened to Captain Alex Gibb, marine duty officer for Search and Rescue in Wellington, tell him that the missing trimaran *Rose-Noëlle* had turned up wrecked on Great Barrier Island.

Gibb wanted him to check out the story by interviewing the four crew once they were brought back to Auckland by helicopter. Search and Rescue was already anticipating an investigation as to why *Rose-Noëlle* was not found during the official search.

Bowen had been involved in just about every aspect of the sea, ships, and boating over the past thirty years. His wide responsibilities kept him busy and office-bound much of the day, and he welcomed this interruption as a chance to use some of that knowledge and experience. Methodical, organized, and clear-thinking, Bowen sat down immediately and drew up a list of questions he thought he should ask the crew. He rang Shane Godinet at Great Barrier and established that the first helicopter was bringing in Rick, Phil, and Jim at 3:30 P.M. and that I was arriving later in a second helicopter.

197

Bowen spent the next hour completing work that couldn't wait and rearranging his diary. He went into the next-door office and asked Captain Jack Lyon, the deputy superintendent of mercantile marine, to join him at the interview. One of Lyon's portfolios was receiver of wrecks, and, thinking ahead, Bowen thought there could be a problem with looting and with establishing to whom the remains of the *Rose-Noëlle* belonged. At that stage Mel Bowen had no idea just how little remained of *Rose-Noëlle* after stormy winds and waves had crushed her into little pieces overnight.

Jack Lyon listened while Mel Bowen briefly told him what he knew. "John Glennie," Jack exclaimed. "I know him. We met up in the islands years ago."

In fact, David and I met Jack Lyon in Rarotonga in 1965 when he was master of the island trader *Bodmer*, and we were cruising in *Highlight*. Because of our link with the sea and the Pacific Islands, our paths were to cross on a number of occasions over the next few years. There was another connection. Lyon had met Kalo Siutaka in Auckland in 1961 and lived with her there for a couple of years until they returned to the islands in 1963. Kalo travelled to Fiji with him on the *Bodmer*, and they parted company at the end of that year. David and I met Kalo in Apia two years later when she joined us on *Highlight*.

Privately Mel Bowen thought the fact that Jack Lyon knew me was a stroke of good luck. He was well aware that he would be in a difficult position, having to ask probing and pointed questions of four exhausted men who would only want to be reunited with their families.

At 3:15 P.M. Bowen and Lyon drove the short distance to Mechanics Bay on the waterfront to wait for the helicopter. Already the tarmac was thronged with newspaper, television, and radio reporters and cameramen. Bowen introduced himself to the helicopter line staff, who offered to set up a meeting with us before letting the reporters near. Bowen and Lyon helped the helicopter staff arrange tables and chairs in a side room as the crew's flight touched down outside. The only other people in the room were two policemen and a small group of medics.

*   *   *

Mel Bowen frowned a little to himself as first Phil, then Jim and Rick, walked through the door. Rick looked dazed and stumbled a little. Phil was clean shaven. They appeared well dressed, and their skins were clear of any sores. Phil Hofman placed a yellow-handled knife on the table in front of him, and that appeared to be the only possession the men had with them.

Jack Lyon thought for a moment that the men before him were not the survivors from the *Rose-Noëlle* but residents of Great Barrier who had accompanied us across.

"These guys," Mel Bowen thought to himself, "look like they've just walked off the Waiheke Island ferry." The first seed of doubt formed in his mind. He decided to keep the questions brief and informal, giving the impression of a discussion rather than an interrogation.

The three men seemed a little taken aback after spotting the crowd of media waiting outside. Rick and Jim were dazed and vague in their answers, and after a while Bowen was aware that Jim was becoming irritated by the line of questioning. Phil Hofman answered most of the questions and did not seem to mind Bowen's probing; at times he even appeared to be enjoying himself.

Bowen knew that with the media facing their own deadlines, he was short of time. How did the capsize occur? When and how was the EPIRB deployed? Did they attempt to rig a jury sail/mast?

At the end of the ten-minute interview, Mel Bowen was still unconvinced that our story was true. He had read plenty of shipwreck survival stories and knew to expect gaunt, haggard frames. Phil, Rick, and Jim looked too fit and neatly presented. There was no sign of sunburn, saltwater sores, or cuts on their hands. Where was the proof that *Rose-Noëlle* had in fact been wrecked after floating upside down for 119 days? Could it in fact have been on its way back from a mission when it was wrecked on the Barrier? A trimaran like *Rose-Noëlle* could travel a long way in four months.

Bowen considered that Rick, Phil, and Jim had been vague with their answers, although in hindsight he concluded that the three men had been in a state of shock and still dazed by the attention they were creating. For their part, the three men simply wondered what all the fuss was about. They did not consider they had done anything special. They had survived, and now all they wanted to do was to get home.

As Mel Bowen and Jack Lyon left Mechanics Bay they saw the *New Zealand Herald* helicopter approach, but already the media were closing in, so they decided to interview me the following morning. In the meantime Bowen was mulling over something Phil Hofman had said when asked about ships and aircraft sighted during the voyage. He had mentioned the light aircraft that had circled over us the day we hit Great Barrier. Bowen had flown light aircraft as a hobby for the past twelve years and had contacts within civil aviation. He knew it would be relatively easy to track down the pilot and get an eyewitness account of the capsized *Rose-Noëlle* to help verify our story.

An assortment of television crew and radio and newspaper reporters were busy interviewing Rick, Phil, and Jim when the *Herald* helicopter touched down. I simply couldn't face the thought of a barrage of questions at that stage and asked Pat Hanning to explain to the media that I wasn't up to it.

However, one of the TVNZ Paul Holmes news team, Mike Valentine, was persistent and even followed me up to Auckland Hospital when the four of us were taken there by ambulance. Paul Holmes wanted me to appear live on his current affairs show at six-thirty that night, and eventually I agreed.

As a result I could not wait around long enough at the hospital to be checked over other than to have my blood pressure taken. Blood tests done on Phil, Jim, and Rick showed mild anemia, and Rick complained of constipation. Jim also had a slight reduction in serum sodium levels, but doctors decided no treatment was necessary, and all three were discharged. Somehow my diving knife was left behind at the hospital, and I never did find it.

When I arrived at the television studio, Paul Holmes beamed and announced he had arranged a live satellite linkup with my brother David and with Danielle. Some fast work on the part of the Australian media had them flown by helicopter to a television studio in Brisbane. Suddenly there I was, still huddled inside a donated TVNZ sweatshirt and jacket, exhausted and overcome, looking at David and Danielle with little Alexandra sitting on her knee. It was such a shock, and I didn't know what to say.

Millions of viewers, and no doubt Paul Holmes, were expecting us to say loving words to each other, but our reunion was stiff and contrived. The memory of our parting was still there, smarting, and beyond the knowledge of those looking on.

David broke down, and I fought for control. Danielle kept her composure and searched for something appropriate to say. We had much to discuss, but this was not the moment. Alexandra played and smiled and did recognize the haggard man on the screen as her daddy.

I was not the only one to find reunions with loved ones difficult. Rick and Jim and their respective partners responded in a way we were told later by trauma experts was to be expected. Those close to us had suffered their own stress, their own grieving, and now were faced with "degrieving." We all needed help and support but perhaps were in no fit state to give it to each other.

While we were adrift the four of us discussed the fact that we did not miss our partners in a physical way. It was as though the sexual urge had just shut down, yet another part of us in automatic survival mode. Once we returned, the thought of entering into a sexual relationship immediately was threatening; it took a while for us and our partners to adjust to that. After spending four months in the company of men I needed the companionship of women but no more. I needed to be around people who brought laughter back into my life without the pressure of responding to a physical relationship. Jim and Martha Bell eventually parted company three months after our return when Martha left for Canada. Jim had weeks of counselling to help him cope with the effects of the *Rose-Noëlle* ordeal, and he eventually left New Zealand to spend time with his family in the United States.

By the time Pat Hanning collected me in a taxi to take me back to the *Herald* office for an interview, I was exhausted. I had apparently been linked with current affairs presenter Jana Wendt of Australia's Channel 9, an interview I still to this day cannot remember taking place. I sat with Pat at his desk, eating a big plateful of food from the staff cafeteria and answering his questions. I was so glad to be there.

That night there were pockets of celebrations in Blenheim, Picton, and Anakiwa—in fact all over New Zealand, where family and friends had ended their agonizing wait for news over the past four months.

At Picton wharf my friends Rod and Karol Lovatt had spent the afternoon on their yellow-and-white trimaran *Afternoon Delight*, talking to yachting friends about our return. Earlier in the day Rod had been using a bulldozer on his section at Anakiwa when an instructor from the Outward Bound School ran across the paddock and breathlessly began shouting words at him above the noise. "They're all right, they're back. They got washed up . . . on the Barrier," the instructor babbled.

"Who did? What are you talking about? Slow down," Rod told him.

"The *Rose-Noëlle*. They're back."

With that Rod switched off the bulldozer and heard the full story. After the instructor left, he tried to continue working but finally gave up. He couldn't concentrate, and he wanted to get back to Picton to share the glad tidings with the yachting community. As the day wore on and the news filtered through Picton, people began arriving at *Afternoon Delight* bringing with them something to eat and drink. They were in the mood for a celebration.

The party went on until the early hours of the morning. Rose Young dropped by and so did Karen Hofman.

Cartoonist Tom Scott captured the mood—and my profile—after the live satellite linkup with Danielle and David on the Paul Holmes television show.

Perched high in the cabin was a small television set, and the only time the noise level dropped was to listen to the news flashes and interviews with the four of us throughout the night.

Newsreaders kept describing the four of us "perched on the upturned hull for four months eating seaweed and seabirds." No wonder when people saw our clear skin and clear eyes they doubted our story. We looked too healthy to have gone through that sort of hardship. The party on Rod and Karol's boat rocked with laughter when they saw me talking to David and Danielle and blowing my nose vigorously. The sound reverberated through the microphone connected to my jacket, deafening the listening audience. Russell and Maureen were not in Picton to hear the news of our return, but they held their own private celebration in the United States when a friend they were travelling with rang his brother in New Zealand and heard the news the day we returned.

In a hall out at the Outward Bound School a party was in full swing, with instructors, farmers, and retired people contributing to a spontaneous potluck dinner washed down with French champagne.

Heather Hellreigel, Matthew and Martha Bell spent part of the night waiting at Wellington Airport for a connecting flight to Auckland. As they sat in the departure lounge watching the television news their faces erupted in delight and laughter when Rick and Jim appeared on the screen, the first time the two women had seen their partners in four months.

Up in Auckland we were too tired to party that night. Rick and Jim were resting at the home of Rick's parents in Rothesay Bay, and Phil stayed with his sister in South Auckland. I spent that night at Pat Hanning's home, where I slept fitfully, and I was up early the next morning. The telephone rang; it was Paul Holmes's breakfast show wanting a radio interview with me in half an hour. The man never gave up, and I admired him, so I agreed again.

Listening to the Paul Holmes show that morning was my old friend Penny Whiting, whom I had not seen since my days cruising New Zealand on *Highlight*, and who now ran her own sailing school in Auckland. Penny, according to her television-producer husband, Doc Williams, got a "bee in her bonnet" about contacting me. "You get the children off to school," she instructed Doc. "I'm going to find John and bring him home."

And she did. She arrived at Pat's house just as I remembered her, full of gusto and ready to help in any way she could. She gave me a hug and said cheerfully, "Come on, I've just made a batch of blueberry muffins, and I thought you might like some."

I never went back to Pat's. He and his partner worked different newspaper shifts, whereas Penny was at home that week with her six-year-old daughter Erin and eight-year-old son Carl. It was meant to be, she told me later. Right through the sailing season her diary was full, except for one week—the week I returned.

She offered me her home and family as a refuge, a place to rest, a place to belong. I felt safe, and I knew Penny and Doc would protect me. Looking back, I owe her a tremendous debt. Penny is the sort of person who gives and gives, and when there is nothing left to give she gives some more.

She and her family enveloped me with their love and attention, spoiling me, feeding me up five times a day, making me cups of tea, listening to me repeatedly purge the frustrations and anxieties that had peaked since coming ashore. Erin and Carl treated me like one of the family, hugging and kissing me each morning as though they had known me all their short lives.

One morning shortly after my arrival, Penny came into the bedroom carrying a plateful of steaming scrambled eggs. I took one look at her and broke down. I wept because of Penny's gesture, I wept because of the memory of indulgences like breakfast in bed, I wept because I felt like it.

It didn't take much then to make me burst into tears. I had suffered another disturbed night of waking in a blind panic, drenched in sweat, not knowing where I was. That week Penny, in her no-nonsense manner, shielded me from the scores of media representatives constantly wanting to speak to me by phone, and when she thought I had taken enough called the interview short. Three weeks later my co-author, Jane Phare, took over as my minder, shielding me from outside pressure, taking the load of decision-making, listening to me and feeding me up when I went to stay with her and her husband, Byron Ballan.

When Mel Bowen and Jack Lyon arrived at Penny's home that first morning I was sitting in the living room in a recliner chair with my swollen feet wrapped in an electric blanket, munching delicious, freshly baked muffins. Jack Lyon and I exchanged a few words before I continued with a newspaper interview that was already under way. The media had been there since early that morning, and I was managing to eat and talk at the same time quite well.

I was in fact enjoying the attention, although I had earlier broken down during an interview with a *Sydney Morning Herald* reporter while I was telling her about my boat and how she came to be named *Rose-Noëlle*. Both the Rose-Noëlles existed now in spirit only. If I ever wrote a book, I thought, I would call it *The Spirit of Rose-Noëlle*.

A freelance photographer, Rob Tucker, wanted proof of my emaciated state, so I obediently got out of the chair, went outside, and stripped down to my underwear. Then I turned my back and pulled my underpants down a little to show where once my backside had been. The resulting photograph was published in magazines all round the world, including *Time*.

Watching the performance, Mel Bowen was struck by the wasted muscles in my arms and legs and my puny frame. The sudden activity and interviews had left me exhausted, and I slumped back in the chair, with Penny fussing around to make me comfortable. My feet, unused to walking for four months, were swollen and sore after the six-hour hike through bush on Great Barrier. Bowen had a list of formal questions he had prepared but, after witnessing my vague and rambling state of mind, he abandoned them and decided to opt for a gentle and general discussion.

Both men remarked later they thought I was in considerably worse physical shape than Rick, Phil, and Jim. There were various theories offered as to why this was, including the fact that I was the oldest crew member, that I had done strenuous physical work in the form of diving, and that the stress of feeling responsible for the crew had taken its toll. I personally don't have a theory. All I know is that I lost no time in putting back on the thirteen kilograms I had lost—with a vengeance. I realized two months later, while staying with my coauthor, that I was the heaviest I had ever been.

Bowen and Lyon spent about twenty minutes talking to me, filling in the gaps that Rick, Phil, and Jim had been unable to answer—mostly to do with navigational aspects of the drift. Mel spread out a chart of New Zealand and the Pacific Ocean and asked me to outline what I thought had happened and our likely course. Unbeknown to me, he was interested to see if my answers tallied with those of the three others. The fact that they did, and the sight of my poor physical and mental state, helped to ease any doubts that remained.

Out on Great Barrier at about this time a television helicopter once again collected Shane Godinet and his boss Graeme Rounthwaite to make a search of the wreck site. The two men were particularly interested in the logbook, which Godinet mistakenly thought was hidden in a cave above high-water mark. No one is quite sure where this rumor started, but it could be that, having described the ledge where our floating bundle rested (it was lodged under a ledge), I could have given the impression that our possessions were safe and sound and just waiting to be collected.

As he was searching the foreshore of the bay where *Rose-Noëlle* had first foundered, Shane Godinet spotted an orange buoy in among a mass of rope, clothing, and wreckage. He pulled at it and found it was attached to the carry handles of a sail bag. Of the bag itself there was no sign; it had long been ripped away by the sea. Godinet did not realize at the time how close he had come to finding my possessions. He cut the buoy free and took it to give to the local museum, which collects souvenirs from Great Barrier shipwrecks.

After searching unsuccessfully for the log, the two men collected some samples of the wreckage and arranged for them to be flown to nearby Whangaparapara Harbor on the west coast of Great Barrier and put aboard the Customs launch *Hawk* for transport to Auckland. As they were about to leave, Godinet spotted a new rubber thong sitting on a rock; a couple of meters away on another rock he found the matching thong. He gathered them up and salvaged a stainless-steel pocketknife and a pair of dividers. He thought I might like them as mementoes.

By the time Mel Bowen finished his interview with me and returned to his office late that morning, he found that he was under siege. The story had captured the attention of media around the world, and it seemed they all wanted a statement from him. He couldn't get through to Search and Rescue in Wellington, and they couldn't get through to him.

The next day, 3 October, the Ministry of Transport appointed an outside investigator, Captain Peter Kershaw, to conduct a preliminary investigation as to whether there should be a formal inquiry into the *Rose-Noëlle* saga. Kershaw had spent twenty-eight years of his forty-five-year nautical career in charge of marine search and rescues and preliminary inquiries. Recently retired, he was the ideal man for the job, and his appointment took pressure off already-overloaded maritime staff.

The night before Kershaw had sat watching television news coverage of the *Rose-Noëlle* story at his home on Auckland's North Shore. During his years as a nautical surveyor he had seen a number of survivors of shipwrecks, and now he was skeptical. "I don't know what those men have been doing for 119 days," he said to his wife, "but they haven't been shipwrecked."

On the morning of 4 October the Customs launch *Hawk* docked at the Auckland waterfront, and the crew offloaded a selection of debris from *Rose-Noëlle*, salvaged from Great Barrier. Peter Kershaw had temporarily moved back in to his old office next to Mel Bowen. The two men went downstairs together to examine the first pieces of the wreckage they had seen. While much of the fiberglass had been ground clean by the huge, smooth boulders at Little Waterfall Bay, there was evidence of marine growth inside pieces of aluminium deck track. Neither of the men knew enough about marine biology to determine just how long the tracks had been underwater. But Kershaw planned to find out.

That afternoon the two men arranged to fly out to Great Barrier to visit the wreck site themselves. Kershaw was keen to get there before the northeasterly blows that had battered the exposed coastline in the past two days further smashed the remains. He knew that with each tide the evidence was gradually being washed away.

THE AUSTRALIAN

RIDDLE OF THE GREAT SEA ESCAPE

WEDNESDAY, OCTOBER 4, 1989   Printed and published by Nationwide News at the office of the company, 2-4 Holt St., Surry Hills 2010

Mel Bowen invited me to join the flight to Great Barrier. He knew how important it was for me to find my log and personal possessions, and he thought I might be of some help in identifying the pieces of wreckage. That was the first time I met Peter Kershaw, and once again it was the sight of my physical appearance that caused him to reconsider his initial disbelief over our survival story. Kershaw later told my coauthor how he watched me get into the helicopter, a stooped, tired figure with flesh and loose skin hanging from my gaunt frame. He looked at my badly swollen legs and feet. He saw the expression on my face, the look in my eyes, and listened to me trying to string a sentence together. It was only then he became convinced that he was in charge of an inquiry concerning a genuine survival saga.

At Great Barrier we touched down in the paddock outside the police station so that Shane Godinet could join us. It was good to see him again, and he remarked that I looked better already. He handed me the thongs, which only just fitted my bare, swollen feet, the pocketknife, and the pair of dividers I had used during my boatbuilding apprenticeship.

As we approached the wreck site the helicopter pilot obligingly hovered over the house on Windy Hill so that I could take photographs before heading down to Little Waterfall Bay. As we flew low along the rugged coastline Peter Kershaw was struck with the same thought that had occurred to Shane Godinet the first time he flew over the site. He concluded that Rick, Phil, Jim, and I would not have survived had the *Rose-Noëlle* drifted ashore either side of Little Waterfall Bay. Either we would have been smashed with the boat against the rocks and drowned, or we would have died of exposure, being unable to climb up the sheer cliffs.

As the helicopter prepared to land, I wasn't prepared for the scene below. *Rose-Noëlle* had all but vanished; from the air the little cove looked as if a piece of foam had been crumbled and scattered over the beach and rocks. There was scarcely a piece of fiberglass that I could not pick up with one hand.

After taking photographs of what he saw, Mel Bowen put on a wet suit and skin diving gear and began to search underwater for anything that might be of use in the investigation. He was well aware of the strength of the sea, but he was still surprised to see a rubber tire off my bicycle stretched tightly around a huge boulder beneath the water.

The swell was too high for Bowen to risk swimming out and around the headland into the little bay where we had first grounded and where much of the wreckage now lay underwater. The helicopter pilot solved the problem by skilfully hovering over the area, one skid touching the rocks so that Bowen could scramble out.

As Bowen dived into the water and scanned the sea bottom, the scene struck him as though someone had taken a house, turned it upside down, and shaken it. There were tools scattered everywhere, a wok wedged beneath a boulder, the two-horsepower outboard off the dinghy. He wouldn't be surprised, he thought to himself, if he came across a lawn mower. He was looking at the contents of a man's home, a lifetime's collection of possessions, scattered across the seabed.

That day Mel Bowen found both *Rose-Noëlle*'s anchors, a Danforth and a CQR. Shane Godinet, knowing the scavengers and treasure hunters would be combing the wreck once the weather settled, hid them both in the bush until he could arrange for them to be transported out.

Two days later Godinet returned by boat with local men Charlie Blackwell and his son Johnny to collect the anchors. They sifted through the ever-changing array of debris on the beach in the hope of striking it lucky. Johnny Blackwell spotted a writing compendium with "very important papers" embossed on the front, but it was empty. Ironically I had removed its contents—the ship's papers, licenses, and Customs documents—the day before we landed and put them with my other personal possessions in the plastic containers to be taken ashore.

Local carriers kindly transported the anchors across Great

Barrier and back to Auckland, where Penny Whiting collected them from the wharf. She took them home to grace her backyard while I decided what to do with them; they were no good to me now without a boat, yet I could not bear to part with them straightaway.

During the early interviews I was asked why we had not anchored as we drifted close to Great Barrier. I replied that the anchors were stowed in a bow locker which, when upside down, was beneath the waterline and inaccessible. When *Rose-Noëlle* began to break up on the rocks, the anchors would have fallen out and sunk straight to the bottom, too heavy for even the swell to shift.

While the investigators searched for pieces of wreckage at Little Waterfall Bay, I hobbled among the debris looking for pieces of my past life that I could take with me: a plastic Tahitian lei, a teapot stand, a scrap of pareu—a Tahitian sarong.

Peter Kershaw, his assistant Alex More, and Mel Bowen had collected a range of wreck samples, which they loaded in the helicopter to take back for testing. I was a little bemused at the trouble to which everyone was putting themselves over this investigation, but I was confident of the outcome and decided to let them get on with it.

Shane Godinet was keen to help me find the logbook and spent a couple of hours half-submerged searching for any signs of our bundle of gear. I described the sail bag, the plastic containers, the buoy tied to the bundle. Godinet shook his head. "I found the buoy yesterday, mate. There was nothing left," he told me. I thought of the hours, days, weeks, and months I had spent writing. I thought of Geordie's drawings, my cycling medals, my apprenticeship papers and photographs. I just could not believe they were lost.

By the end of that trip I was exhausted. The three days of questions, media interviews, reunions with friends and family had taken their emotional and physical toll. Within half an hour of being on the beach I could no longer walk but had to sit resting on a rock, watching the others hunt among the wreckage that had been my home.

The following day Peter Kershaw and Mel Bowen took fourteen pieces of wreckage from *Rose-Noëlle* to be examined by Brian Foster, associate professor of zoology at Auckland University. Foster told them he would need a little time to examine and identify the stalked barnacles and to file a report. However, he said at that meeting that the marine growth looked to him as though the wreckage had been in the water for several months.

In the subsequent report Foster concluded that the scientific evidence was consistent with the drift of the wreck from the south, within a pocket of seawater of southern origins, generally well offshore, and for a minimum time of sixty to ninety days.

He identified the *Lepas australis* barnacle, a species not recorded north of 39°S. Three related species he identified were not commonly encountered south of Cook Strait but were common foulers of floating objects in the northern, temperate seas. It seemed plausible that the *Rose-Noëlle* drifted northward within a body of surface water of southerly origin. The absence of acorn barnacles, tubeworms, or molluscs characteristic of coastal seas suggested a drift well offshore.

"The fact that the barnacles were damaged could be explained by physical dislodgement on the grounding of the craft, but some of the stalks were without internal tissues, which suggests that the decapitation could have occurred while adrift (e.g., biotic removal, including human harvest)." That last bit amused me, as I thought of Jim and I raiding the barnacles off the hull to add to fish soup or to flavor Jim's culinary delight of the day.

The same day that Professor Foster examined the wreckage, Peter Kershaw and Alex More paid me a visit at Penny Whiting's home. I was in bed after a restless night of dreams, waking up drenched in sweat and having to change my bedclothes and sheets. Penny's daughter Erin

had vacated her bedroom for me, so there I was in this
lacy bedroom full of dolls and toys with Peter Kershaw
perched on a little chair trying to interview me. I didn't
particularly want to talk to him, and we didn't get off to
a good start when he asked me in an official voice, "What
is your name?" When he asked me my address, I replied,
"*Rose-Noëlle*, Great Barrier Island."

A local Herne Bay doctor, Peter Cairney, had examined
and spoken to me before Kershaw arrived. He told Kershaw
he did not think I was in any state to be interviewed, but
Kershaw was keen to get the inquiry under way. However,
after a while he conceded that the interview should wait. He
concluded that I was "a physical and mental wreck" and that
I was not capable of responding rationally to an interview.

Malcolm and Christabel flew up from Blenheim the next
day, arriving at Penny and Doc's home full of smiles and
hugs—just as I remembered them. I had so much to tell
them, and there was so much I wanted to know. How was
Glenrose? What was happening in Picton and Blenheim?
How was everybody? They spent the next four days with
me, and Penny took us out sailing on her yacht, *Endless
Summer*. Even in my emaciated state I thought I was doing
quite well winching in the headsail until Penny took over
and ground the handle at twice the speed.

Meanwhile Peter Kershaw was attempting to get statements from Rick and Jim. He drove out to the Hellreigels'
home in Rothesay Bay, where Jim, Martha, Rick, and Heather were staying, and Rick gave him a full statement. But Jim
refused to be interviewed, saying that he would consider
doing it once he returned to Picton. However, he changed
his mind, on Rick's advice, and the following week gave
Alex More a full statement. After his brief meetings with
Jim, Kershaw sensed a deep emotional bond between Jim
and Rick, to the point where he considered Jim was relying
on Rick to do a lot of his thinking for him. In the end Jim
gave an open, honest statement, assuming that it was to be a
confidential document. A month later he was appalled to read
parts of what he had said, particularly personal observations

about the four of us, in the newspapers after the preliminary inquiry was published.

Phil Hofman gave his statement the week after we returned, when he visited Kershaw in his office on the waterfront. Kershaw thought Phil had recovered well both mentally and physically, and Phil even made light of some of the incidents that had occurred during our trip.

Kershaw visited me once again at Penny Whiting's home on 10 October, and this time found my condition much improved. I was able to give him a full statement about *Rose-Noëlle*, her equipment, the weather, and incidents leading up to the capsize and how we survived after that.

After reading the four statements Kershaw privately concluded that the capsize would never have happened had we sailed through the storm as I had originally planned. He knew I was confident that the boat could handle the conditions and that the storm was not bad enough to cause damage to a boat the size and weight of *Rose-Noëlle*. However, the fact that I was persuaded by a panicking crew into lying ahull and setting the parachute anchor was a mistake, and as skipper of the craft I should have trusted my initial judgment.

Kershaw also concluded that we were indeed fortunate to find ourselves surviving on a large, stable platform with an unusually large supply of food aboard, much of which was accessible.

In the meantime Mel Bowen had tracked down the young pilot, Mark Hughston, who confirmed over the phone what he had seen on 30 September. It was not until he watched the television news on the night of 2 October and heard about *Rose-Noëlle* that Hughston realized he had in fact flown over a trimaran about to be shipwrecked. He later sent a full written report, a copy of his flight plan, and a diagram of where he had seen the boat in relation to Great Barrier.

The week after we returned, Mel Bowen flew himself from Dairy Flat to Great Barrier in a two-seater Cessna. He landed at Claris and was picked up by Shane Godinet in his wagon. The two men planned to retrace our steps from Little Waterfall Bay up through the bush to Windy Hill. Mel Bowen was a keen tramper, fit and wiry for his age. He saw the expedition as an opportunity for some relaxation and exercise as well as another chance to check for the log, which he knew would be invaluable to Peter Kershaw for the inquiry. If it was there, he was determined to find it. He also planned to take back the box of old clothing we had left with Shane Godinet in case it, too, was needed for the inquiry. The box had been stored in his generator house, and Godinet kidded me later that he could smell it every time he opened the door even after the clothing had gone.

The two men left the wagon at Windy Hill and set off on foot, using a direct route with the help of Bowen's orienteering compass. It took them a little over an hour to get down to Little Waterfall Bay, where Bowen again put on a wet suit to search for sunken treasure. One of the first things he spotted was my bicycle, minus its wheels, wedged beneath a boulder. He pulled it free and, in a lighthearted gesture, perched the bike up on a large rock and pretended to peddle. Shane Godinet captured the moment with a photograph.

The two men spent about two hours on the beach, Godinet wearing his customary rugby shorts and shirt to fossick in the shallow water. They searched the immediate coastline thoroughly but found no sign of the contents of my missing sail bag. I wasn't to realize until much later the extent to which various people went to find it; although they were unsuccessful, I will never forget their kindness.

When Bowen and Godinet set off through the bush back up to Windy Hill, they were hoping to stumble across our campsite of the night of 30 September. As Godinet, the larger and slower of the two men, moved steadily through the bush, Bowen darted about trying to find a clue in the form of empty food cans. He soon realized that without constant reference to the compass in the thick foliage they would easily be lost. It took the two men just over an hour to get back up the track. Although none of us wore a watch, it had taken Rick, Phil, Jim, and me something like six hours to reach the house. We had taken a long and circuitous route the morning after our night in the open. We backtracked, argued, walked round in circles, and argued some more until we eventually found the track and road that led to the house. The bush we went through was not as thick as that which Bowen and Godinet tramped through, hence our lack of scratches two days later when we were rescued.

In the second week of our return the weather became calm, and the Customs boat *Hawk* once again visited the wreck site. This time its scuba divers were able to dive in deeper water out near the flat reef where *Rose-Noëlle* had first grounded. That day they salvaged heavier pieces from the boat—a crumpled color radar set, a radio, tape deck, and, luckily, the EPIRB, which was sent straight to Wellington to be tested by the Department of Scientific and Industrial Research.

The beacon was wired up and found to work perfectly well. Officials continued to insist they could not understand why the beacon signal had not been picked up, although they acknowledged that flights in the area were scarce and detection depended to a certain extent on whether the flight crew were listening at the time. I am convinced it was not detected because we were simply out of range.

While we were adrift, one of the yachts taking part in the South Seas Regatta required assistance after its satellite navigation system broke down and one of its crew became badly seasick. An RNZAF Orion on a routine patrol searched for the yacht to guide it to a rendezvous with a Tongan fishing boat. The yacht's skipper activated the EPIRB, a signal that was picked up by the Orion only once it was within ten miles of the yacht.

A couple of weeks after we came ashore, two old-timers from Great Barrier Island, Dave Medland and Charlie Blackwell, went to fish at one of their favorite spots. They had fished together regularly for years, but in the past few weeks the island had been buffeted by easterly onshore winds, the same wind that had pushed *Rose-Noëlle* into Little Waterfall Bay. On this day the weather was unusually fine and the seas calm, so Medland decided to go ashore and hunt among the wreckage of *Rose-Noëlle* while Blackwell stayed with the boat.

There wasn't much left on the beach; he picked up an aluminum porthole, its glass long gone, some stainless-steel blocks and rigging wire, and an electric drill before walking round to rocks near the headland. There he saw something glinting in the sun and stopped to collect some American coins—part of $20 in change I had been given when we sold *Highlight* in Los Angeles—from the crevices in the rocks.

He picked up four round brass objects, which at first glance he thought were old coins but were in fact cycling medals—two of mine and two belonging to my father. Dave Medland later handed the medals in to Shane Godinet, who posted them back to me in Auckland. I was thrilled to see them, one of the few items of sentimental value left from my past life.

A month later, when I went back to Great Barrier with my coauthor, I stopped in to see Dave Medland to thank him personally. Coincidentally he used to live in Picton during the 1950s and 1960s and remembered David and me cycling for Marlborough. He took me into his garage and showed me the electric drill he had salvaged; the day he found it he cleaned it up, plugged it in, and was amazed to find that it still worked. That drill had been underwater for more than four months.

One of the aspects of our voyage that intrigued everyone, including Rick, Phil, Jim, and me, was exactly where we had drifted over the past 119 days. Because I was unable to navigate and knew we could not sail the boat, I accepted from the start that we were at the mercy of the winds and currents.

Shortly after we returned, the *New Zealand Yachting Magazine* asked the Auckland Weather Office to track *Rose-Noëlle*'s path based on weather reports—only the wind was taken into account, not the currents. Because of time constraints the study was limited, but the resulting drift chart is fascinating and is shown on page 221.

Forecaster Greg Reeve took on the job of plotting a rough course for our 119-day drift, starting from the position at which we capsized on 4 June and basing his chart on a midday average of the wind direction and speed in the area. Reeve decided to make an educated guess at our drift speed and came up with an average of half a knot an hour for a twenty-knot wind.

He laid out a pile of weather charts dating back to June and sat down to work. As the line of track progressed Reeve thought to himself, "No way can these guys have ended up back in New Zealand." The line was heading east, straight across to South America. By his calculation we should have still been on our way to Chile.

It wasn't until he had worked for hours that Reeve realized he was mistakenly using weather charts from the previous year. Cursing himself for the hours of wasted work, he repeated the exercise using 1989 weather information, and this time the line of drift looked quite different.

Up until 25 June our track zig-zagged in a generally easterly direction for about 270 nautical miles. During that time gales (winds averaging thirty-four knots and above) occurred about once every four days.

At first Reeve thought the result was going to be similar to the 1988 chart, but then the weather, and the resulting drift, changed. Over the next week winds from the southerly quarter drove us northward to about the same latitude as East Cape. In the following two-week period, during which time there was a southerly gale on 6 July, the trimaran drifted in a loop to the south and east and by 16 July lay roughly near 174°W. A week of south-to-southwest winds pushed *Rose-Noëlle* to the furthest point east on about 25 July, about 420 nautical miles east-northeast of East Cape, at which point we gradually began to be pushed back toward New Zealand.

From late July *Rose-Noëlle* rode with east-to-northeast winds toward East Cape for two weeks, and in August we drifted in a counterclockwise loop before picking up south-erlies and moving northward. In the following three weeks running into September we were pushed in a figure-eight. In the final two weeks winds from the northeast quadrant pushed *Rose-Noëlle* to her final resting place, which was, by Greg Reeve's calculation, somewhere inland near Raglan—on the west coast, south from Auckland.

There were a couple of errors in Reeve's initial informa-tion. He based the track on a 120-day drift, not 119 days, and his capsize point of 40.5°S, 179°E was about fifty miles southwest. But in terms of where we eventually struck land compared with Reeve's diagram, the errors scarcely made any difference. His calculations still showed quite clearly our line of drift.

In the preliminary inquiry report Peter Kershaw concluded it was difficult to establish a drift pattern for *Rose-Noëlle* for the entire time. From weather information supplied by the New Zealand Meteorological Service he theorized that we would initially have been blown east of East Cape and then up north, well offshore. In August and September we entered an area of predominating easterly winds that returned us to New Zealand.

The New Zealand Oceanographic Institute was asked to comment on ocean currents as they might relate to the drift of *Rose-Noëlle*. The institute stated that data on the mean currents in the area were scarce and it was possible that ocean currents would have had a relatively small effect on the trimaran, because for much of the time it was in areas well offshore from the strong current systems such as the East Cape Current. Offshore currents could well have carried it north before the easterly winds blew it back toward New Zealand.

The direction of surface currents is determined by the prevailing wind, and in the year 1988/89 the Southern Oscillation moved from an extreme negative phase (El Niño) to a positive phase (La Niña), upsetting traditional current patterns and winds.

While data on the currents is inconclusive, there was one very simple and interesting experiment carried out

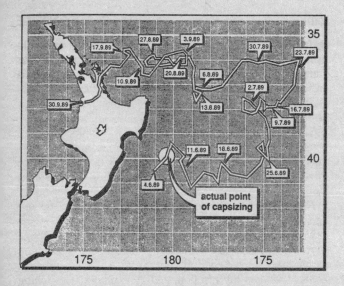

The map shows markers at various positions:

27.8.89 · 3.9.89 · 30.7.89 · 23.7.89
17.9.89 · 20.8.89 · 6.8.89 · 2.7.89 · 16.7.89
10.9.89 · 13.6.89 · 9.7.89
30.9.89 · 11.6.89 · 16.6.89 · 25.6.89
4.6.89

actual point of capsizing

35 · 40 · 175 · 180 · 175

The Auckland Weather Office tracked our path based on wind only. Commissioned by *NZ Yachting* magazine

involving a message in a bottle, the results of which were included in Kershaw's report. Strangely enough it was Jim Bramwell's son, Daniel, who put the sealed bottle overboard off the *Argonauta* at 39° 24.23′S, 177° 21.51′E off Hawke's Bay and not too far from our capsize point. Jim Bramwell took a fix on the position with his satellite navigation and recorded the date—27 June 1989.

The bottle floated along with the currents, and on 21 September, nine days before *Rose-Noëlle* hit Great Barrier, a sixteen-year-old Aucklander, Caren Shrubshall, found the bottle washed up on Mangawhai Beach, just fifty miles west of Little Waterfall Bay. Caren Shrubshall wrote to Daniel Bramwell to tell him where and when she had found the bottle, and Jim Bramwell forwarded the letter to Kershaw.

The preliminary inquiry covered various other aspects of the *Rose-Noëlle*'s disappearance and concluded that the events had happened the way we had described. Kershaw made a list of recommendations to the minister of transport, Bill

Jeffries, including that all New Zealand yachts departing overseas be fitted with an EPIRB and a single-sideband marine radio, and that the New Zealand government install a local user terminal to join the international distress satellite reporting system. His final recommendation was that no formal inquiry be held.

The minister described our voyage as "testimony to the benefits of a sound vessel, ample provisions, and the determination of its crew. If there was ever any question that the *Rose-Noëlle* was not overturned and drifting for 119 days then this investigation dispels those doubts."

News that Kershaw's report completely backed up our version of the 119 days we were missing leaked to the news media before the report was released. The telephone started to ring at my coauthor's home and did not stop for the next three days. Reporters from Australia and New Zealand wanted my reaction, and their line of questioning suggested that I had been holding my breath until the report was released. In fact, most of the doubt over our story had started with the media in the first place, ranging from the subtle questioning to open disbelief. It was they who had created the issue, not me.

While the inquiry was in progress I had been concentrating on the book and hadn't given the inquiry another thought. I knew what the outcome would be and was therefore not surprised by the verdict. Kershaw had struck me early on as a fair man, and I trusted him to report honestly and accurately from the information he gathered, and that is what he did.

The media were also quick to pick up on hints of disharmony that had emerged in our personal statements. "Of course there were personality problems," I told an Australian television station during a live interview. "What do you expect if four men are living in a space like the underneath of a low table for four months and every now and then have a bucket of water chucked over them?"

I thought my young son Geordie summed up the whole business rather well in a poem he wrote shortly after I returned entitled "John":

John is my father,
that does not want to drift any farther.
He went through an ordeal
that some people think is not real.
Mum, Dad and I doubt that it was a lie;
if he was fibbing, the molluscs would not be living,
in the aluminum pipe on a trimaran type.

EPILOGUE

I first met John Glennie on 10 October 1989 in a conference room at the *New Zealand Herald* offices in Auckland. He was sitting hunched at the conference table in his donated clothing, looking gaunt and tired, listening to discussions about coauthoring a book with a *Herald* journalist. With him was his literary agent, a gentleman—in the true sense of the word—named Ray Richards, who had been approached by Penny Whiting to look after John's interests. John wanted to write a book and tell his story, but at that stage he was in no condition to make decisions on his own.

I was asked at short notice if I would like to write a book with the skipper of the *Rose-Noëlle*. Once John and I met and agreed to work together, we were to begin straightaway. I knew nothing about John Glennie apart from what I had learned from my journalist colleague Pat Hanning, now working at the *Herald*.

When John first went missing, the feature writers at the *Herald* shared with Pat the sense of loss he felt, the absence of a longtime friend, someone for whom he had the deepest respect. Pat would have been out there with John had he accepted an invitation to cruise on *Rose-Noëlle*; instead, a mortgage and work commitments kept him "shore-shackled," something John had always been at pains to avoid.

When John was declared missing, Pat rang Search and Rescue headquarters in Wellington to tell them what he knew about *Rose-Noëlle*, a boat he watched being built at the peach orchard in West Pennant Hills near Sydney.

When the search was abandoned, Pat wrote a feature on

John and his cruising life, an article he could write almost off the top of his head after *Playboys of the South Pacific* and his long friendship with John. Pat wrote the feature not as an obituary but as a tribute; like others who knew and loved John, he never really believed he was gone.

Pat agreed with John's sister Christabel that it would take a catastrophe in the form of a massive gas explosion or collision with a container ship to cause the disappearance of *Rose-Noëlle*. He knew also that John was meticulous about keeping watches and that the boat was equipped with sophisticated gas-warning devices. Both scenarios were unlikely but still possible.

"With thousands of John's friends around the Pacific," Pat wrote at the end of the article, "I wish and pray with his and the crew's families that they could keep on searching, to find some piece of evidence. . . . Please, God, he never did anyone any harm and did many a little bit of good."

Pat later told me he would always be grateful to John for his friendship and for the lessons he had learned from him, both in a personal and practical sense. John and David Glennie were extremely well known throughout the Pacific during their days of voyaging in an old-style trimaran. From real novices, they had become superb seamen. Every lesson they had learned the hard way, and they were generous in passing on the easy way to others.

John doesn't suffer fools easily, Pat told me. He would be endlessly generous with his time and patient to someone who was prepared to listen and learn, but he knew that he had learned about certain things because he had done it that way so often before. He would quickly lose patience with a know-it-all and in that event could be a hard character to get on with.

In August Pat travelled to Britain to cover the Admiral's Cup and the start of the Whitbread round-the-world yacht race. He later visited a mutual friend of his and John's, a Western Australian named Mal Beilby, now married to a French woman and living in France. One of the first things that Mal asked Pat when he picked him up from the airport was, "How is John Glennie?" Mal had not heard that *Rose-Noëlle* was by then two months overdue, and Pat had to break the news to him. Mal listened and replied simply, "He'll be all right."

While researching this book John and I twice visited the Marlborough Sounds; he wanted me to see for myself those special places of which he talked so lovingly. We visited his friends the "live-aboards" at Picton, flew over the picturebook beauty of Queen Charlotte Sound and Kumutoto Bay, walked the streets of Blenheim, where every now and then someone would stop and say something like, "Hi, John, you won't remember me, but we used to go to school together. I'm glad you made it."

Closer friends who knew John's sailing reputation and his outlook on life were more philosophical. "We knew you'd be back," they told him.

We revisited all his old haunts—the steep roads around Picton where he and David cycled on the weekend; the Glennie Rhododendron Dell at Waterlea Park in Blenheim, full of azaleas and rhododendrons donated from the garden at Glenrose, Picton waterfront, and the nearby bays where the Glennie family holidayed.

We visited an old family friend of John's, Charlie Saunders, now in his eighties, who had represented New Zealand as a rower at the 1930 Empire Games in Ontario and the 1932 Olympic Games in Los Angeles. Charlie Saunders had some rare film footage showing the launching of *Highlight* in 1964 on the banks of the Opawa River. Saunders had taken a keen interest in John and David's planned cruise of the South Pacific and had worked hard to coax sponsorship and donations toward the boat from local companies.

We had a yarn with Jack Morgan, with whom John did his boatbuilding apprenticeship, and the two talked boats nonstop. We visited John's mother, Jean, at her Picton rest home. She knew her elder son had been gone a long time but needed a gentle reminder as to the reason.

*   *   *

As we travelled about Picton and Blenheim, John laughed off the persistent rumors that the story of *Rose-Noëlle* was a hoax but was more annoyed at suggestions that the crew had been drug-running, an insult to someone who holds strong views against drug-taking of any kind, does not smoke, and drinks little.

When the results of Peter Kershaw's preliminary inquiry were released, John couldn't understand what all the fuss was about from the media. He had known all along what the result would be and thought the comment should be coming from those who had doubted their story.

While researching this book we immersed ourselves in survival stories. The more I read of those tales of hardship and endurance, the more I realized how blessed the four men aboard the *Rose-Noëlle* had been. If anything, it was a story of good luck.

They were lucky that no one was on deck when the trimaran capsized and that no one was injured. Throughout the 119 days they managed to stay healthy. While they suffered periods of extreme hunger and thirst, they were in fact eating quite well toward the end. They were lucky that the boat was so well stocked at the beginning of a cruise that was to last months.

Perhaps the greatest stroke of good fortune was the wind and sea currents that took them back to New Zealand rather than toward the expected destination of South America. And when they did come ashore, *Rose-Noëlle* washed up in the only cove along that part of the Great Barrier coastline with access to the bush and civilization beyond.

For a long time after his return John could not bear to see food go to waste. He would finish up leftovers even when he was no longer hungry and continued to do so until three months after his return, when suddenly he levelled off. He used to joke that he was on a "see food" diet.

In the early days he seemed incapable of making a simple decision . . . what color ice cream he wanted for dessert;

should he have plain toast or raisin bread for breakfast.

His concentration span was limited, and any diversion or interruption would break his train of thought completely, to the point where he simply could not remember what he had been talking about a minute earlier. Even when reminded, his memory drew a blank. He suffered from chronic lapses and had to write everything down the moment it came to mind.

Penny Whiting told me of watching John slowly get up from the recliner chair in the lounge and feel his way down the hall, supporting himself against the wall to the toilet on his badly swollen feet. In the mornings she and Doc used to find little notes he had written in the night, thanking them for their kindness. He had woken in a blind panic, breathless and drenched in sweat, terrified that he would not make it through to the morning.

While working on the book, John relived every day of his time adrift as we went over and over tiny details, building up hours of taped transcriptions. The interviews would leave him exhausted and emotionally spent. Often the memory of a particular incident would leave him shaking and breathless, signs of anxiety. Sometimes I had to extract information slowly and painstakingly; other times it bubbled out of him, and he kept repeating the same things over and over, purging himself of incidents that he had bottled up for four months.

Gradually his room and our garage began to fill with crumpled, salt-encrusted souvenirs salvaged from the wreck site at Great Barrier. The EPIRB sat in pride of place on John's desk, where he spent hours at night, unable to sleep, writing to friends and family.

Six weeks after his return we were in Blenheim at Glenrose when the postman arrived, bringing a bundle of mail returned from the forwarding address in Nukualofa. Among the mail was the box of homemade butter biscuits posted in June by Rose Young. Even though Malcolm, Christabel, and I pointed out that the butter biscuits, by now almost six months old, had seen better days, John insisted on eating every last one—sharing the crumbs in the bottom of the bag with the family labrador, Rhody.

While we were at Glenrose, Karen Hofman telephoned John to thank him for his part in bringing Phil home safely. She was the only person connected with the other three crew ever to ring Glenrose after the *Rose-Noëlle* returned.

It was intriguing to share the process of John reestablishing himself in modern society as though he had a brand-new identity. We collected his new passport from a Blenheim travel agent; we went into a bookshop to buy an address book so that he could start collating a lifetime of contacts and friends on paper once again; we visited the bank to open a new account and claim his money back from the lost traveller's checks.

When John walked out of the bank he stuffed the notes in the pocket of his borrowed tracksuit pants. He had no wallet; he would have to buy one of those, too. He stopped to admire a calendar of the Marlborough Sounds but, he pointed out, he had no wall on which to hang it.

As John slowly regained his health and relaxed, his concentration span improved, he lost the urge to bolt anything edible in sight, and the tormented nights of sweating and breathlessness lessened until they disappeared completely. Hair that had thinned on the top of his head had grown back within three months of returning.

He began to get his sense of humor and fun back, became interested in everything around him, and expressed a yearning to travel. People who visited the house would often ask, "Are you going to build another boat?" or "Are you going to go sailing again?" The answer was always no. He wanted nothing to do with boats; not to design, build, or sail. They were part of a past life.

He used to say to me that he built *Rose-Noëlle* with a woman in mind. He built a beautiful boat with every modern gadget and an enviable galley, and yet he could never find that special person to share his dream. Now that part of his life is over, the boat is gone, and suddenly there are new and special people in his life.

A stream of letters and parcels sent to Glenrose were forwarded to Auckland, each day bringing news from a friend or a message of admiration from a stranger. John's friend, John Hitch, sent $1000 from Australia; Danielle sent a big parcel of new clothes, some of them unfortunately too small since his rapid weight gain; a friend from the Bay of Islands, Connie Hirst, whom John had not seen for twenty years, sent more clothes. Another boxload arrived from local yacht squadron members and still more arrived from the Whiting family.

A few weeks after John's return we visited Dr. Peter Cairney's surgery to collect results of tests, and the doctor remarked that John was already looking ten years younger. In a subsequent medical report on John's condition in those early days, Dr. Cairney described dramatic loss of subcutaneous tissue or fat under the skin and severe ankle edema, or soft-tissue swelling, caused by fluid retention in the area. This was caused by a high level of sodium in the blood and from the trauma of walking a long distance after being inactive for so long. He suffered slight abdominal distension from his prolonged semistarved state, was anemic, and there were other signs of a deficient diet, including a higher-than-normal serum sodium level, probably caused by dehydration as a result of a high-protein diet and high salt intake combined with insufficient fluid; low potassium, again related to high sodium and a deficient diet; and folic acid deficiency (folic acid is obtained from dark green, leafy vegetables).

Two weeks after his return to land John was referred to a psychiatrist, who considered John was not suffering from any serious degree of post-traumatic stress disorder and that he would come through the whole experience with ego intact. Peter Cairney, who had seen John in the very early days, felt then he was perhaps suffering from a moderate degree of post-traumatic stress disorder in the form of insomnia, inability to make decisions, and memory loss for names, places, and recent conversations that had taken place. His condition may have been made worse by biochemical and electrolytic disturbances in the blood that showed up in subsequent tests. However, within a month, Dr. Cairney had noticed a marked improvement in John— both in his physical and his mental condition.

I consider it a privilege to have known and worked with John Glennie, and I, too, have learned from him. The *Rose-Noëlle* story is a tribute to the inner strength and determination of all four men—John Glennie, Rick Hellreigel, Phil Hofman, and Jim Nalepka.

Jane Phare

APPENDIX ONE

The survival notes and articles I wrote while adrift on *Rose-Noëlle* were lost, along with my logbook, when we came ashore at Great Barrier Island. During the 119 days adrift I had plenty of time to think about multihull capsize and how best to cope with it. The four of us learned from our mistakes, by experimenting, by perseverance.

Multihull owners all hope and believe that capsize will never happen, but on the rare occasion it does, it is better to be prepared and make your chances of survival just that much greater. I have reconstructed an abbreviated version of my survival notes in the hope that they will be of help to someone, somewhere in the future.

All important gear on the boat should be individually tied in place with strong cord—particularly equipment such as spear guns, fishing rods, landing nets, and gaffs. It is not good enough simply to store them in a locker. Ropes should be coiled and tied along the gunwale inside the float, not just looped on hooks. Make sure the tool kit is stored in a locker that will not open if the boat capsizes.

A suncover, also tied in place, can be used to collect rainwater. Make sure that lockers, particularly those holding food or drink, are fitted with catches that will not give way should the boat capsize. Stow plastic soft-drink bottles, cooking oil, and vinegar in compartments below the cabin sole.

A plastic tap fitted on the end of the air-breather hoses on the water tanks will stop the water leaking out should you capsize and will double as a tap through which to fill containers if you do turn upside down. When refilling bottles with water, leave an air space, otherwise the water will go foul.

Canned food has always been a problem on boats because the tins tend to rust and the labels fall off once they are wet. Before setting sail, remove the labels and dip the cans in a protective varnish. Label or code the cans with a waterproof marker pen; keep the code list in a safe place or memorize it.

Organize a long-term dried-food locker in which food is kept in double-sealed plastic bags under a screw-down hatch. This emergency locker would have the dual purpose of acting as a food reserve in the hurricane season or when times are hard and you have no money. Stash away freeze-dried foods, milk powder, and the like. Large containers of rice will store well; we found that parboiled rice cut down on boiling time and was edible uncooked once it had been soaked. Large packets of boiled glucose sweets and barley sugars for energy are also useful and should store well in airtight containers.

Most modern multihulls are now fitted with escape hatches in the hull that can be opened from both inside and out, and I support the idea of these. If you have a ham radio, store it in a cupboard that will be above flood level in the event of capsize. A spare aerial cut to the length of the twenty meter band, which the marine mobile network uses, can be rigged up on a pole. A sealed battery supply and a portable solar panel would be added insurance.

A portable hand-held VHF radio in a waterproof container, kept in a secure locker, is a must. Most ships keep a continuous check on channel sixteen, and if you can see the ship, someone in the radio room should be able to hear you. Big ships are so automated these days that there is usually just one set of eyes scanning the horizon every twenty minutes or so. A capsized and half-submerged multihull without sails is difficult to spot, even in calm weather. In rough or choppy seas it is next to impossible to see.

On 15 June 1989, eleven days after *Rose-Noëlle* capsized, a yacht was sunk by whales six hundred miles off Costa

Rica. The survivors, William and Simone Butler, spent sixty-six days drifting in a life raft during which time they counted forty ships before they were finally spotted and rescued.

Even with all the gadgets and safety devices in the world, there is no such thing as a guarantee. If something goes wrong, a piece of equipment does not work, or you lose it, don't be too disappointed. Keep the faith and hold tight to the belief that you will make it; that attitude is probably the most important piece of survival equipment to have with you. That and a sense of humor.

Below I have divided equipment into two groups—one an emergency pack and the other a list of extras that will help to make life at least a little more comfortable while you are adrift.

Emergency pack

Hand-held VHF radio
EPIRB/emergency flares in waterproof container
Dried food
Water containers
Can opener
Waterproof marker pen/paper and ballpoint pen or pencils
First-aid kit
Book on survival
Plankton net
Boiled glucose sweets
Fishing lines, assorted stainless-steel hooks, lures
Gaff hooks and spear points
Electronic flint lighter
Waterproof matches
Distress V-sheet
Stainless-steel knives, including a floating knife
Sharpening stone
Waterproof torch and batteries
Signalling torch/signalling mirror
Hand-operated water desalination unit
Spoons, plastic cups, and bowls
Survival suits and a space blanket

Secondary items

Small solar panel, secured inside
Rechargeable batteries
Packet of stainless-steel needles and sail thread
Waterproof screw-top containers
Saw, hammer, chisels, and nails
Adjustable wrench and screwdrivers
Small gas camping stove
Underwater camera and film, secured inside
Sunscreen lotion
Hammocks
Air mattresses
Whipping twine and plenty of polypropylene cord
Graduated measuring cup
Cyclist's plastic drinking bottle
Fish identification book
Underwater spear gun
Wool clothing safely stored

APPENDIX TWO

Sail plan of *Rose-Noëlle*

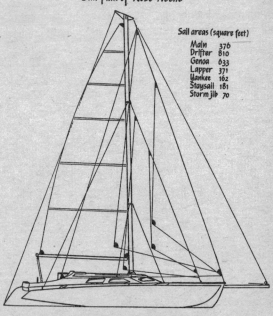

Sail areas (square feet)

Main	376
Drifter	810
Genoa	633
Lapper	371
Yankee	162
Staysail	181
Storm jib	70

Design by John Glennie

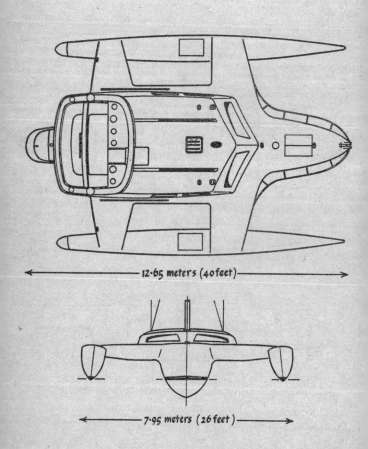

12·65 meters (40 feet)

7·95 meters (26 feet)

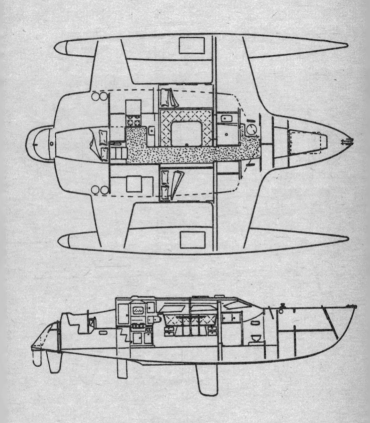

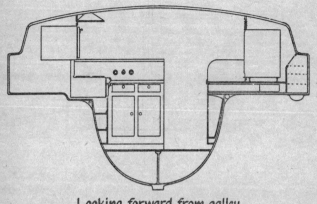

Looking forward from galley

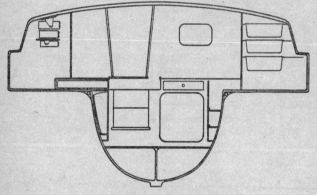

Looking aft from galley

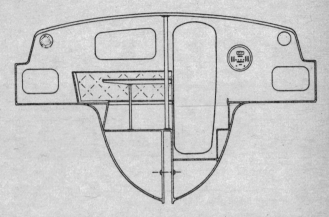

Looking forward from dinette area

About the Authors

JOHN GLENNIE has spent most of his adult life designing, building, or sailing boats. Between 1964 and 1970, John and his brother David explored the South Pacific, Hawaii, Canada, and the United States in their trimaran *Highlight*. John then lived in Sydney for ten years, designing and building multihulls while building his new boat, *Rose-Noëlle*. He arrived in New Zealand on Christmas Eve 1988 and left for the islands on *Rose-Noëlle*'s last voyage on June 1, 1989.

JANE PHARE has been a journalist with the *New Zealand Herald* for fourteen years, including three years as features editor. This is her first book.